T0339418

Lecture Notes in
Behavioral Finance

World Scientific Lecture Notes in Finance

ISSN: 2424-9955

Series Editor: Professor Itzhak Venezia

This series provides high quality lecture note-type texts in all areas of finance, for courses at all levels: undergraduate, MBA and PhD. These accessible and affordable lecture notes are better aligned with today's classrooms and are written by expert professors in their field with extensive teaching experience. Students will find these books less formal, less expensive and also more enjoyable than many textbooks. Instructors will find all the material that they need, thus significantly reducing their class preparation time. Authors can prepare their volumes with ease, as they would be based on already existing, and actively used, lecture notes. With these features, this book series will make a significant contribution to improving the teaching of finance worldwide.

Published:

Vol. 3   *Lecture Notes in Behavioral Finance*
by Itzhak Venezia (The Hebrew University of Jerusalem, Israel)

Vol. 2   *Lecture Notes in Fixed Income Fundamentals*
by Eliezer Z. Prisman (York University, Canada)

Vol. 1   *Lecture Notes in Introduction to Corporate Finance*
by Ivan E. Brick (Rutgers Business School at Newark and
New Brunswick, USA)

Forthcoming Titles:

Lecture Notes in Market Microstructure and Trading
by Peter Joakim Westerholm (The University of Sydney, Australia)

Lecture Notes in Risk Management
*by Zvi Wiener and Yevgeny Mugerman (The Hebrew University of
Jerusalem, Israel)*

World Scientific Lecture Notes in Finance – **Vol. 3**

Lecture Notes in Behavioral Finance

Itzhak Venezia

Tel Aviv-Yaffo Academic College, Israel

The Hebrew University of Jerusalem, Israel

 **World Scientific**

NEW JERSEY · LONDON · SINGAPORE · BEIJING · SHANGHAI · HONG KONG · TAIPEI · CHENNAI · TOKYO

Published by

World Scientific Publishing Co. Pte. Ltd.
5 Toh Tuck Link, Singapore 596224
USA office: 27 Warren Street, Suite 401-402, Hackensack, NJ 07601
UK office: 57 Shelton Street, Covent Garden, London WC2H 9HE

Library of Congress Cataloging-in-Publication Data
Names: Venezia, Itzhak, author.
Title: Lecture notes in behavioral finance / Itzhak Venezia (Tel Aviv-Yaffo Academic College,
     Israel & The Hebrew University, Israel).
Description: 1 Edition. | New Jersey : World Scientific, [2018] | Series: World scientific lecture
     notes in finance ; Volume 3 | Includes bibliographical references.
Identifiers: LCCN 2017045434 | ISBN 9789813231566
Subjects: LCSH: Finance--Psychological aspects. | Investments--Psychological aspects. |
     Stock exchanges--Psychological aspects.
Classification: LCC HG101 .V46 2018 | DDC 332.01/9--dc23
LC record available at https://lccn.loc.gov/2017045434

British Library Cataloguing-in-Publication Data
A catalogue record for this book is available from the British Library.

For any available supplementary material, please visit
http://www.worldscientific.com/worldscibooks/10.1142/10751#t=suppl

Desk Editor: Shreya Gopi

Typeset by Stallion Press
Email: enquiries@stallionpress.com

Printed in Singapore

To my loved ones Dana, Laurie and Irit

PREFACE

Behavioral finance is the area of study that investigates the intersection of finance and psychology and explores how investors' psychology — especially their psychological and cognitive biases — affects their behavior, the functioning of capital markets, the prices of capital assets and the financial actions of firms. This area is the fastest growing area in finance. It was developed as a reaction to evidence from financial markets that did not conform to market efficiency and benefited from findings in psychology showing that decision makers are not as rational as was hitherto believed. Theoretical, empirical and experimental advancements in both finance and psychology, which analyzed the sometimes puzzling behavior of decision makers and market anomalies stimulated the fusion of insights from these two distinct fields to create behavioral finance.

This course provides the basic understanding of behavioral finance and demonstrates many applications of its theories in helping individuals, corporations, analysts, professional investors and legislators make better financial decisions and improving the functioning of capital markets.

This book is self-contained as an introduction to behavioral finance. This area is very dynamic with new discoveries constantly being made — making it impossible to present them all. The book however, does cover the essentials of behavioral finance: the main psychological basics that underlie this area, prospect theory which is the area's main theory of choice, and the most important financial applications. Among the applications we address are: the disposition effect — the tendency of investors to sell winners too fast and to hold on to losers for too long; overconfidence and its effect on investment, trading and mergers and acquisitions; herding and what causes this phenomenon and what its implications are for market stability and for analysts' behavior; overreaction and underreaction of markets to several types of news — what causes investors to react disproportionally to the news they receive and what effect these reactions have on markets; the equity premium puzzle — why equity returns are so high compared to returns on fixed income and whether investors are too timid in their investments; the home bias — when investors tend to invest too much in the stocks of their countries rather than diversify more internationally; and the question of whether stock prices are too influenced by investors' sentiment.

The book is a lecture notes book comprising of 17 lectures most of which are self-contained. It is written in an easy, yet rigorous manner, to make it understandable to students without delving into too many technicalities. Suitable references are provided should the reader need further details. The book however requires the students to critically evaluate some of the theories and findings presented.

By the end of this course, you will have a good understanding of the functioning of capital markets and how cognitive and psychological biases affect them. Being aware of the cognitive biases that lurk around you will enable you to avoid them and give you the tools to apply the knowledge acquired in this book to make better financial decisions.

NOTES TO TEACHERS

Thank you for choosing this book for your course in behavioral finance. I hope this book will make the teaching process of this exciting subject easier, clearer and more instructive to you and to your students.

These notes are based on classes I taught both at the PhD level at Bocconi University in Milan and at the MBA level at the Tel Aviv-Yaffo Academic College. They draw more heavily on my MBA classes, but can easily be adapted for a PhD class. In the PhD class, the same topics were covered but with greater rigor and more attention to statistical and theoretical issues. In the MBA class, these issues received less attention and more consideration was placed on intuition and applicability. Suitable references are provided should the reader need further details.

Although behavioral finance is quite a young field, it has become rather widely studied and therefore, it is impossible (and unwise) to cover all topics. For the same reason, there is no tradition that determines the "must" topics in this area. Therefore, when teaching this course the instructor must make tough choices on which topics to include, which to leave behind, and how much emphasis should be dedicated to each topic This lecture notes book reflects my own personal choices which I have revised through the years according to the feedback I received.

This book is an introduction course and hence it relies quite heavily on the early literature of behavioral finance. Since this is an iconoclastic discipline showing that many well-accepted theories and beliefs in finance are not necessarily true, it requires a great deal of critical thinking on the part of the students — something that I encourage students to do. The field straddles two disciplines: psychology and finance, and it is important for teachers to strike the right balance between the two. This book is intended as a course in finance, but the psychological element is also significant.

In order to make some of the lectures more self-contained, a number of the discussions appear more than once in the book in different lectures. For example, parts of the discussion on conservativeness and representativeness that first appeared in Lecture 3 are repeated in Lecture 9 which deals with overreaction and underreaction. This relieves the readers of the latter lecture from going back and forth between the lecture.

As this is a lecture notes book, some of the text was placed in boxes in order to highlight it and to mark it as suitable for PowerPoint slides. In few of these cases, some of the text was repeated in the text that follows the box in order to keep the text outside the box complete.

The book consists of 17 lectures, each on a different topic and intended for a 90-min lecture. The book is constructed of two parts. The first five lectures (Part 1) provide the psychological and financial foundations of behavioral finance. Lectures 6–17 (Part 2) are applications. I consider Lectures 6–13 to be essential and recommend going over all of them. Lectures 14–17 are special topics and hence could be elective.

In the first lecture, I go over the history of behavioral finance. I present this history as evolving in two almost parallel universes: the financial and the psychological. In the financial one, I stress that the discipline needed alternatives to the traditional economic rationality theory and to the efficient market hegemony due to the prevalence of anomalies, bubbles and crashes. The lectures then proceed to present the efficient markets hypothesis and the capital asset pricing model (CAPM) as the basis for pricing and the yardstick by which normal returns are measured. I also present new theories such as the arbitrage pricing theory (APT) and the Fama–French four factors model and argue that even these theories cannot explain the ubiquity of anomalies.

Next the evolution of decision-making theory is discussed. The Von Neumann Morgenstern (VNM) rationality axioms are presented and utility theory is introduced. From there, the lectures proceed to the early (pre Kahneman and Tversky) paradoxes demonstrating violations of the rationality axioms: The Allais and the Ellsberg Paradoxes. In both cases, it is shown how they violate some of the VNM axioms and exhibit psychological biases. The relevance of these paradoxes is then evaluated.

The following lecture describes the many biases presented by Kahneman and Tversky leading to prospect theory. Shiller's excess volatility puzzle is presented as well as some other relatively "modern" anomalies. It is argued that these then new findings together with those of Kahneman and Tversky were the factors that gave the final push to introducing behavioral finance. The lecture on prospect theory comes next. The following points are emphasized: that prospect theory deals with deviations from a reference point, that it is almost independent of wealth, and that it stresses loss aversion. The pros and cons of prospect theory vs. utility theory are also discussed

The lectures in the second part are applications of behavioral finance. The disposition effect is the first to be introduced for several reasons. First, historically this was one of the first topics that was analyzed using real market data and hence gave the discipline a big push. Second, most people are acquainted with this effect and it does not come as too much of a surprise. Lastly, this is a bias that can be explained by prospect theory and hence provides a good motivation for this theory. The next lecture is about overconfidence. Although most people would acknowledge the prevalence of this bias, its measurement must be clarified in detail. In addition, the implications of overconfidence are surprising and need careful explanation.

The following lecture is on herding. The lecture describes this phenomenon and reviews the many reasons for its emergence showing that they could be either rational or irrational. Two essential theories of herding are presented: Bickchandani, Hirshleifer and Welch's cascade model explaining rational herding by investors, and Scharfstein and Stein's model explaining analysts' herding behavior.

The next lecture deals with overreaction and underreaction. Evidence provided by DeBondt and Thaler showing overreaction is presented first, followed by Jegadeesh and Titman's evidence supporting underreaction. The theories of Barberis, Shleifer, and Vishny and Daniel, Hirshleifer, and Subrahmanyam, which attempt to reconcile the seeming contradictions between the findings of overreaction and underreaction are then debated

The equity premium puzzle is a subject well accepted by students yet its explanation is not that simple. One of the more compelling explanations, that of Benartzi and Thaler, is presented at length. This explanation was highlighted also because it is based on the notion of loss aversion thus successfully connecting prospect theory to real life. The next lecture, the home bias, in addition to describing an important bias is also a great example of how biases may diminish over time either because investors become aware of their existence or due to external factors.

It seems that the following lecture, limits to arbitrage should have appeared earlier in the book. If this topic is described only at this stage, it is because the models explaining limits to arbitrage are rather complicated and cover specialized situations. Schleifer and Vishny's model (excellent for a PhD class) is nevertheless (briefly) presented because of its elegance and the insights it provides. The next lecture about market (investor) sentiment is a good sequel to its predecessor as the two of them involve the analysis of noise traders

The subsequent lectures are elective and can be condensed into a few classes. By now, the students have been exposed to quite a large number of cognitive biases and new ones might seem a little *déjà vu*. I therefore ask students at this stage to present these topics in class and we then conduct a class discussion. This elevates interest in the topics and challenges the students, providing them with a higher sense of control over the material. The lecture on cognitive biases in savings and insurance contains some lesser-known materials but the issues covered — such as the $1/N$ rule, nudging for higher savings, and the full-coverage puzzle — are quite important. The hot hand anomaly was briefly covered in one of the early lectures as an example for representativeness or the law of small numbers. However, students love to hear related stories and to go over the many arguments for and against the hot hand. This lecture also provides more material on the business aspects of the hot hand. The lecture on accounting anomalies requires some accounting background. Most students and some professors of finance do not know much about the accruals anomaly but I find this anomaly important for practitioners. The very important subject of post-earnings announcement drift was mentioned briefly in Lecture 9 but is covered in more depth here.

I chose to conclude the book with the lecture on the appearance and disappearance of anomalies because anomalies are an important *raison d'etre* of behavioral finance. Their volatile nature adds to the excitement of this field.

ACKNOWLEDGMENTS

The financial support of the Tel Aviv Yaffo Academic College in funding the *First and Second Israel Conferences in Behavioral Finance* is gratefully acknowledged. I also thank Professor Shlomo Biderman, President, and Professor Israel Borovich, Dean of the School of Business and Economics, at the Tel Aviv-Yaffo Academic College for their encouragement and support, and Avner Arroyo for excellent research assistance.

Itzhak Venezia
Tel Aviv Yaffo Academic College
May 2018

CONTENTS

Preface   vii

Notes to Teachers   ix

Acknowledgments   xv

Part I. Psychological and Financial Foundations of Behavioral Finance   1

Lecture 1. Introduction: The History of Behavioral
            Finance and the Impetus for Its Emergence   3

Lecture 2. A Review of Traditional Decision Theory:
            The Mean–Variance Rule and Utility Theory   19

Lecture 3. Critique of Utility Theory, the Assumption
            of Rationality and the Efficient Markets
            Hypothesis   39

Lecture 4. Kahneman and Tversky's Essential
            Cognitive Biases   59

Lecture 5. Prospect Theory   69

Part II. Applications of Behavioral Finance   81

Lecture 6. The Disposition Effect   83

Lecture 7. Overconfidence   99

Lecture 8.   Herding   115

Lecture 9.   Overreaction and Underreaction   129

Lecture 10. The Equity Premium Puzzle and Myopic
             Loss Aversion   145

Lecture 11. The Home Bias   157

Lecture 12. Limits to Arbitrage   167

Lecture 13. Market Sentiment   177

Lecture 14. Biases in Savings and Insurance   187

Lecture 15. The Hot Hand   203

Lecture 16. Accounting Anomalies   215

Lecture 17. Appearance and Disappearance of Anomalies   223

Readings by Chapters and References   235

Index   257

Part I

Psychological and Financial Foundations of Behavioral Finance

INTRODUCTION: THE HISTORY OF BEHAVIORAL FINANCE AND THE IMPETUS FOR ITS EMERGENCE

Agenda

➤ What is Behavioral Finance?
➤ The Topics we'll Cover in the Course
➤ The History of Behavioral Finance and the Impetus for Its Rise
➤ Review of the Efficient Market Hypothesis (EMH) and the Capital Asset Pricing Model (CAPM)
➤ Profitability Measures
➤ Market Inefficiencies/Anomalies
➤ CAPM Extensions and Multi-Factor Asset Pricing Theories

In this lecture, we will first explain what is the area of behavioral finance and we will then briefly describe the main topics to be covered in this course. Subsequently, we will discuss why and how this new area of finance evolved over time. To better understand the evolution of behavioral finance and its contribution to the more general field of finance, we will review the concepts of market efficiency, the capital asset pricing model (CAPM) and some more advanced pricing theories. I will also give a short review of some well-known stock market anomalies.

What is Behavioral Finance?

Behavioral finance is the area in finance that studies the intersection of finance and psychology and explores the effect of cognitive biases on the behavior of market participants, on the functioning of capital markets and on the prices of capital and other assets.

Behavioral finance is the fastest growing area in academic research in finance. It started its meteoric rise circa the mid-1980s and it is by now an important part of finance in investments and in corporate finance. Finance is a dynamic area and it has developed many sub-areas over time either because of new theoretical findings, market developments and legislation. For example, the market for options grew in the 1970s, in part, because of the theoretical advances in the pricing of options. Likewise, the area of behavioral finance was developed as a reaction to theoretical findings in psychology and to evidence from financial markets that did not sit well with market efficiency. These findings prompted the fusion of insights from the two distinct fields to create behavioral finance. The new area, as we shall see during this course, contributes considerably to the understanding of the behavior of capital markets and capital markets participants. Behavioral finance has many applications that help individuals, corporations, analysts, professional investors and legislators to make better financial decisions and to improve the functioning of capital markets.

Since behavioral finance explores biases, it may seem that it mainly points at activities that decision makers need to avoid. However, revealing the cognitive biases of decision makers and becoming aware of flaws in their judgments, allows us to find ways to overcome these biases and to design policies to improve financial decision making and the functioning of capital markets. Authors such as Ariely (2008, 2010), Kahneman (2011), and Thaler and Sunstein (2009), popularized behavioral finance by making the concepts of this area more accessible to academics, analysts, professional investors and laypeople.

List of the Topics Covered

➤ Efficient Markets, Rationality and Utility Theory
➤ Prospect Theory
➤ The Disposition Effect
➤ Overconfidence
➤ Herding
➤ Overreaction and Underreaction
➤ The Risk Premium Puzzle and Loss Aversion
➤ The Home Bias
➤ Limits to Arbitrage
➤ Market (investors) Sentiments
➤ Biases in Savings and Insurance
➤ The Hot Hand
➤ Accounting Anomalies
➤ Appearance and Disappearance of Anomalies

Although the list of topics is extensive, it does not exhaust all topics in behavioral finance. While this area is relatively new, it has become quite large, and covering all topics is not only prohibitive but also counterproductive. Instead, this course will cover the most important theories and issues. We will emphasize the broad significance of the psychological and financial concepts rather than go in detail over their statistical and theoretical fine points.

The History and Evolution of Behavioral Finance and the Impetus for Its Emergence

It is hard to pinpoint when exactly behavioral finance started, but its origins however can be traced to sometime in the mid-to late 1980s. During the 1970s and 1980s, there was a growing dissatisfaction and frustration in finance from the failure to deal with findings (anomalies) that did not match the Efficient Market Hypothesis (EMH) and the assumption of investors rationality. These anomalies in addition to numerous financial crises and well-documented bubbles (a bubble is an occurrence where the prices of assets rise without apparent reasons and eventually crash) posed a major challenge to main stream finance that extolled the EMH and investors rationality. Examples for bubbles and crashes that preceded the birth of behavioral finance abound, but we will mention only the following: The Dutch Tulip Mania aka "Tulipomania" of 1634–1637, the Stock Market Crash of 1929, the Mississippi Bubble (1716–1720), the Florida Real Estate Bubble of the 1920s, the savings and loan crisis of the 1980s and Black Monday — the Stock Market Crash of 1987 (which reinforced behavioral finance in its early days).

For brevity, we will go over just few of these phenomena: Tulips, because of their rarity and beauty became favorites of the Dutch high society and speculators in the 17th century, causing their prices to soar to "insanely" high levels. At some point, according to British journalist Charles Mackay (cited in Thompson, 2007), 12 acres of land were offered during that period for a Semper Augustus bulb. Some tulip bulb prices became worth the equivalent of tens of thousands of dollars (in current values) and many Dutch tulip speculators became fantastically wealthy. However, when prices fell to their "sane" levels many investors were ruined and Dutch commerce suffered a severe shock throwing the Netherlands into a mild economic depression that lasted for many years.

Black Monday refers to Monday, October 19, 1987, when stock markets around the world crashed. The Dow Jones Industrial Average (DJIA) fell by 22.61%, the largest one day percentage fall of the DJIA. There were no apparent reasons for such a crash, and despite the efforts of many researchers to explain this event, no explanation prevailed. Following the stock market crash, a group of 33 eminent economists from various nations met in Washington, D.C and collectively predicted that "the next few years could be the most troubled since the 1930s" (see The New York Times, 1987). However, the economy was barely affected and growth actually increased throughout 1987 and 1988, with the DJIA regaining its pre-crash closing high of 2,722 points in early 1989.

The failure to explain phenomena, such as those described above, implied that either markets were not efficient or that theory was lacking or both, and that people could systematically behave irrationally and markets inexplicably. New pricing theories were offered, but also these theories could not explain all anomalies.

While in finance researchers were struggling to explain anomalies via traditional economics, in the psychological sphere, important new strides were made. Kahneman and Tversky published their paper on prospect theory in 1979. This theory together with the many cognitive biases which Kahneman and Tversky, and their many colleagues and students have discovered, started to grab the attention and approval of many financial economists in the early 1980s. One of the main attractions of their theory was that they were able to identify some large classes of cognitive biases and showed the prevalence of these classes of biases. The world of psychological and cognitive biases, which until then seemed chaotic, suddenly started to make sense.

The fusion of these two developments is how behavioral finance was born. It was not until the mid-1980s and early 1990s that main stream finance journals started to publish papers by leading financial economists that favorably viewed behavioral finance concepts and that were critical of the EMH. Acknowledgment of phenomena that previously seemed heretic by mainstream finance such as "market inefficiency", "limits to arbitrage", "overreaction" and "market sentiment" became acceptable in the early 1990s.

The emergence of behavioral finance did not, of course, eliminate bubbles and anomalies that continued to appear also in later periods, nor could behavioral finance fully explain these phenomena. Hence, behavioral finance's work is not yet done.

On the persistence of anomalies even beyond the 1980's, we will talk in Lecture 17. As for later days' bubbles (we mentioned earlier just pre behavioral finance ones), the dot-com bubble of the period 1995–2001 and the sub-prime crisis of 2007–2009 are worth mentioning here. During the early days of the dot-com bubble stock markets in many countries rose rapidly mainly due to the growth in values of technology firms. During that period many new firms were established with fantastically high prices even though they could not provide credible financial evidence or promise for future growth that would warrant such prices. Adding the suffix "com" or a prefix "e" to the firm's name would give the firm a "tech" aura and would add to its market value. Consequently, the average P/E of NASDAQ firms reached 200. The party started to crash in the late 1990s and early 2000s, as many firms that saw a spectacular growth, such as pets.com and Webvan, went bankrupt and many others fell considerably (for example, Cisco's price per share fell by 86% and Amazon's fell from $107 to $7, it rebounded eventually and reached $768.7 on December 12, 2016).

The sub-prime crisis refers to the sub-prime mortgage market collapse that caused a major banking crisis in the US and worldwide during 2007–2009. One of the triggers for this crisis was the bursting of the housing bubble, a sharp decline in housing prices after a long period where they steadily rose. The fall in prices led to a great number of mortgage delinquencies and foreclosures and the devaluation and default of housing-related securities such as mortgage-backed securities (MBS) and collateralized debt obligations (CDO), which were central in the financing of household debt. These instruments seemed to offer attractive rates of return, but these returns were specious since they overlooked the CDOs lower credit quality. Ultimately, these defaults caused the collapse of several major financial institutions in 2008 (e.g., Lehman Brothers) and caused a major economic crisis. This crisis is beautifully described in Michael Lewis' (2010), book: "The Big Short: Inside the Doomsday Machine" and the motion picture, "The Big Short" based on it that appeared in 2015.

Review of Market Efficiency and the Capital Asset Pricing Model (CAPM)

To explain the shortcomings of traditional finance that paved the way for the emergence of behavioral finance, we will start the course with a review of the Efficient Market Hypothesis (EMH).

Markets are considered efficient if the prices of assets reflect all information (see, e.g., Berk and DeMarzo, 2007).

There are three forms of market efficiency: weak efficiency, semi strong efficiency and strong efficiency. According to the first form of efficiency, current prices reflect all information provided by past prices, semi-strong efficiency means current prices reflect all published information (past prices and other public information), and strong form efficiency means prices reflect all information (including also insiders' information).

The EMH says that markets are by and large informationally wellfunctioning. The belief in this hypothesis has been the leading theme in mainstream financial theory and still is quite dominant (this is evident in almost any text book in introduction to finance, see, e.g., Brick, 2017, Berk and DeMarzo, 2007). Behavioral finance on the other hand, contends that the deviations from this hypothesis are significant and cannot be dismissed as mere peculiarities.

Efficiency Criteria

Markets are considered efficient if it is impossible to make above-normal profits, based on the available information. Thus, to make this definition concrete, normal profits must be described. "Normal" profits are defined as those ascribed by some pricing theory (say, the CAPM; see, e.g., Berk and DeMarzo, 2007). According to the CAPM, the firm's total risk can be divided into two parts: the risk due to the firm's correlation with the market (the systematic risk, or "beta") and its idiosyncratic risk which is firm-specific. The CAPM then argues that in equilibrium, only the firm's "beta" affects its expected returns. The idiosyncratic risks are not rewarded with a risk premium since investors can diversify them away. The normal returns, or expected returns, according to the CAPM are shown below:

The CAPM

$$E[R_i] = R_f + \beta_i[E(R_m) - R_f]$$

where:

$E[R_i]$ is the expected return on the stock of firm i,

$E(R_m)$ is the expected return on the market,

(*Continued*)

(Continued)

R_f is the risk free interest rate,
β_i is firm i's measure of systematic risk,
$E(R_\mathrm{m}) - R_f$ is the market risk premium.

We then say that there are inefficiencies if the returns on a stock are systematically higher than those predicted by the above formula for $E[R_i]$. We would also argue against efficiency when there are arbitrage opportunities, and when we observe behavior conflicting with well-accepted axioms or rationality, the correct way of calculating probabilities or with common sense.

Mispricing can exist because of limits of arbitrage. If arbitrage (the simultaneous purchase and sale of the same, or essentially similar securities in two different markets for advantageously different prices) opportunities were not limited, then the astute arbitrageurs would pounce on the underpriced securities buying such assets, possibly financing them by selling overpriced (or even correctly priced) assets, thus making above-normal profits.

Profitability Measures

In addition to normal profits defined by the CAPM, one can find some other profitability measures that are popular with practitioners and academics alike, where earning returns above them, and could constitute evidence against efficiency.

Non Risk Adjusted Measures

$$R_i - R_F$$

This measure is the "plain" risk premium, that is the return on asset i above the risk-free rate. It is too elementary since it disregards the firm's riskiness.

Risk Adjusted Measures

Lintner's ratio: $(R_i - R_f)/\beta_i$

Lintner's ratio measures the risk premium of the asset, $R_i - R_F$, relative to its systematic risk. It is appropriate for evaluating the performance of well-diversified portfolios.

Sharpe Ratio: $(R_i - R_f)/\sigma_i$

Sharpe's ratio measures the risk premium relative to the total risk of the asset σ_i. Since this measure is defined over total risk, it is better suited for the evaluation of non-diversified portfolios.

Jensen's α

Jensen's α of a security (or its alpha) is another measure of its profitability. It is defined as the estimate of the intercept in the following regression:

$$R_{it} - R_{ft} = \alpha + \beta_i[R_{mt} - R_{ft}]$$

In the above formula, we added a time index t to the already defined variables: R_i, R_m and R_f. In this regression, $R_i - R_f$ is the dependent variable, and $R_m - R_f$, the market risk premium, is the independent (explanatory) variable.

The logic behind this measure is the following: According to the CAPM,

$$E[R_i] = R_f + \beta_i[E(R_m) - R_f]$$

This can be rewritten as

$$R_i = R_f + \beta_i[R_m - R_f] + \text{Errors},$$

Or, by subtracting R_f from both sides, as

$$R_i - R_f = 0 + \beta_i[R_m - R_f] + \text{Errors}$$

Accordingly, if the profits are "normal" and we run the regression,

$$R_{it} - R_{ft} = \alpha + \beta_i[R_{mt} - R_{ft}]$$

the estimate of α should be zero (more precisely, not significantly different from zero). A positive (negative) α indicates that asset i earned above (below) normal profits. Assuming the current situation continues, above normal profits could be made by buying the asset (going long) if the alpha is positive and by selling it short if the alpha is negative.

Market Inefficiencies/Anomalies

Consistent market inefficiencies are situations where, contrary to market efficiency, investors could make above-normal profits, and hence are dubbed anomalies. We will go over market anomalies in greater detail later in the course. For now, we will mention just a few: The weekend effect, the January effect, size anomalies, P/E anomalies, momentum anomalies.

During the 1960s and 1970s, many scholars and practitioners found that above-normal profits could be made based on the above factors. For example, according to the weekend effect returns on Mondays are lower than in other days of the week. Since this is known, why don't arbitrageurs devise strategies of buying on Mondays and selling on other days and make easy profits. The debates around this effect usually ran along two lines: first, whether or not the effect is true or spurious (just a statistical artifact), and second, if the effect is genuine, why does it persist? The January effect refers to the phenomenon where many (mostly small) firms earn above-normal profits in January. According to the size anomaly, firms earned returns above those justified by their betas if they were small. Again, if this is a fact (and apparently known to all), then one could easily make above-normal profits by buying small firms prior to January. Their prices will then rise and their expected returns will fall until equilibrium is reached. Similar findings were discovered about the other above-mentioned factors. Observations of stocks that exhibited extreme P/E ratios or prolonged periods of rise in prices (momentum) provided investment strategies yielding above-normal returns.

In addition to the above anomalies, there developed in the 1960s and 1970s a whole industry of research examining the validity of the EMH in its semi-strong sense by using the methodology of event studies. These studies examined how asset returns react to public information such as earnings and dividend announcements, corporate announcements, corporate events, analysts' newsletters, Wall Street Journal articles, etc. EMH adherents used these methods to claim that markets are efficient as stock returns behave as expected according to theory, while their opponents argued the opposite (see, e.g., Bodie *et al.* 2013). Michael Jensen who used to be one of the more influential academics arguing for the EMH conceded in 1978: "taken individually many scattered pieces of evidence on the reaction of stock prices to earnings announcements which are inconsistent with the [Efficient Market] theory don't amount to much. Yet viewed as a whole, these pieces of evidence begin to stack up in a manner which make a much stronger case for the necessity to carefully review both our acceptance of the efficient market theory and our methodological procedures."

The existence and persistence of these anomalies has been one of the main issues contributing to the emergence of behavioral finance. They led researchers to suspect that the investors may not be as rational as the efficient markets aficionados claimed, or that markets do not behave as if all investors are rational, and hence that studies probing the behavior of decision makers without assuming they are perfectly rational are needed.

Market Efficiency/Inefficiency Findings Critique

➤ The joint hypothesis issue
➤ Insufficient data
➤ Anomalies could be temporary

Market efficiency tests and or market inefficiency findings could be flawed because of the following reasons, and both proponents and opponents of the EMH used them one against the other.

- *The joint hypothesis issue*: When measuring normal returns, we assume a pricing model, so when testing the anomaly, we test both the theory and that the profits are above those implied by the theory. For example, if we use the CAPM as our theory (pricing model), deviations from the normal profits prescribed by the CAPM could stem either from inefficiency or from the fact that the CAPM is not the correct theory. Hence, one cannot be sure which of these factors is responsible for these deviations.
- *Insufficient data*: For reliable inference, a long history of prices is needed and such data are not always available.
- *Anomalies could be temporary*: Above-normal profits may emerge, disappear and reemerge.

There also exist the more general methodological questions, which are true for all research and also for both sides of the efficient markets debate, and these are the issues of data snooping, data mining and of the 5% significance rule. Authors tend to focus on "surprising" or "interesting" results since these are easier to publish. Authors also like to publish evidence for their theories rather than against them. These authors may look at the same or similar data as those preceding them finding corroborating evidence for the initial "surprising" or "interesting" results, although really they did not find anything new. In the same vein, because of the prevalent use of the 5% significance level requirement, which is the common yardstick according to which researchers deem their results significant or not, 5% of regressions could be found significant even if based on nothing. Researchers usually just report successes (tests that are significant), but do not disclose information on all the experiments that they conducted. It is hence possible that some of the significant results reported in the literature, and maybe some of the reported anomalies, are just the product of this type of practice.

However, the defense against opponents of market efficiency based on statistical and data issues became increasingly harder over time as the evidence against this hypothesis piled up. Instead, other researchers suggested that the markets were efficient, but that the inefficiency findings were due to the use of inappropriate pricing theories, and that these theories should be revised.

Extensions of the CAPM and Multi Factor Asset Pricing Theories

➤ The APT
➤ Fama–French multi-factor asset pricing model
➤ Fama–French five factor asset pricing model

As previously noted, findings of abnormal profits could be attributed to market inefficiency, but they could also be spurious and due to misspecification of the theory. Since it was found that the CAPM could not explain prices and that above-normal profits according to this model could be made, some researchers concluded that the CAPM could be insufficient, and that there are more sources of risk in addition to the firm's beta that should be considered. New theories were hence proposed to replace it. Some theorists suggested to look at consumption betas rather than market betas (see, e.g., Breeden *et al.*, 1989), and others (see, e.g., Levy, 1980) suggested extensions of the CAPM, generalized CAPM (or GCAPM), taking into consideration limits on the number of assets in investors' portfolios.

The Arbitrage Pricing Theory

$$E[R_i] = R_f + \gamma_{1i}F_1 + \gamma_{2i}F_2 + \cdots + \gamma_{ni}F_n$$

One of the more influential and compelling theories was the Arbitrage Pricing Theory (APT), proposed by Ross (1976) and Roll and Ross (1980). This theory posits that there exist some non-diversifiable factors $F_1, \ldots, F_n$ that determine firm's returns. Firm i's expected returns are hence given by

$$E[R_i] = R_f + \gamma_{1i}F_1 + \gamma_{2i}F_2 + \cdots + \gamma_{ni}F_n$$

where γ_{1i} is firm i's sensitivity to factor 1, γ_{2i} is firm i's sensitivity to the second factor and so on to factor n. We note that the CAPM is a special case of the APT where F_1 is $[E(R_m) - R_f]$ and $\gamma_{1i} = \beta_i$. Roll and Ross suggested factor analysis methods to find these factors.

Fama French Four Factor Asset Pricing Model

$$E[R_i] = R_f + \gamma_{1i}F_1 + \gamma_{2i}F_2 + \cdots + \gamma_{4i}F_4$$

where

F_1: Returns on the market,

F_2: SMB: Relative returns of "small" firms vs. "large" firms (Small Minus Big),

F_3: HML: Relative returns of high vs. low book to market firms (High Minus Low),

F_4: MOM: The extra returns earned by high momentum firms relative to low momentum firms.

Although the APT presented an improvement over the CAPM, it was hard to apply and inaccessible to the layperson because the factors were somewhat abstract. Fama and French (1992, 1993) simplified this model by replacing the abstract factors by more concrete ones and by making these factors available to all, free of charge, in Prof. Ken French's website. They introduced a four-factor pricing model, which is similar to the original APT, but with the following definition of the factors explaining the returns of the individual firms:

The size portfolio return/factor (SMB) is approximated by the difference in monthly returns on the small cap index and the large cap index. The book-to-market factor (HML) is approximated by the return difference between high value portfolios and growth portfolios. The momentum factor (MOM) is the difference in monthly returns between a group of stocks with recent above-average returns and another group of stocks with recent below-average returns.

The group with above-average returns is defined as, say, the top 30% of stocks from the S&P index over the past 11 months and the below-average group contains the lowest 30% of stocks from the same index over the same time period. Professor Ken French maintains these factors in his website: http://mba.tuck.dartmouth.edu/pages/faculty/ken.french/. A more detailed description of the above variables can be obtained from this website.

Fama French Five Factor Asset Pricing Model

As the four factors model could not explain all inefficiencies, the exploration for new factors continued. In 2014, Fama and French introduced a new model with two additional factors:

RMW: a profitability factor, Robust Minus Weak,

CMA: an investment factor, Conservative Minus Aggressive.

The new five factor model is now given by the following equation:

$$R_{it} - R_{Ft} = \alpha_i + \beta_i(R_{Mt} - R_{Ft}) + \sigma_i \mathrm{SMB}_t + \eta_i \mathrm{HML}_t$$
$$+ \rho_i \mathrm{RMW}_t + \chi_i \mathrm{CMAt} + \varepsilon_{it}$$

This model is similar to the four-factor model, except that the MOM factor has been removed and that two new factors were introduced: RMW and CMA. For full details, see Fama and French (2014).

While we concentrated above on financial economists' attempts to explain the behavior of capital markets by rationality and efficient markets, in the next lecture, we will discuss the progress psychologists made in looking for and finding examples of individuals behaving irrationally and providing theories to explain such behavior.

Conclusion

➤ Behavioral finance was described.

➤ Market efficiency, arbitrage, the CAPM and more advanced pricing theories were reviewed.

➤ Early period (1970s and 1980s) anomalies were reviewed.

➤ The vacuum in finance theory that behavioral finance was meant to fill and the impetus for its rise were explained.

A REVIEW OF TRADITIONAL DECISION THEORY: THE MEAN–VARIANCE RULE AND UTILITY THEORY

Agenda

➢ Risk Aversion and the Mean–Variance Rule
➢ Utility Theory and the Definition of Rationality
➢ The Effect of Wealth on Decision Making Under Uncertainty

Market efficiency and traditional economic theory assume that people (economic agents) are rational, although purists of the efficient market hypothesis would say that people are not rational all the time, yet markets behave as if they were. Psychologists strongly suggest that people generally act on many psychological biases that should not be dismissed when we analyze economic markets.

One of the difficulties in taking sides in this debate is the difficulty to define what it means to be a rational person. Traditional economists have converged on von Neumann and Morgenstern's (VNM) axioms of rationality, which they developed as early as 1944 and became the accepted yardstick for rationality (we'll discuss them below). Utility theory, which is based on these axioms, has become the leading theory that explains decision making under uncertainty.

In contrast, Kahneman and Tversky's (1979) prospect theory, which is an alternative to utility theory and is one of the cornerstones of behavioral finance, does not assume rationality in the VNM sense.

In this lecture, we will review some of the existing theories of decision making under uncertainty and describe their advantages and shortcomings. This provides the background for showing in what respects behavioral finance can be considered a more appropriate theory than traditional rationality-based theories.

We will start with some of the more rudimentary rules used in decision making under uncertainty, such as the mean and the mean–variance criterion. We will critique these rules and then introduce VNM axioms of rationality and utility theory.

I assume that students are familiar with the mean–variance decision rule, so we will review it quickly, just to make sure that all students are on the same page. We will also emphasize the shortcomings of this rule for decisions that are not relevant for portfolio choice, which will bring us to recognize the advantages of utility theory.

Choosing between Alternatives According to Their Mean

Faced with several uncertain alternatives, this rule recommends that we select the alternative with the highest mean return/profit. Choosing between alternatives according to their mean return/profit is quite popular, but it is a very elementary rule. Its main drawback is that it disregards differences in the riskiness of the alternatives and the fact that decision makers are typically risk averse.

Risk Aversion and the Mean–Variance Rule

Risk aversion

A decision maker is risk averse if she always prefers a certain value, W_0, over any uncertain alternative with an expected value of W_0.

(Continued)

(Continued)

The mean–variance rule

The mean–variance rule says that choices between risky alternatives are made according to their means and variances. If one alternative has the same mean but a lower variance than the second alternative, the first alternative is preferable. Also, if an alternative has the same variance and the same or higher mean, then it is preferable.

The mean–variance rule is superior to choosing between alternatives according to their means because it does not disregard the riskiness of the alternatives in question. In fact, since its introduction (Markowitz, 1952, 1991), the mean–variance rule has become the primary tool for portfolio diversification used by investors, the majority of pension and mutual funds globally. It is quite popular in decision making in general because it is simple, reasonable, and appropriate for many applications. Let's illustrate how this rule is applied and then discuss some of its pitfalls.

We should note that risk aversion and the mean–variance rule are quite closely related concepts.

Applying the Mean–Variance Rule

Set 1:

Alternative A: Receive $1,000 with certainty.
Alternative B: A 50% chance of receiving $500 and a 50% chance of receiving $1,500.

Set 2:

Alternative C: Receive $1,000 with certainty.
Alternative D: A 50% chance of receiving $500 and a 50% chance of receiving $2,000.

In Set 1, both alternatives have the same mean, but Alternative B is more risky (it has a greater variance) and hence it is less preferable.

In Set 2, Alternative C is the less risky option, but it offers a lower mean return. In this case, the mean–variance rule cannot help us determine whether Alternative C is better than Alternative D.

Below, we discuss the deficiencies of the mean variance rule. These must be interpreted cautiously relative to its importance.

The Mean–Variance Rule has Some Problems

Problem #1: It gives only partial ordering of the alternatives.

Problem #2: It fails theoretically because it mainly applies to relatively symmetric distributions and quadratic utility functions.

Problem #3: It sometimes leads to unreasonable conclusions.

Problem #1: It gives only partial ordering of the alternatives

In many choices between alternatives, the mean–variance rule cannot determine the best alternative (this is what we mean by partial ordering). For example, if one alternative has both a higher mean and a greater variance than the other, the rule cannot determine the preferable alternative. This was the case in Set 2 in our example above.

Problem #2: It fails theoretically because it mainly applies to relatively symmetric distributions and quadratic utility functions

Although the mean and the variance are two very important features of the distribution of profits and/or returns, the mean–variance rule ignores other important properties including asymmetry, maximal loss, and minimal profits. As a result, the rule is appropriate only under certain conditions: when returns are normally distributed or investors have a quadratic utility function. An examination of returns of several asset classes shows that traditional instruments such as stocks or bonds do demonstrate distributions that are more or less approximated by normal, but in many other cases, the mean–variance rule is inappropriate (for example, derivatives which show a high level of irregularity, such as skewness and kurtosis excess), most hedge funds (which generate asymmetrical returns), and insurance decisions (where losses are quite skewed and far from normal). One therefore must be very cautious about when to use the mean–variance rule and when to avoid it.

Problem #3: It sometimes leads to unreasonable conclusions

In some cases, application of the mean–variance rule will yield non-sensical results!

The Mean–Variance Rule Can Lead to Bad Decisions

Consider the following decision sets which are slight variations of Sets 1 and 2 above:

Set 3:
Alternative E: Receive $1,000 with certainty.
Alternative F: Receive $10,000 with a probability of 95.5% or $0 with a probability of 0.5%.

Set 4:
Alternative G: Receive $1,000 with certainty.
Alternative H: Receive $1,000 with a probability of 50% or $2,000 with a probability of 50%.

Using the mean–variance criterion, we cannot decide between E and F since E has a lower mean than F ($1,000 vs. $9,550) and also lower variance (0, vs. a positive variance in F). And yet, almost all reasonable decision makers will choose F!

If we add a colorful narrative, we can see how the preference for Alternative F might be justified in some circumstances: Suppose the decision maker needs $1,000 to buy a life-saving medication. In this case, he will prefer Alternative E, since any amount above $1,000 is useless to him. Obviously, this is a very unique scenario.

An automatic application of the mean–variance rule to choose between Alternatives G and H might lead to even more illogical decisions. In Set 4, Alternative H dominates G since it yields the same or higher returns than alternative G in all cases — and yet, the mean–variance rule does not rule in H's favor because H is riskier! Paradoxes like these that result from an application of the mean–variance rule prompted the introduction of the stochastic dominance ordering principle, which does not allow them (see Levy, 2015).

Utility Theory

➤ Utility theory is a more elegant and theoretically sound theory of choice than the mean–variance rule.

➤ Utility theory is not plagued by the three deficiencies of the mean–variance rule.

➤ This theory has its own deficiencies.

➤ Let's start with its origins and move on to discuss its applications.

The Origins of Utility Theory and Bernoulli's Paradox

The origins of utility theory can be traced back to Bernoulli's Paradox (or the St. Petersburg Paradox). This problem was discovered by the 18th century Swiss mathematician Nicolaus Bernoulli and was published by his brother Daniel in the St. Petersburg Academy Proceedings (1738, English trans. 1954), which explains why it is also known as the St. Petersburg Paradox.

The theory was further developed by VNM in their 1944 book. Since then, despite some criticism, utility theory has been used as the basis for the most economic theory. In their book, VNM present several axioms that define rationality and show that for rational decision makers, a utility function exists such that the optimal decision rule for choosing between alternatives is to choose the alternative with the highest expected utility.

The Bernoulli (St. Petersburg) Paradox

Players are offered the following game: A fair coin with an equal chance of heads (H) or tails (T) is flipped. The player receives a prize according to the number of flips until the coin comes up T. If a T comes up on the first flip, the player receives \$2, if a T comes up on the second flip, she receives \$4, if T comes up on the nth flip, the player receives $\$2^n$ and so on.

How much would you pay to participate in this game?

Bernoulli introduced this paradox to illustrate the limitations of choosing between alternatives according to their expected values, and he proposed an alternative method of choice based on this experiment. Although Bernoulli's theory is not as elegant and self-contained as the later version developed by VNM and therefore did not prevail, Bernoulli's achievement is definitely no mean feat keeping in mind that it was made two centuries before VNM published their own work.

Let's return to the game: Bernoulli found that the average price players were willing to pay to participate was, on average, \$4. This is surprising because the expected value of this lottery is infinite, as can be seen from the following calculation:

$$V = E[X] = \sum 2^n \times (1/2)^n = \infty$$

Why were people only willing to pay \$4 for a game in which they might win an infinitely large sum of money? One possible explanation is that people are overwhelmingly risk averse. Bernoulli, though, had an alternative explanation for the unexpected choices of the participants of his experiments.

Bernoulli's Theory

Bernoulli suggested that the value of lotteries like this (in decision making under uncertainty, uncertain alternatives are often called lotteries) is given by the expected value of the natural logarithm of the proceeds the lottery yields. Therefore, decision makers decide how much they are willing to pay to participate in the game based on the expected value of the natural logarithm of the proceeds from the game. In the case of the above lottery, the expected utility of a participant is given by

$$V = E[\ln(X)] = \sum \ln(2^n) \times (1/2)^n$$

In this formula, X is the random variable denoting the proceeds from the lottery, n is the number of flips of the coin until T appears, P_n is the probability that T will appear after n flips of the coin. To support his theory, Bernoulli brought his empirical finding that people were willing to pay no more than four ducats on average (the currency they used in his experiment was ducats) for his lottery. The expected value of the natural logarithm of the proceeds of this lottery can be shown to equal $\ln(4)$. Bernoulli thus concluded that $\ln(x)$ is a good representation of the utility function.

This argument of course is hardly convincing evidence as the basis of a well-founded theory. It is too much *ad hoc* and based on one very specific lottery. Surprisingly, the amount offered for this lottery in many experiments was not that far from what Bernoulli obtained.

The Definition of Utility Theory

Utility theory posits that, provided that decision makers are rational, their preferences can be described by some utility function such that decision makers choose between alternatives according to their utility's expected value:

$$V = E[u(X)] = \sum u(Xi)P_i$$

Instead of the logarithmic function proposed by Bernoulli, which is somewhat arbitrary, utility theory asserts that if decision makers are rational, their preferences can be represented by some utility function $u(x)$, such that the decision makers choose between alternatives according to their expected value or expected utility. Accordingly, a decision maker prefers alternative X to alternative Y if

$$V_X = \Sigma u(x_i)p_i > V_y = \Sigma u(y_j)p_j$$

In the above formula, V_x and V_y represent the expected utility of alternatives X and Y, respectively, $u(x_i)$ and $u(y_j)$ represent the utilities from the possible realization of the uncertain alternatives, and p_i and p_j represent their probabilities.

In some sense, the utility function describes the welfare, satisfaction, or happiness that the DM obtains from each alternative. The utility function represents just an ordinal ordering (the alternatives are only ranked and there is no meaning to the scale of the utility): The higher the expected utility/welfare of an alternative, the more desirable it is. According to utility theory, decision makers choose the course of action that yields the highest level of expected welfare or satisfaction and not the option that will generate the greatest expected wealth.

Unlike Bernoulli who specified the exact form of the utility function, VNM only argued that such a function exists for rational decision makers. On the other hand, VNM were the first to formulate the requirements (or axioms) that define rational decision making and showed that if people are rational (if they conform to the axioms), their preferences can be described as a utility function. Empirically, however, there are some restrictions on the possible form that a utility function can assume.

The Properties of a Typical Utility Function

Figure 2.1 shows a typical utility function. The horizontal axis measures the decision maker's final wealth, w, that is, her wealth after resolving the uncertainty. The vertical axis represents her utility, $u(w)$, and each point on the function represents an alternative that the decision maker can choose. The function is *increasing in wealth*, meaning that more wealth is always preferable to less wealth. It is also *concave*, which means it reflects diminishing marginal utility: the wealthier you are, the less each additional dollar adds to your utility. It can also be shown that diminishing marginal utility implies risk aversion and vice versa, but we'll skip the proof.

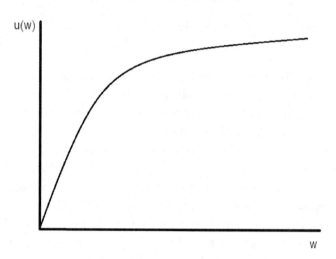

Figure 2.1. A typical utility function.

More on the Properties of the Utility Function

(1) Decisions are made based on one's final wealth.

In utility theory, utility (or welfare) is defined on the decision maker's final wealth, or his absolute situation after making the decision, and not on the profits that each alternative generates, which typically are independent of the decision maker's wealth.

Final wealth is thus composed of the initial wealth (the wealth prior to making a decision) plus the profits/losses that the decision generates. This implies that initial wealth is central to the decision-making process.

The main reasons for defining utility on the decision maker's final wealth rather than on her profits is that the decision maker's final wealth, not her profits, determines her consumption/savings opportunities and consequently her welfare. The implications of a risky project involving the possibility of losing, say, $100,000 are much more serious for less wealthy people. A rich person may therefore be more willing than a less wealthy individual to engage in the risky project.

We stress the point that in utility theory, utility is defined on wealth because this is one of the main differences between utility theory and prospect theory, which, as we shall see later, is one of the cornerstones of behavioral finance. In prospect theory, the preferences of the decision maker are defined on profits/losses and not on final wealth.

(2) People are generally risk averse.

The assumption of risk aversion is well accepted by utility theory, although the proponents of utility theory disagree on some of the specifics of the effects of wealth on risk aversion. (Prospect theory has serious reservations about the assumption of risk aversion and contends that in many situations, people are not risk averse but rather risk loving.)

Pratt, 1992, defined relative and absolute measures of risk aversion in the following manner: Relative (absolute) risk aversion measures the extent to which decision makers are averse to a small lottery that proportionally (absolutely) affects their wealth. Empirical tests designed to show the effects of wealth on these measures offer inconclusive results.

Unfortunately, it is impossible to determine the exact form of people's utility function. Most researchers in finance theory assume a constant relative risk aversion (CRRA) function. The usual argument in favor of this assumption is that since it measures aversion to relative changes in wealth, the absolute level of wealth is immaterial. The CRRA functions became popular among academic scholars also due to their convenience for model formulation and obtaining theoretical results. In many applications, however, diminishing absolute risk aversion seems to make sense: Extremely wealthy people are not likely to be afraid to take small risks.

For decades, researchers have been puzzled by the phenomenon that people can simultaneously exhibit risk-averse and risk-seeking behaviors, for example, by buying both insurance policies and lottery tickets. The best explanation for this phenomenon seems to have been proposed by Friedman and Savage as early as 1948, and I haven't encountered a better one yet. They suggest that people are risk averse when it comes to decisions that might cause them to experience a drop in their wealth, but are risk seeking with respect to decisions that offer the possibility of gains that would put them in a higher economic class.

Incidentally, several economists (for example, see Dunn and Norton, 2012) using income rather than wealth have argued that although "more" is preferable to "less" for most people, there is a point between $60,00 and $75,000 (but not in current $) where additional income does not increase happiness significantly. From that point on the income scale and upwards, people's happiness depends more strongly on how they spend their money rather than on how much they earn. This argument implies that if the utility function represents happiness, we can expect it to plateau at a surprisingly low level of income. But a lot more research is needed to explore just how generalizable these findings are.

Using Utility Theory for Decision Making: The Effect of Wealth

A student has to decide whether to enroll in a graduate program in finance. The cost of the program is $25,000 (to be paid immediately). The present value of the salary increases that he expects after graduating from the program are uncertain and could be either $50,000 at a probability of 50% or $2,000 at a probability of 50%.

Should the student enroll in the program?

This example is important for two reasons. First, it shows how utility theory can be applied in practice, and second, it highlights the importance of wealth in decision making. This will stand in contrast to prospect theory, which practically ignores initial wealth and concentrates on gains and losses.

Solution of the Decision Problem

The expected net present value of the project is:

$$-\$25,000 + (\$50,000 \times 0.5) + (\$2,000 \times 0.5) = \$1,000$$

The program thus seems a good one as it provides a positive net present value. But are the benefits worth the risk?

Let us see what utility theory says about this.

Assume first that the student's utility function is given by $u(w) = \sqrt{w}$ and that his initial wealth, w_0, is \$200,000 (we will then examine how the solution changes when his initial wealth is lower). The assumption concerning the utility function is somewhat arbitrary (not being able to specify the exact form of the utility function of a decision maker is one of the major obstacles to the application of utility theory). This function is, however, consistent with the concept of CRRA used in most research in finance and the same qualitative results are expected with other utility functions of the same family.

If the student forgoes the graduate program in finance, his expected utility will be

$$E[u(w_0)] = u(200{,}000) = 447.21$$

If the student enrolls in the program, his final wealth will be w_1 in the case his salary increase is \$50,000, or w_2 if it is \$2,000, where

$$w_1 = 200{,}000 - 25{,}000 + 50{,}000 = \$225{,}000$$

$$w_2 = 200{,}000 - 25000 + 2{,}000 = \$177{,}000$$

The student's expected utility in this case will be

$$E[u(w)] = 0.5\sqrt{w_1} + 0.5\sqrt{w_2} = 0.5\sqrt{225{,}000}$$
$$+ 0.5\sqrt{177{,}000} = 447.53$$

The student will therefore enroll in the program because he enjoys a higher expected utility than if he forgoes the program.

But What if the Student is Less Wealthy?

Suppose now that the student's initial wealth is lower, say \$75,000. We repeat the above process, except that we replace \$200,000 by \$75,000.

If the student does not enroll in the graduate program in finance, his expected utility will be

$$E[u(w_0)] = u(75{,}000) = 273.86$$

If he enrolls, his final wealth will be w_1 if the salary increase is $50,000, or w_2 if it is $2,000, where

$$w_1 = 75{,}000 - 25{,}000 + 50{,}000 = \$100{,}000$$

$$w_2 = 75{,}000 - 25{,}000 + 2{,}000 = \$52{,}000$$

and his expected utility is

$$E[u(w)] = 0.5\sqrt{w_1} + 0.5\sqrt{w_2} = 0.5\sqrt{100{,}000}$$
$$+ 0.5\sqrt{52{,}000} = 272.13$$

In this case, the student will decline the opportunity to earn an advanced degree.

The moral of this example for decision makers is that initial wealth affects decisions. Those interested in social justice and education might infer that (higher) education increases income inequality because wealthier students would invest in the graduate program that provides a positive net present value, but poorer students would not, and the gap between the two groups would grow wider.

What does it Mean to be a Rational Decision Maker?

There are many definitions of rationality, but we use VNM's axioms to define rational behavior. They showed that if a person conforms to these axioms of rational behavior, then there exists a utility function that describes her decision making.

Rationality axioms

1. **Ability to choose**: Given any two alternatives, A and B, a rational decision maker can decide whether $A \succ B$, $B \succ A$ or $A \approx B$ (note that the symbol $\succ$ represents "preferable to" and the symbol $\approx$ represents "equivalent to").

This axiom may seem trivial, but actually it is not. Often people do not find it easy to decide among several alternatives and therefore they may procrastinate or decide not to choose.

Tversky and Shafir (1992) expand on option overload or choice overload — the difficulty to make a choice when there are numerous alternatives. They show that when the set of alternatives is enlarged, people increasingly tend to choose the default alternative. In an experiment they conducted, participants could choose between a default prize of $1.5 and a specific prize (a pen known to be valued at $2). One-quarter of the participants chose the default prize. When another prize was added to the choice set, the number of participants who chose the default rose to 53%. When many equivalent choices are available, decision making becomes an overwhelming and mentally draining task due to the numerous potential risks and outcomes resulting from the wrong choice. As a result, the satisfaction that the decision maker gains from the availability of a greater range of choices may decrease as the number of added alternatives increases, to the point at which some decision makers may be paralyzed and unable to make any decision.

2. **Transitivity**: If $A \succ B$, and $B \succ C$, then $A \succ C$.

Transitivity in preference is similar to transitivity between numbers. It says that if we prefer apples to oranges and oranges to bananas, then we should prefer apples to bananas. However, it is not a universally accepted axiom when A, B and C represent non-monetary alternatives. Transitivity is not what we have in elections or in sports competitions: team A might beat team B, and team B might beat team C, and yet team C might beat team A. Also, in the above "fruity" example, transitivity need not hold.

We can, however, make a positive argument that transitivity is beneficial for the decision maker. Let us use an example adapted from Raiffa (1993): Suppose that a decision maker (DM) does not comply with transitivity, say her preferences are: $A \succ B$, $B \succ C$, but $C \succ A$. Assume she already owns A. Since C is preferable to A, the decision maker would be willing to pay some small amount, say \$1 to replace A with C. The DM now has C. Since she prefers B to C, she would be willing to replace C by B and pay a small amount, say \$1, for the exchange. The DM now has B. However, since she prefers B to A she will be willing to replace B with A and pay \$1 for it. The DM is back where she started, except that she is \$3 poorer.

3. **Continuity**

   Let x, y and z denote different alternatives such that $x \succ y \succ z$. Continuity means that there is some probability p such that the decision maker will be indifferent between receiving y for certain or receiving x with a probability p, or z with the complementary probability $(1 - p)$.

4. **Independence of Irrelevant Alternatives** (IIRA)

   This axiom means that if we choose x over y from the set of alternatives (x, y) then we choose x over y also from the set (x, y, z). That is, adding the possibility of choosing z does not alter the preference between x and y.

   This, as we shall see in future classes, is the most controversial of all axioms, and most examples of decision makers' deviations from rationality stem from violations of this axiom (that is, enlarging the set of alternatives changes the preference between the original ones).

   We intuitively understand that this axiom does not hold in all situations. In elections, this axiom would not hold because the addition of additional candidates (alternatives) often alters the preference between the original candidates. For example, assume an election with two candidates, A and B, and 100 voters. In the case that 60% of the voters prefer A and 40% prefer B, A wins the election. Now, assume that a new candidate C enters the race, and "steals" voters from A. The preferences now become 30% for A, 40% for B and 30% for C. In this case, B wins the election.

   Here is another example of dependence of alternatives:

A woman sitting at a table in a restaurant is offered a steak or a hamburger. She orders the steak. Upon receiving the order, the waiter says that he forgot to mention that fish was also available that day. The woman then says, "In that case, I will take the hamburger." The logic behind this dependence is that the availability of fish on the menu may signal that the restaurant does not specialize in meat, and in that case, a hamburger may seem a safer choice than a steak.

Axioms that VNM did not include

Many people think that preferring more wealth to less is always rational, but this kind of thinking is not required in the VNM axioms (it is perfectly rational for people to donate money or even to throw away money if it pleases them). People also often identify rationality with risk aversion, but also this is necessary neither according to utility theory nor according to prospect theory.

Can Individuals Make Rational Choices?

➤ In their innovative and somewhat provocative 2009 book, "Nudge," Thaler and Sunstein (TS) argue that sometimes decision makers need some "help" or need to be "nudged" into making good decisions, especially when some individuals lack self-control. According to TS, a nudge is anything that influences our choices.

➤ Dividends and self-control.

Given that many people choose the default alternative when making choices, defaults can be designed to steer people toward a specific (desirable) outcome. A well-known example is to make the default option on a person's driver's license state that the driver agrees to be a donor, rather than requiring her to check a box. In this "nudge," a person has to make a conscious effort to opt out of being an organ donor. But nudging people in a good direction involves more than default options. TS recommend the use of "choice architecture," which involves the design of the context in which people make choices. A school wishing to nudge kids into making healthy choices in the cafeteria should consider what foods to put in the most visible and accessible locations, and what foods to make less accessible, or, in other words, design the setting in which the kids make their food choices. Of course, supermarkets (and restaurants) have been using "choice architecture" for years, but they were not nudging consumers to buy healthy food — their goal was to encourage people to buy products that would maximize the stores' profits.

The cafeteria could have easily banned all unhealthy food simply by not ordering it from its suppliers, but to TS this seems too much of an infringement of the kids' freedom of choice. TS would like policy makers to use choice architecture to improve people's lives without making decisions for them.

The difference between nudging and deciding for others is subtle. TS could have suggested a more traditional method of inhibiting actions: a pricing scheme where taxes are levied on the unhealthy items (these items would then be priced higher), but they prefer nudging. They do not, however, demonstrate that their method is more effective. TS consider nudging a good, feasible compromise between leaving people completely free to make decisions on alternatives they have little knowledge of and policy makers forcing people to make specific decisions.

Nudging involves influencing people who might lack self-control (cannot say no to junk food well aware it is not good for them). Behavioral finance scientists used lack of self-control to explain some phenomena in corporate finance. For example, Shefrin and Statman (1984) argue that many investors lack self-control and therefore adopt some decision rules to overcome the tendency to succumb to temptation and spend frivolously non-steady income. They suggest that individuals' preference for dividends, in spite of the tax disadvantages of dividends vs. capital gains, can be explained by self-control. One rule that households sometimes use to prevent overspending is to only spend the dividends and not touch capital gains. Dividend-paying firms thus help them adhere to this rule.

Conclusion

➤ We defined risk aversion.

➤ We reviewed and critiqued the basic decision-making rules — the mean and mean–variance rules — and assessed their limitations.

➤ We introduced utility theory and demonstrated how to apply it in practice.

➤ We explained what it means to be a rational decision maker based on VNM's axioms.

➤ We showed the effect of wealth on decision making.

➤ We discussed the role of choice architecture and nudging in decision making.

CRITIQUE OF UTILITY THEORY, THE ASSUMPTION OF RATIONALITY AND THE EFFICIENT MARKETS HYPOTHESIS

Agenda

➤ Early Examples of Rationality Violations:

  ✓ Allais Paradox

  ✓ Ellsberg's Paradox

➤ Critique of the Early Paradoxes

➤ The "new wave" Evidence (late 1970s early 1980s) in Finance and Psychology Leading to Behavioral Finance:

  ✓ Excess volatility

  ✓ Siamese Twin Shares Royal Dutch/Shell Transport

  ✓ Index inclusion

➤ Kahneman and Tversky's Examples of Cognitive Biases — I:

  ✓ Representativeness

  ✓ Conservatism

The Allais Paradox illustrates that there are some circumstances in which decision makers behave in a manner inconsistent with utility theory.

The Ellsberg Paradox illustrates that in some circumstances, especially when faced with ambiguity, decision makers' decisions cannot be explained by utility theory.

The Allais Paradox

Participants (subjects) are given two sets of choices:

Set 1:

Participants are asked to choose between two urns, A and B, which are filled with balls. Participants may pick at random one ball from the selected urn and receive a prize according to the ball's color. The urns differed in the composition of balls they contained:

Urn A contains: 100 black balls (prize is $1,000,000)

Urn B contains: 10 red balls (prize is $5,000,000)
                    89 black balls (prize is $1,000,000)
                    1 yellow ball (prize is zero)

Most subjects chose Urn A.

Set 2:

Similar to Set 1 except that participants were asked to choose between:

Urn C contains: 11 black balls (prize is $1,000,000)
                    89 yellow balls (prize is zero)

Urn D contains: 10 red balls (prize is $5,000,000)
                    90 yellow balls (prize is zero)

Most players chose Urn D.

How do these Choices Violate Utility Theory?

The Allais Paradox, based on an experiment conducted by Allais in 1953, demonstrates that people behave irrationally by illustrating the inconsistency between utility theory and human reasoning. Here is a formal proof:

We assume that a utility function exists and show that the decisions illustrated above are inconsistent or lead to a contradiction.

Note first that the utilities can be calibrated so that $u(1) = 1$ and $u(0) = 0$.

When A is preferred to B in Set 1, we infer that

$$u(1) > 0.1u(5) + 0.89u(1) + 0.01u(0)$$
$$\rightarrow 0.11u(1) > 0.1$$
$$\rightarrow u(1) > 0.1/0.11$$

When D is preferred to C in Set 2, we infer that

$$0.11u(1) + 0.89u(0) < 0.1u(5) + 0.9u(0)$$
$$\rightarrow 0.11u(1) < 0.1u(5)$$
$$\rightarrow u(1) < 0.1/0.11$$

This inequality is the opposite of the inequality obtained from the choice in Set 1, which implies a contradiction.

Possible Explanations for the Allais Paradox

➢ Regret
➢ Certainty premium
➢ Which axiom is violated in Allais Paradox?

· *Regret*

By choosing A, a person guarantees his welfare, and by choosing B, he may jeopardize this by being overly greedy. If he chooses B and it turns out that his prize is zero, he will regret having made the wrong decision because he knows that had he chosen A, he would have guaranteed a millionaire status, albeit not as comfortable as with a $5 million prize. This decision might haunt him for the rest of his life. He avoids this possibility if he chooses A.

Certainty premium

In alternative A, the prize is sure. It has been argued by psychologists (as we shall see later when discussing prospect theory) that sure prizes receive higher weights than uncertain ones in the subjective expected utility calculation of individuals. The special weight the sure prize receives in Allais' experiment is not reflected in the utility calculations and this leads to the paradox.

Which axiom is violated in Allais Paradox?

Notwithstanding the intuitive appeal of the explanation for the paradox and its formal proof, they do not point out which VNM axiom is violated. According to VNM, if their rationality axioms prevail, then a utility function representing the preferences of the decision makers exist. Since apparently it does not, the question arises: the violation of which of the axioms is the culprit?

It can be shown that it is the independence of irrelevant alternatives (IIRA) axiom which is violated in Allais Paradox. Note in Table 3.1 that by replacing 89 black balls in Urns A and B with yellow balls, we obtain urns A' and B' (see Set 1') which are the same as Urns C and D, respectively. However, according to the IIRA, if we delete the same number of "good" balls both from A and B, this should not alter the preference between them, hence if A is preferred to B, C must be preferred to D. In practice however the participants reverse their preference and prefer D over C.

Most people will choose B over A, but at the same time choose C over D. These choices illustrate that there are circumstances in which people do not behave as predicted by utility theory.

The Ellsberg Paradox — Ambiguity Aversion

This paradox is another example of choices that don't follow expected utility theory.

Participants face an urn containing 30 red balls (Red) and 60 balls that are either yellow (Yellow) or green (Green) balls. Participants

Table 3.1.

Set 1

Urn A	Urn B
100 B ($1 m)	10 R ($5 m)
	89 B ($1 m)
	1 Y ($0 m)

Set 2

Urn C	Urn D
11 B ($1 m)	10 R ($5 m)
89 Y (0$ m)	90 Y ($0 m)

Set 1′

Urn A′	Urn B′
~~100 B ($1 m)~~	10 R ($5 m)
11 B ($1 m)	~~89 B ($1 m)~~
89 Y (0 m)	90 Y ($0 m)

do not know how many of the 60 non-red balls are yellow and how many are green.

Two sets of experiments were run: In each experiment, the player must choose between two gambles:

Set 1:

A: Get a $100 prize if you draw a red ball

B: Get a $100 prize if you draw a yellow ball

Set 2:

C: Get a $100 prize if you draw either a red ball or a green ball

D: Get a $100 prize if you draw a yellow ball or a green ball

Most players chose A over B, and D over C.

Where is the paradox?

From Set 1, we infer that the probability of Red is higher than that of Yellow because the same prize is awarded when the participant picks

Red or Yellow and hence, the choice of A over B implies that the participant believes Red is more probable than Yellow. Thus, from Set 1: $P(\text{Red}) > P(\text{Yellow})$.

From Set 2, we infer that the probability of the aggregate of a yellow ball or a green ball is higher than that of red or green balls because the prize awarded when the participant picks D is higher than C. That is, $P(\text{Red or Green}) < P(\text{Yellow or Green})$. However, since the number of green balls in C is the same as that in D, the choice of D implies that the participant believes there are more yellow balls than red ones, that is he believes that $P(\text{Red}) < P(\text{Yellow})$. A contradiction has thus been reached.

The choices of the participants were probably guided by ambiguity. The preference of Red over Yellow in Set 1 can be attributed to the fact that the probability of Red is known to be $1/3^{\text{rd}}$ whereas the probability of Yellow is ambiguous (although it is reasonable to assume it is also $1/3^{\text{rd}}$). The participants presumably also prefer the aggregate Yellow and Green in Set 2 because the probability of this aggregate is known whereas that of Red and Green is ambiguous.

The paradox, or contradiction, emerges as a result of a violation of the independence from irrelevant alternatives (IIRA) axiom. As in the case of Allais Paradox, once the same change has been introduced to the two alternatives, the preference between the alternative has changed. In the Ellsberg Paradox, the same number of green balls were added to the alternatives causing the preference between them to reverse.

There are many variations on the Ellsberg Paradox. Here is one

Suppose there are two urns. Urn A contains 50 red balls and 50 black balls and Urn B contains a mixture of both red and black balls, but you do not know how many of each color are there. You have to choose either Urn A or Urn B and then draw a ball at random from it. If you pick a red ball, you win a prize.

If you are like most people you will choose Urn A. This choice implies that you believe that the probability that Urn B contains a red ball is less than 50%. Now, the same experiment is repeated, but you are promised a prize if you draw a black ball from the urn you pick. Again, you will most likely prefer Urn A, implying that the probability that Urn B contains a black ball is less than 50%. It hence follows that you believe that the probability that Urn B contains a black ball is less than 50% and at the same time, you believe that the probability that Urn B contains a red ball is less than 50%! This is impossible because the two probabilities must add up to 100%.

People seem to be averse to ambiguity; they prefer alternatives that have well-defined probabilities over alternatives that have ambiguous probabilities.

Heath and Tversky (1991) suggest that people prefer to bet on alternatives over which they have more control or about which they are more competent to bet. Since the players in this experiment feel more knowledgeable about the bet when they know the probability for certain, their choices are in line with Heath and Tversky's hypothesis, but may be inconsistent with VNM's axioms.

Critique of the Early Paradoxes

➤ Unrealistic situations
➤ Prize size

Unrealistic situations

Are the situations described in these two paradoxes realistic? The answer is no, especially for Allais Paradox. The options given to the players (in millions of dollars) are somewhat contrived and therefore are not strong enough to disprove utility theory.

Prize size

The size of the prizes offered in these alternatives magnifies the effect of regret because of the size of the prizes. In real life, people do not get such opportunities worth millions. Ellsberg Paradox does not involve huge sums of money and hence in this respect, it is fine, yet it is too particular to be able to overthrow utility theory.

> Advances in psychology and finance in the late 1970s and early 1980s paving the way to behavioral finance

In the first part of this lecture, we discussed the state of the art in the early 1970s in decision theory. Utility theory and rationality seemed to be good representatives of individuals' decision making. Mainstream finance researchers felt that the few paradoxes that were discovered were not serious enough to discredit rationality and besides there were no alternative theories. The above-mentioned anomalies, according to mainstream finance, did not warrant rejecting the efficient market hypothesis.

Things have changed in the late 1970s and early 1980s. New evidence in a new style emerged against the market efficiency, and the research of Tversky and Kahneman not only added new evidence against utility theory but also provided prospect theory as an alternative to utility theory.

> ### The New Wave of Market Efficiency Criticism
> ➤ Excess volatility
> ➤ Siamese Twin shares Royal Dutch/Shell Transport
> ➤ Index inclusion

In the early 1980s, more evidence refuting the efficiency of the market appeared. Notable among them was the evidence presented by Shiller (1981), showing that the stock market is excessively volatile. Shiller's studies were published almost concurrently with the new understanding of psychological biases discovered by Kahneman and Tversky (see below), whose accomplishments were the impetus for the development of behavioral finance.

This section presents only some examples of the evidence that emerged in the late 1970s and early 1980s. More will be presented in Lecture 12.

Excess volatility

In an efficient market, the value of stocks should equal the present
value of the cash flows they provide. The volatility of stocks should
therefore equal the volatility of the present value of the stocks' dividends. Shiller (1981) challenged the efficiency of the market by showing that the volatility of the (entire) stock market is much greater
than the volatility of the dividends, i.e., the cash flows the stocks
included in the stock market produce. Shiller demonstrated this rig-
orously in his paper, but a visual inspection of Figure 3.1 adds an
intuitive appeal. In this figure, one observes that real stock prices
were much more volatile than PDV, the present discounted value of
the dividends.

Additions to the S&P 500 index

Several researchers showed that when a stock is added to the S&P500
index, its price increases. According to Harris and Gurel (1986) and

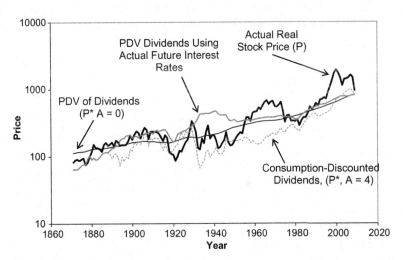

Figure 3.1. Comparing actual real stock prices with three alternative PDVs of
future real dividends.

Source: Data from Robert Shiller's Website: http://www.econ.yale.edu/~shiller/
data.htm.

Shleifer (1986), the increase is 3.5% on average; when Yahoo was added to the index, its price jumped by 24% in a single day. Since such additions to the index do not represent an increase in cash flows, these price increases seem to violate efficiency (although such increases could be justified by an increase in the stock's liquidity and the information that this change in status conveys).

Twin shares

Another example of findings presented as evidence that the stock market was inefficient involves twin shares. In 1907, Royal Dutch and Shell Transport, completely independent companies at the time, agreed to merge their interests on a 60:40 basis, while remaining as separate entities. Shares of Royal Dutch, which are primarily traded in the US and the Netherlands, received a 60% stake in the total of the two companies, and Shell, which trades primarily in the UK, has the remaining 40%. Therefore, after the merger, we could expect the price of Royal Dutch shares to be exactly 1.5 times the price of Shell shares. One can see however from Figure 3.2, which plots the deviations of the actual prices of these firms from the theoretical 1.5, that this was not the case for many periods.

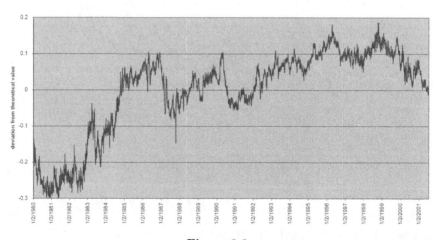

Figure 3.2.

Source: Ritter (2003).

Almost concurrent with the above-mentioned developments in finance, Kahneman and Tversky and many of their students and colleagues made important strides in psychology which cast doubt on the generality of the rational behavior of decision makers.

Kahneman and Tversky (KT): The New Wave of Paradoxes

Cognitive biases á la Kahneman and Tversky (since the early 1970s):

➤ A new version of Allais Paradox.
➤ A wide variety of new biases.
➤ Biases are classified into a small number of categories.

There are several important attractions to KT's paradoxes and biases. First, unlike the Allais Paradox, they typically deal with real-life situations. Therefore, their claim that they represent how people actually behave is credible. Second, they provide an extensive list of real life biases, thus highlighting the prevalence of cognitive biases, and third, they classify cognitive and psychological biases into several broad categories. This classification brings order to the world of biases, since in principle, there are infinite ways in which people can be irrational. Or to rephrase the opening line in Anna Karenina (Tolstoy, 1877) which says: "All happy families are alike but each unhappy family is unhappy in its own way": All rational people behave the same, but there are infinite ways to be irrational. By introducing some order to the chaotic world of biases, KT enabled the possibility of a more productive analysis of cognitive biases. Incidentally, since Tolstoy's time, advances have also been made in the marital (un)happiness knowledge and researchers were able to classify and narrow down considerably dysfunctional marital relationship styles.

The first KT bias presented here is a version of the Allais Paradox that KT framed using thousands of dollars instead of millions. This demonstrates how KT worked carefully to ensure that their paradoxes were better aligned with real-life situations. Hence, their criticism of utility theory is more convincing. We then introduce several new paradoxes developed by KT and their colleagues.

KT's version of Allais Paradox

The experiment conducted by KT is similar to Allais' experiments but with smaller prizes. This version is designed to address the criticism that the Allais Paradox uses unrealistically high rewards and therefore, its results can be explained by regret. Since KT's version of the Allais Paradox uses smaller rewards (no greater than $2,500), their scenario is more realistic, and the regret effect is smaller.

Set 1

Urn A:

      100 black ball (get $2,400)

Urn B:

      33 red balls (get $2,500)

      66 black balls (get $2,400)

      1 yellow ball (get nothing)

Most players choose A.

Set 2

Urn C:

      34 black balls (get $2,400)

      66 yellow balls (get nothing)

Urn D:

      33 red balls (get $2,500)

      67 yellow balls (get nothing)

Most players choose D.

Like Allais Paradox, this result also contradicts utility theory, but the result is shown to emerge in a more realistic scenario and cannot as easily be attributed to the regret effect.

Formal Proof of Inconsistency with Utility Theory

Scale: $u(2{,}500) = 1$ and $u(0) = 0$

Preference of A over B implies:

$$u(2{,}400) > 0.33u(0) + 0.66u(2{,}400)$$

$$\rightarrow u(2{,}400) > 0.33/0.34$$

Preference of D over C implies:

$$0.33 > 0.34u(2{,}400)$$

$$\rightarrow u(2{,}400) < 0.33/0.34$$

A contradiction is reached.

Which axiom is violated?

Like the Allais Paradox, the KT version also illustrates a violation of the IIRA axiom as can be inferred from Table 3.2. By replacing 66 of the black balls both in Urn A and Urn B in Set 1, we obtain Set 1′ which is exactly the same as Set 2. According to the IIRA, if participants prefer Urn A, to Urn B in Set 1, they should also prefer Urn C to Urn D. Since on the contrary, they prefer D to C, a violation of the IIRA axiom has been demonstrated.

KT's Examples of Cognitive Biases — I

➢ Representativeness (Law of small numbers)
➢ Conservatism

These biases were presented to justify prospect theory and to point to the deficiencies of utility theory and challenge the assumption that all decision makers are rational.

Moreover, KT claim that these biases are widespread and systematic. As we shall see later in this course, cognitive biases can also help explain some important phenomena in finance.

Table 3.2.

Set 1	
Urn A	**Urn B**
100 B ($2,400)	33 R ($2,500)
	66 B ($2,400)
	1 Y ($0)

Set 2	
Urn C	**Urn D**
34 B ($2,400)	33 R ($2,500)
66 Y ($0)	67 Y ($0 m)

Set 1′	
Urn A′	**Urn B′**
~~66 B ($1 m)~~	33 R ($2,500)
34 B ($2,400)	~~66 B ($1 m)~~
66 Y ($0)	67 Y ($0)

Representativeness

Representativeness is the bias where people make judgments by a general idea of what the data represent rather than by the data's true implications and significance.

As a result of representativeness, decision makers make inferences based on small samples and identify patterns out of very little (or insufficient) evidence:

In business, for example, several successful quarters can induce people to believe that a firm is profitable.

The "hot hand" fallacy in basketball (or the corresponding "hot" fund manager) — a player is considered "hot" after making few good shots and has a better chance of continuing to make good shots.

This bias causes deviations from rationality in three main ways:

1. Insensitivity to sample size (sarcastically dubbed as "the law of small numbers"): People draw conclusions based on too few observations.
2. Insensitivity to prior probabilities of outcomes: People do not revise their assessment of probability correctly (according to the Bayesian interpretation of probability). They attach too little weight to prior probabilities and attach too much weight to striking new information.
3. Misconceptions of chance: People are not good in distinguishing between sequences of events that are the result of pure chance and those that are systematic. People see patterns in what are actually random sequences. (This can explain some of the popularity of technical analysis).

Representativeness I: Sample size

Consider two hospitals: 45 babies are born each day in one hospital and 15 babies are born each day in the other hospital. Experimenters recorded the number of days on which more than 60% of the babies born in each hospital were boys.

Which hospital had more such days?

When more than 60% of the babies born in a hospital in one day are boys, this is an extreme event, and such events are more likely if the sample size is small. When the sample size is large, the law of large numbers starts to kick in and the chances that the average of a sample will deviate from the actual average become negligible. In this example, this means that as the number of births in a sample increases, the chances that the average percentage of boys born in a day will differ significantly from 50% approach zero.

This logic also explains why weird statistics (such as a high incidence of a strange disease) are often found in small villages and towns. Extreme average occurrence of such diseases is due to the small number of inhabitants in these communities. In large cities, the average incidence of these diseases converges to its statistical mean.

Representativeness II: Misconceptions

Example 1: A fair coin is tossed six times. On each toss, either H (Heads) or T (Tails) shows up.

Which sequence is more likely: HTHTTH or HHHTTT?

More people said the first sequence is more likely although they are equally likely $(1/2^6)$! People look at what each sequence represents. The first one is representative of randomness because we see no order in the appearance of the Hs and Ts. In contrast, the second sequence represents some order or logic.

Example 2: **The Linda Problem**

Participants were presented with the following description of Linda: "Linda is 30 years old, single, outspoken and bright. As a student, she was deeply concerned with issues of social justice and participated in anti-nuclear demonstrations."

The Participants were then Asked to Rank the Following According to Probability:

a. Linda is a teacher in an elementary school.
b. Linda works in a bookstore and takes yoga classes.
c. Linda is an active feminist.
d. Linda is a psychological social worker.
e. Linda is a bank teller.
f. Linda is an insurance saleswoman.
g. Linda is a feminist bank teller.

People rank g higher than e.

That is, people believe that the probability that Linda is a feminist bank teller is greater than the probability that Linda is a bank teller. But of course, the latter option is more probable because the event "is a bank teller" already includes the event "is a feminist bank teller." People apparently focus on what the description represents (a social activist) rather than on the true probabilities. People believe that (g) is more likely than (e) because (g) seems to be more "representative" of Linda, even though it is clearly less likely to happen than (e).

Representativeness III: Underestimation of Base Rates (Overreaction)

In a city, there are 15% blue taxis and 85% green taxis. A taxi was involved in a hit and run, and a witness identified the offender as a blue taxi. It is, however, known that witnesses are reliable only 80% of the time.

What is the probability that the taxi that caused the accident is a blue taxi?

On average, people said 65%, but they were overreacting to the new information about the offender by the witness. According to Bayes' theorem, the correct answer that the offending vehicle was a blue taxi is 41%:

According to Bayes rule, the posterior probability that the hitter is a blue car having heard the witness say it is blue ("blue") is given by the following formula (which is the ratio of the probability that the hitter is blue and the witness declares "blue" and the probability that the witness will declare "blue").

Prob(blue/"blue")

$$= \frac{\text{Prob}(\text{"blue"}/\text{blue})\text{Prob}(\text{"blue"})}{\text{Prob}(\text{"blue"}/\text{blue})\text{Prob}(\text{blue}) + \text{Prob}(\text{"blue"}/\text{green})\text{Prob}(\text{green})}$$

$$= \frac{0.8 * 0.15}{0.8 * 0.15 + 0.2 * 0.85} = 0.41$$

But, people responding to this question usually gave a higher estimate, 65% on average, possibly because they did not consider the low percentage of blue taxis in the city (the prior probability). They underestimated the importance of the base information and overreacted to the information given by the witness.

Conservatism

A conservatism bias may look like the opposite of representativeness: Decision makers suffer from conservatism bias when they give greater weight to their initial beliefs and fail to sufficiently adjust to new information.

The following example taken from KT was first introduced by Edwards (1962):

Players were shown two urns: Urn A contained seven red balls and three black balls, and Urn B contained three red balls and seven black balls.

One of the urns is randomly chosen by the experimenter, and the players do not know which urn was chosen. 12 balls are randomly drawn from the chosen urn (with replacement after each draw). In this draw, eight red balls and four black balls were drawn. What are the chances that the draw was taken from Urn A?

According to a Bayesian calculation (see below), the probability that the draw was taken from Urn A, Prob(A/8R), is almost certain (0.967). Most players however underestimated this probability considerably and gave an average estimate of 0.7.

Apparently, players were quite conservative and did not adjust their prior probability of 0.5 that Urn A was chosen to extract the correct inference from the results of the draw.

The Bayesian calculation is as follows:

$$\text{Prob}(A/8R) = \frac{\text{Prob}(8R/A)\text{Prob}(A)}{\text{Prob}(8R/A)\text{Prob}(A) + \text{Prob}(8R/B)\text{Prob}(B)}$$

$$= \frac{0.231 * 0.5}{0.231 * 0.5 + 0.008 * 0.5} = 0.967$$

Is Conservatism the Opposite of Representativeness?

➤ Technically representativeness and conservatism are opposites.
➤ Representativeness, however, relates more to extreme cases, while conservativeness concerns cases in which new data are not very representative.

In the hit-and-run taxi example, we saw that players gave too little weight to base information (the distribution of blue and green taxis in the city), but in the last example, we came to the opposite conclusion, that players gave insufficient weight to the prior probabilities.

KT argue that if the data are representative of an underlying model, then people give greater weight to the new data (as in the taxi example, where relying on the witness' opinion is the representative model), but if the data are not representative of any salient model, as in the coin toss, people will underreact to it.

Griffin and Tversky (GT) (1992) attempt to reconcile conservatism with overreaction and to determine when would decision makers behave according to the first bias and when with the latter.

They argue that when people assess the likelihood of an event, they not only consider the statistical elements of the available evidence but also attach importance to the salience and extremity of the information. GT classify new information according to two features: strength and weight. By strength, they mean how salient and extreme the information is, and by weight they mean statistical informativeness, such as sample size. GT give an example of a recommendation letter: The strength of the letter refers to how positive and warm it is, while the weight represents the letter writer's credibility.

According to GT, when people revise their initial prediction, they tend to focus too much on the strength of the evidence, and too little on its weight, relative to a rational Bayesian. In the hit-and-run taxi example, players focus too much on the strength of the evidence (the witness saw a blue car). As a result, they overreacted to this information. In the coin toss example, people were conservative: they paid too little attention to the weight of the evidence (the statistical properties of the problem).

Conservatism is likely when the evidence has low strength but high weight. When facing evidence with high strength but low weight, people will overreact. In fact, we can think of representativeness as excessive attention to the strength of particularly salient evidence, despite its relatively low weight.

Conclusion

➤ Early criticism of utility theory (Allais and Ellsberg Paradoxes) did not offer a strong challenge to utility theory.

➤ In the 1970's, new style of market anomalies and especially Shiller's findings of excess market volatility put a further dent in the Efficient Market Hypothesis.

➤ Kahneman and Tversky offer evidence of more general biases in more realistic situations.

➤ Their examples constitute more compelling and unified evidence against utility theory.

➤ These developments paved the way for behavioral finance.

KAHNEMAN AND TVERSKY'S ESSENTIAL COGNITIVE BIASES

Agenda

➤ Kahneman and Tversky's Cognitive Biases — II

✓ Framing

✓ Anchoring

✓ Mental Accounting

✓ The Isolation Effect

✓ Small Probabilities Effect

➤ Factors Affecting Biases

In the previous lecture, we presented two important biases introduced by KT (Kahneman and Tversky, 1979) and Kahneman, 2011: Representativeness and Conservatism. In this lecture, we will continue in presenting biases introduced by these authors. As we shall later see, these biases together with those presented before are central in explaining some important financial phenomena and in the development of Prospect Theory, KT's alternative for utility theory.

**Framing: How Alternatives are Presented Affects
the Decision**

Story #1:
A person faces a 1% risk of losing $20,000 and she can buy a policy
that gives her full insurance coverage for $90 or a policy with a
$500 deductible for $20. Which should she choose?

Story #2:
A man faces a 1% risk of losing $500. He can avoid the risk alto-
gether if he pays $70. What do you recommend?

In Story #2, the answer is simple. Very few people would recommend paying $70 to avoid a lottery with an expected value of $5
and a maximum loss of $500. However, this lottery is exactly the
same as the one presented in Story #1. In the insurance problem
presented in Story #1, however, the answers were divided with many
people opting for the full-coverage option although it is equivalent to
the current lottery. When choosing full coverage, you pay extra $70
(compared to choosing the policy with a deductible) to avoid losing
the deductible ($500) in case an accident that has a 1% chance of
happening.

The above example from the field of insurance highlights the
importance of framing for individuals' decisions. This example was
used by KT to explain people's tendency to buy full-coverage insurance, when such insurance is much more expensive and inferior to
buying insurance with some deductible.

Anchoring

When forming estimates, people often start with some initial, possibly arbitrary value — an anchor — and arrive at their estimate
by making some adjustments to the anchor.

The arbitrary anchor may influence the final estimate since the
adjustments may be insufficient.

Kahneman and Tversky (1979) offer the following illustration of the anchoring effect: They asked subjects to estimate the percentage of African countries in the United Nations. However, before giving their answer, the subjects were presented with a randomly generated number between 0 and 100 and were asked whether their guess would be higher or lower than that number. The estimates that people gave were heavily dependent on the random numbers provided to them. The average estimate of those who were given an anchor of 10 was 25%, whereas the average estimate of those who were given an anchor of 60 was 45%.

Another close concept to the anchoring bias is the availability bias. According to the availability bias, when making estimations, people use the more available information.

Yet, another close concept is priming. Technically, priming refers to the activation of particular representations or associations in memory just before an action or task is performed. For example, if we show someone green pictures, she will more easily recognize tea given to her later as green tea. In this case, the memory anchors on "green," the prime. In the above UN example, the participants were primed by the random numbers shown to them prior to their estimation task. Priming is also used to put people in a special mood in order to influence their actions.

Mental Accounting

➤ The special way in which decision makers divide a decision into distinct, separate mental accounts although the decision is non-separable.

➤ People tend to segregate different types of gambles into separate accounts and ignore possible interactions.

The Theater Goer Example

Story #1

An individual purchases a theater ticket in advance for $100. On the day of the show, he takes a taxi to the theater. When he reaches the entrance, he discovers that he left the ticket in the taxi. The taxi has gone and he has no way of retrieving the ticket. The box office is open and there are still good tickets for $100. Should the person buy a ticket or go home.

For most people, whether or not to purchase a ticket is a dilemma.

Story #2

A man takes a taxi to see a show. When he reaches the box office, he notices that he lost $100 in the taxi. Nonetheless, he has enough cash to buy a $100 ticket. What should he do?

Most people do not see much of a dilemma in this case, and they will buy the ticket.

Financially, the two situations are the same. Why are people's reactions so different? Possibly, in the first case, the theater goer has divided his decision into compartments: entertainment expenses and other expenses, and he is reluctant to switch money between the "accounts".

One aspect of mental accounting that is exemplified by the above story is "narrow framing": The first individual contemplating whether or not to buy a new theater ticket may have narrowed his focus to his "entertainment account" which he considered separately from his other accounts and therefore did not consider his entire wealth when contemplating the purchase of another theater ticket.

Shefrin and Statman (1984) use mental accounting to explain why firms pay dividends despite their tax disadvantages. Firms that pay dividend rather than retain their earnings make it easier for investors to segregate gains into several "compartments" and thus increase their utility. For example, consider a firm with a profit of $100. The firm could choose to distribute $100 to the individual investor as a capital gain, and this would all go into her "capital gains account" increasing her utility by $u(100)$. In contrast, if the firm gives the investor a dividend of $20 and a capital gain of $80, the investor will mentally attribute $20 to her "dividends account" and add $80 to her "capital gains account," thus increasing her utility by $u(20)+u(80)$ which is larger than $u(100)$ because the utility function exhibits decreasing marginal utility of wealth (hence, the marginal utility of $20 added to $80 in the "capital gains account" is lower than the marginal utility of the first $20 in her "dividends account"). The investor therefore would prefer the same sum from the dividend-distributing firm rather than from the non-dividend-paying firm.

The Isolation effect — I (Sequential Decisions)

The following two-step decision problem as we shall see exemplifies the isolation effect. The isolation effect refers to decision makers' tendency to focus on the elements that distinguish between alternatives and disregard the elements they have in common.

A Two-step Decision Scenario

Individuals were faced with the following two-step decision scenarios and were required to state in advance, before seeing the results of Step #1 what they would choose to do in Step #2.

Step #1: You have a 75% chance of getting nothing and a 25% chance of moving on to Step #2 (no choice here).

Step #2:
Choose between receiving:

A. $4,000 with 0.8 probability
   0 with 0.2 probability
B. $3,000 with certainty

Most people choose B.

In the sequel, KT's notation is often used: The alternative $(x, p; y, q)$ means that the decision maker receives x with a probability p, y with a probability q, or 0 with the complementary probability $(1 - p - q)$. For example, $(1{,}000, 0.5; 500, 0.3)$ means receiving 1,000 with probability of 0.5, 500 with probability 0.3 or nothing with a probability of 0.2.

Note that choosing in advance to take the certain $3,000 if you get to the second stage is the same as getting $3,000 with probability of 0.25 (this is the probability of reaching Step #2) and 0 with a probability of 0.75. This lottery can be written as $(3{,}000, 0.25)$.

Choosing in advance the lottery (4,000, 0.8) in Step #2 is the same as winning 4,000 with a probability of 0.2 (0.25×0.8) or nothing, which is actually the lottery (4,000, 0.2).

According to their choices, it appears from the above scenario that people prefer (3,000, 0.25) to (4000, 0.2).

The Isolation Effect — I (Sequential Decisions) — Continued

People were given the following alternatives:

Choose between receiving:

C: $4,000 with 0.2 probability
　 0 with 0.8 probability
D: $3,000 with probability 0.25
　 0 with .75 probability

Most people chose C.

In this setting, people prefer C to D, exactly the opposite of their preferences when they chose between alternatives A and B, although they are exactly the same. People apparently ignored Step #1, which is the same for the two alternatives A and B in the former scenario and just focused on Step #2 which distinguishes between them.

The Isolation Effect II (Reference Point)

People were given a choice between the following alternatives:

Set 1: In addition to what you have, you get $1,000 and then choose either

A: (1,000, 0.5) or
B: 500

Set 2: In addition to what you have, you get $2,000 and then choose either

C: (−1000, 0.5) or
D: −500

In the alternatives above the pair (A, B) is the same as (C, D) because at the end you have exactly the same amount of wealth, but in the experiments, people exhibited a reversal of preferences: They preferred B to A but C to D.

The moral of the story is the same as in the previous case: It is important how you get to the wealth (or how the alternatives are framed) and not merely how much wealth the decision maker ends up with. In this example, each set of alternatives had a different reference point, and these led to different conclusions.

Small Probabilities Effect

Violation of the substitution axiom (independence of irrelevant alternatives)

The substitution principle is another form of the independence of irrelevant alternatives (IIRA) axiom (their equivalence can be shown but we'll skip it here). It states the following: Assume the alternative (x, p) is preferable to the alternative (y, q), then for any probability r, the alternative (x, pr) must also be preferable to the alternative (y, qr).

In words, if in the above alternatives (x, p) and (y, q), we change the probabilities both of prize x and prize y by the same percentage (r), then the preference between the alternatives should not change.

Some of the paradoxes (the Allais Paradox and the Ellsberg Paradox) presented earlier stem from violations of the independence of irrelevant alternatives axiom (which KT call the substitution axiom). The current example adds insights on decision makers' handling of small probabilities and also shows that individual attitudes toward such probabilities may also lead to the IIRA.

Consider the Following Sets of Alternatives Involving Small Probabilities

Set 1: Choose between
A: ($6,000, 0.45) and B: ($3,000, 0.9)

(*Continued*)

(*Continued*)

Set 2: Choose between
C: ($6,000, 0.001) and D: ($3,000, 0.002)

Most people prefer B over A and C over D.

In this example, you can see that alternative C is the same as receiving alternative A with probability of 1/450, and alternative D is the same as receiving alternative B with a probability of 1/450. Thus, rationality requires the same preferences when choosing between A and B as when choosing between C and D, but decision makers' attitude toward small probabilities apparently do not conform to VNM's axioms of rationality.

People probably discount the small probabilities in this case and do not see much difference between a probability of 0.001 and 0.002 lumping the two into the category of "remote chances". Thus, receiving $6,000 with a small likelihood is better than receiving $3,000 also with a small likelihood albeit twice as large. Although the relative difference between the probabilities is the same in the two sets, the absolute difference between the probabilities is larger in the first set, and this leads to preferring to receive $3,000 with the higher probability.

Moreover, the expected value of the alternatives in Set 2 is $6 (6,000 × 0.001 for A and 3,000 × 0.002 for B) with a maximum value of $6,000. This makes investing much thought in deciding between the alternatives undeserving.

The Lessons from the Above Effects

✓ Alternatives can be composed and then be decomposed in various ways without altering their final outcomes. They may be judged differently, however, depending on the way they are constructed and presented.

✓ This stands in contrast to utility theory, which contends that all that matters are final outcomes and their probabilities.

From a normative point of view (that is, understanding how individuals should behave) decision makers should be cautious to avoid biases and consider carefully the way alternatives are presented to them in order to make good decisions and to circumvent being taken advantage of. In a utopian world, people and agencies of power will not use these biases to take advantage of others, but in the real world, this is something to be aware of.

From a positive point of view (that is, understanding how individuals actually behave rather than how they should behave), we should be aware that individuals are susceptible to the above (and other) biases. Utility theory is deficient as a positive theory since it ignores such biases.

Factors Affecting Biases

Are all decision makers susceptible to biases in the same way? Research shows that not since there are several different factors that lead to behavioral biases and since individuals differ in the degree they are influenced by them.

Some factors that have been shown to affect biases:

✓ Gender
✓ Media
✓ Sophistication
✓ Culture
✓ Experience
✓ Professionalism

Behavioral finance acknowledges a large, but manageable, number of common and well-defined biases. This naturally leads to the following questions: what are the factors that determine whether these biases come into play or not? Which investors are more or less susceptible to biases? And, do biases vanish overtime?

There are quite a few controversies regarding whether or not biases persist. Proponents of the efficient market theory argue that biases will eventually disappear once the decision maker becomes aware of them. Behavioral scientists, however, maintain that most of the biases are stable. Venezia (2016) proposes several theories on the origins of biases. Factors that contribute to the prevalence of biases suggested there include gender, media, sophistication, culture, and experience. Discussions of these factors however are beyond the scope of this book.

Conclusions

➤ We have seen how framing, mental accounting and anchoring affect decisions.

➤ We have seen that people tend to focus on the elements that distinguish between alternatives and disregard the elements that they share.

➤ Contrary to the assumptions of utility theory, these biases show that decision making is based on more than just the final outcomes.

➤ People exhibit behavior inconsistent with rationality when facing alternatives involving small probabilities

In the next lecture, we will present prospect theory, an alternative to utility theory that acknowledges the fallibility in individuals' rationality.

PROSPECT THEORY

Agenda

➤ The Reflection Principle
➤ The Two Stages of Prospect Theory: Editing and Evaluation
➤ Prospect's Theory Value Function
➤ The Weighting of Probabilities

The Reflection Principle — I

Preferences for negative outcomes are mirror images of positive outcomes:

Positive domain	Negative domain
$(4{,}000,\ 0.8) \prec 3{,}000$	$(-4{,}000,\ 0.8) \succ (-3{,}000)$
$(4{,}000,\ 0.2) \succ (3{,}000,\ 0.25)$	$(-4{,}000,\ 0.2) \prec (-3{,}000,\ 0.25)$
$(3{,}000,\ 0.9) \succ (6{,}000,\ 0.45)$	$(-3{,}000,\ 0.9) \prec (-6{,}000,\ 0.45)$
$(3{,}000,\ 0.002) \prec (6{,}000,\ 0.001)$	$(-3{,}000,\ 0.002) \succ (-6{,}000,\ 0.001)$

Recall: The complementary probability corresponds to receiving zero. The $\prec$ and $\succ$ signs stand here for less preferable and more preferable, respectively, and not as inequality signs.

The reflection principle states that decision makers are risk averse in the positive domain (profits) and are risk seekers in the negative domain (losses), which is illustrated in the above examples obtained experimentally by Kahneman and Tversky (KT).

The Reflection Principle — Scenario 1

Your country is preparing itself for a plague that might kill 600 people unless it undertakes one of the following alternatives:

Alternative A: This action will save the lives of 200 people.
Alternative B: There is a 1/3 chance of saving everyone and a
              2/3 chance of not saving anyone.

Most people choose Alternative A (saving 200 people), exhibiting risk aversion.

The Reflection Principle — Scenario 2

Your country is preparing itself for a plague that might kill 600 people unless it undertakes one of the following alternatives:

Alternative C: 400 people will die.
Alternative D: There is a 2/3 chance that everyone will die
              and a 1/3 chance that no one will die.

Most people choose Alternative D.

In both scenarios, the same number of people are saved and die, with the same probabilities. The scenarios only differ in the way the outcomes are framed. In the first scenario, the outcomes are framed by positive results (the number of saved people). The second scenario is described by negative results (the number of people who will die). People choose among the alternatives in each scenario in line with the predictions of the reflection principle.

This is also an example of framing: You can alter people's decisions by framing the alternatives in a particular way. In this case, the alternatives were framed using the reflection principle by framing the alternatives either positively (to induce risk aversion) or negatively (to induce risk taking).

Prospect Theory

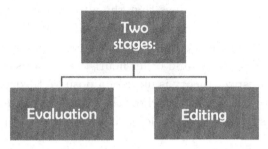

Prospect theory was first proposed by Kahneman and Tversky, who intended to develop a theory that explains some violations of utility theory. The theory builds on some general observations and is not as precise as utility theory, but it has the advantage of being more representative of real life. Its main disadvantage is that it relies on some *ad hoc* assumptions.

In utility theory, decision makers need to know all possible final outcomes and their probabilities, and then they proceed to evaluate the alternatives. In Prospect theory, there is an additional stage that precedes evaluation, which is absent in utility theory, where the alternatives are first edited. Only after the editing stage do decision makers proceed to evaluate the alternatives.

As we shall see, the theories also differ in how they describe the evaluation stage.

Stage 1: Editing

➢ In this stage, the decision maker reduces the decision problem into numerical profits, losses and their probabilities.

➢ The editing process takes into account the effects of mental accounting, framing, reference points and other heuristics of decision making.

Editing is a stage in decision making that does not exist in utility theory. Utility theory assumes that the alternatives are well defined in terms of their outcomes and probabilities and that no editing is necessary. Prospect theory considers the effects of mental accounting, framing, reference points and other heuristics on decision making. In this respect, prospect theory is more of a positive theory: it describes how people behave rather than how they should behave. Utility theory, in contrast, plays a dual role both as a positive and a normative theory.

The Editing Stage — I–Coding and Combination

The following actions are separately applied to each prospect, or alternative outcome:

➤ Coding: The prospect is defined in terms of gains and losses relative to a reference point.
➤ Combination: The prospect is simplified by combining probabilities of identical outcomes.

Example: (200, 0.25; 200, 0.25) => (200, 0.5)

The editing stage is what makes prospect theory completely different from utility theory. Utility theory makes no room for considerations of editing and coding since the only things that matter in decision making are the final outcomes and their probabilities. There are no reference points in utility theory and all monetary values refer to final wealth rather than profits and losses.

The Editing Stage — II–Segregation and Cancellation

➤ **Segregation**: The certain element is segregated from the risky element:

Example: (300, 0.8, 200, 0.2) is converted to: 200 + (100, 0.8).

(Continued)

(*Continued*)

➤ **Cancellation**: Discarding of common elements:

Example: The choice between

A: (200, 0.2; 100, 0.5; −50, 0.3) and
B: (200, 0.2; 150, 0.5; −180, 0.3)

becomes the choice between

C: (100, 0.5; −50, 0.3) and
D: (150, 0.5; −180, 0.3).

Note that segregation and cancellation stem from the isolation effect: People tend to focus on the elements that distinguish the alternatives and disregard the common elements.

The Evaluation Stage — I

This stage in prospect theory is different from utility theory:

➤ Evaluation is based on the difference of each alternative outcome from a reference point. It is not based on the final (absolute) wealth as in utility theory.
➤ Probabilities are weighted.
➤ The value function has a particular shape.

The existence of reference points is one of the main issues that separate prospect theory from traditional decision theory, and their impact on financial decisions is well documented. In many cases, but definitely not always, the reference point is the *status quo* point.

In a recent paper, Zapatero (2016) argues that the significance of reference points extends far beyond the status quo points of prospect theory and that reference points are not always exogenous to the decision-making system. Their pervasiveness can be explained by their benefits to society according to Zapatero. A decision-making system in which decision makers use reference points, either given to them by nature or by other principals, is quite effective in incentivizing and motivating economic activity. To support this argument, Zapatero presents examples of the use of reference points in habit formation, relative wealth concerns, benchmarking, performance evaluations, managerial compensation decisions, and other decision-making systems.

Furthermore, if the reference points are not entirely exogenous, this prompts the question of the link between a decision maker's personality and the way she determines her reference points. If economic agents can influence reference points or select specific reference points, will all of them make the same choice? If not, what are the factors that influence their selection? These are questions that the original prospect theory does not address. Some of these issues are explored in Venezia (2016).

The Evaluation Stage — II

➤ Attaching a value v (similar to utility) to each outcome, a value V to each prospect, and choosing the prospect with the highest V.

➤ The value V is obtained as a special type of a weighted mean of the values of the possible outcomes.

We arrive at this stage after the alternatives have been edited and the outcomes and their probabilities are well defined. From this point, decision making proceeds as in utility theory. A value function $v(x)$ attaches a value to each outcome x and a weighted average of all the possible outcomes is obtained which is the basis for comparing between alternatives. The main difference between utility theory and prospect theory is that in utility theory, the weighted average is calculated on the basis of the probabilities of the outcomes x_i but in prospect theory the probabilities p_i are replaced by some weighted probabilities $\pi(p)$.

The Evaluation Stage — III

$$V = \Sigma v(x_i) \times \pi(p_i)$$

where

x_i is the monetary outcome of event i (deviation from the reference point),

p_i is the probability of event i,

$\pi(p_i)$ is a weighting function for probabilities such that $\pi(p_i) \neq p_i$ for some p_i's.

Note that V is a function of the probabilities, p, only indirectly through $\pi(p_i)$, the weighting function. There must be some $\pi(p_i) \neq p_i$, otherwise the weighting function is redundant.

It is important to stress that the existence of a weighting function for the probabilities does not assume that the decision maker errs in the probability assessment. The weights of the probabilities are influenced by how desirable each outcome is or how important the decision maker thinks that each is. The weighting of the probabilities is a controversial assumption because it can easily lead to contradictions, as KT also acknowledged.

Properties of the Value Function

➢ More is preferable to less: $v' > 0$

➢ Risk aversion, $v'' < 0$, for gains

➢ Risk seeking, $v'' > 0$, for losses

Wealth is not completely irrelevant (but its role is usually limited to extreme situations).

The value function is concave ($v'' < 0$) for gains, representing risk aversion in this region and convex ($v'' > 0$) in the loss domain. The shape of the value function agrees with the reflection principle.

Prospect theory does not directly refer to wealth, but considerations of wealth are not irrelevant. In extreme situations, in which

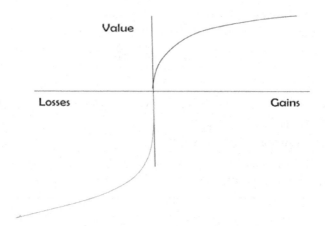

Figure 5.1.   Form of a typical value function.

heavy losses would be devastating to decision makers, decision makers may exhibit risk aversion.

In Figure 5.1, we present a typical function. It has an S shape and reflects loss aversion: it is steeper for losses than for gains, which means that a given loss hurts more than the joy of a similar gain.

The function flattens as the losses increase: A move from −100 to −200 is considered to be a worse outcome than a move from −1,100 to −1,200 (but as was mentioned earlier, this is true up to a point beyond which losses would be unbearable).

Note that, in the case of losses, the value function contradicts the common economic assumption of diminishing marginal utility, according to which a dollar is always appreciated less as a person becomes wealthier. This property of the value function stems from the assumption of risk seeking in the losses domain because diminishing (increasing) marginal utility implies risk aversion (seeking). It also stems from the assumption that people concentrate on deviations from a reference point rather than on the final value of wealth.

Evidence for loss aversion abounds. For example Coval and Shumway (2005) discovered this property among Chicago Board of Exchange traders and showed that this bias had an effect on stock prices.

Kahneman and Tversky (KT)'s Empirical Utility Function

Based on the decisions of participants in some of their experiments, KT found that the following utility function best fits people's actual decision making behaviors:

$$v(x) = x^\alpha \quad \text{if } x > 0$$
$$= -\lambda(-x)^\beta \quad \text{if } x < 0$$

KT found the following parameters most suitable:

$$\alpha = \beta = 0.88, \lambda = 2.5$$

In the positive region, this function is the same as the popular constant relative risk aversion (CRRA) function: $U(w) = (1/(1 - \gamma))w^{(1-\gamma)}$ with a risk aversion parameter γ. This parameter is called the Arrow Pratt relative measure of risk aversion (see Pratt, 1992). As we shall later see these types of utility functions have been used in most of the economic research in behavioral finance, albeit not necessarily with the same values for the parameters α, β and γ.

A Typical Weighting Function of the Probabilities

➤ Certain prospects with low probabilities are assigned a special (higher) value.
➤ The weighting function is not well behaved around the end points, and a typical function is presented in Figure 5.2.

Prospect theory also makes some assumptions concerning the weighting of the probabilities function, as shown in Figure 5.2, loosely based on KT.

We see that the typical weighting function is not defined for probabilities of 1 or 0. This is due to the special attention and importance people ascribe to certain events.

The weighting function is also characterized by overweighting of small probabilities and underweighting of large probabilities (as long

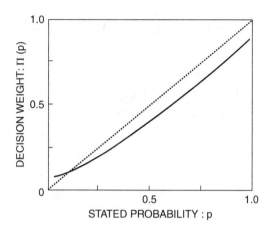

Figure 5.2.   Decision weights as functions of the stated probability p.
Source: Kahneman, *et al.* 1979.

as they are not too close to 1), but this topic is tricky. Even Tversky and Kahneman were not too certain how small probabilities should be treated. When discussing insurance decisions, they say (Kahneman and Tversky, 1979, p. 286): "Indeed there is evidence from both experimental studies, survey research, and observations of economic behavior e.g., service and medical insurance, that the purchase of insurance often extends to the range of medium probabilities and that small probabilities of disaster are sometimes entirely ignored."

Russian Roulette The Nonlinearity of π

You are forced to play Russian roulette. There are n bullets in the chamber that holds up to six bullets.

When would you be willing to pay more for removing one bullet: when there are four bullets in the chamber ($n = 4$) or when there is just one ($n = 1$)?

Most people prefer to pay more when there is just one bullet left in the chamber because of the certainty effect. By removing one bullet in this case, you guarantee that you will survive. However, when there are four bullets and one bullet is removed, your chances to survive and enjoy your money are still not that high (just 1/2) and hence you care less about spending money. The expected value of what you pay to remove the bullet is lower in this case than when only one bullet remains in the chamber. Rationally, you should be willing to pay more when there are four bullets in the chamber.

To better understand this argument, consider the extreme case where there are six bullets in the chamber. In that case, you would be willing to pay everything you have to remove one bullet, since otherwise you will certainly die. This may explain why people with terminal diseases are willing to pay huge sums of money for medications and procedures that offer minimal therapeutic chance of success.

Conclusions

Prospect theory was introduced as an alternative to utility theory. We emphasized that in prospect theory:

➤ Decision makers edit prospects taking into consideration people's biases before proceeding to the evaluation stage.

➤ Prospects are valuated according to the extent to which they deviate from a reference point.

➤ Risk aversion exists in the gains domain while risk seeking exists in the domain of losses.

➤ Decision makers exhibit loss aversion: Losses hurt more than the satisfaction generated by gains.

In the following classes, we review the evidence for the existence of behavioral biases in capital markets, analyze their effects, and discuss their practical implications.

Part II

Applications of Behavioral Finance

LECTURE 6

THE DISPOSITION EFFECT

Agenda

➤ What is the Disposition Effect (DE) and why is it Important?
➤ How is it Measured?
➤ The DE in US Markets
➤ Evidence for the DE among Amateur and Professional Investors and the Distinction between Them
➤ The DE in Real Estate Markets

The Disposition Effect

The disposition effect is investors' reluctance to realize losses and their eagerness to realize gains — the disposition to "ride losers" too long and to sell winners too early. The term was coined by Shefrin and Statman (SS) (1985) and has held since. The disposition effect stands in contrast to standard theory (given the US tax code) that prescribes quicker realization of losses in order to capture tax benefits and delaying or even reducing tax payments by postponing the sale of winners.

Why is the Disposition Effect Important?

➤ The DE may conflict with optimal tax planning and hence hints at irrationality.

(Continued)

(*Continued*)

> ➤ The DE implies that decision makers base their decision on sunk costs.
> ➤ It has implications for investment strategies.
> ➤ It has effects on prices.
> ➤ The DE was one of the first behavioral bias explored with large-scale data from real investors.
> ➤ The DE was one of the first phenomena explained by prospect theory.

Tax considerations in the US dictate that the investors sell winners later so as to pay capital gains taxes rather than the higher ordinary tax rate. Investors are better off selling losers sooner to capture tax benefits earlier. Constantinides (1984) was the first to formally consider the effects of the DE on taxes.

The eagerness to sell winners faster and delaying the sale of losers may also indicate that sellers take their sunk costs (the purchase price) into consideration, although these costs are irrelevant for the decision to sell or hold. The purchase price would be relevant if prices were negatively correlated, for example, if a drop in prices is expected after an increase. In that case, investors would be wise to sell soon before the expected fall occurs. There is, however, no evidence that prices behave in this manner.

The disposition effect is important since it affects investment decisions. Therefore, investors should always be aware of whether they are susceptible to this effect and whether it may lead them to adverse decisions based on poor tax planning or wrong timing of investments.

From the macroeconomic perspective, the disposition effect is not necessarily bad. The disposition effect may behave as an automatic stabilizer. According to this effect investors are quick to sell when prices increase, which creates downward pressure on prices mitigating the price increase. Similarly, investors are slow to sell when prices fall, which mitigates the drop in prices. Furthermore, in a market crash, the disposition effect might prevent investors from acting too quickly and from selling at the bottom. Under the influence of the DE, investors would wait for the storm to pass and sell only after the market rebounds.

The above rationale led some researchers (e.g., Baker and Sesia, 2007) to suggest that the DE may contribute to momentum: a positive correlation between prices where prices continue to rise slowly after the arrival of good news, but do not rise fast enough to reach the correct price justified by the news. According to this argument, after the arrival of good news investors "inflicted" with the DE will sell too soon without any informed justification and thus counteract the effect of the news.

Note that KT's prospect theory was based almost exclusively on controlled experimental settings. The studies covered in this lecture were among the first to explore behavioral biases (such as the disposition effect) based on largescale evidence of decision making by real investors.

In this diagram, p denotes the current price of the stock. The reference point is the purchase price of the stock.

Suppose an investor bought the stock for $10 and suppose p is $15, which is in the upper right quadrant (profits). According to prospect theory, the investor is mentally in the winning zone. If she

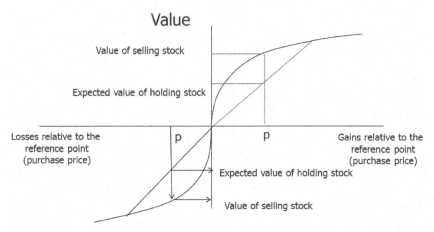

Figure 6.1. Prospect theory explanation of the disposition effect.

holds on to the stock she is taking a risk whereas if she sells she will have $15 for certain. Therefore, if the expected value of holding the share is $15 or even lower, she might sell.

On the other hand, if the purchase price was $8 and the current price, p, is lower than the purchase price, the investor is in the losing zone. According to prospect theory, in this zone, investors are risk seeking. The investor will be induced to sell the stock only if the expected value obtainable from selling the stock is greater than the expected value of holding the stock in order. In this case, the chances for the investor to sell the stock are lower.

DE and Other Cognitive Biases

➤ Mental accounting
➤ Reference points
➤ Regret

Mental accounting

The minute you purchase a stock, your mind opens a new mental account that records all the profits and gains from this stock. The account is separate from your mental portfolio account. Shefrin and Statman (SS) (1985) acknowledge that people might want to hold on to losers because of the DE, but found that investors are even reluctant to swap stocks to capture tax losses. They proposed that investors do so because they invoke mental accounting. Suppose you sustained a loss on a stock, you can sell the stock, take the capital loss and obtain the related tax benefits earlier, you could then buy a similar stock to replace the stock you sell and maintain the structure of your portfolio. SS offer the following example: Suppose you own the shares of Citigroup. You suffered a loss on this stock, and therefore, you can sell it and obtain tax benefits. In order not to alter the structure of your portfolio, you buy shares of JP Morgan. But these shares are monitored by you in a different mental account, forcing you to admit that you made a loss in the Citigroup account. Thus, conclude SS, because of the effects of mental accounting and regret, investors might not engage in these transactions even though they are beneficial.

Reference point

In DE, the working assumption is that the purchase price is the reference point.

Regret

The human desire to avoid regret causes investors to sell their winners, while holding on to their losers. As long as the loss is not finalized, through a sale, for example, the regret about buying the losing stock is less painful. On the other hand, the joy of winning is strong and investors would prefer to experience it as early as possible.

Evidence for the DE: US Data

➤ Odean (1998), compares the propensity to sell winners to that of losers.

➤ In his study, Odean sampled the daily transactions of 10,000 investors from 1987 to 1993 in a big discount brokerage house.

Evidence for the DE among US investors was presented by Schlarbaum, Lewellen and Lease (SLL) as early as 1978, before the term 'DE' was coined and before the publication of prospect theory. SLL did not frame their findings in terms of a cognitive and psychological bias and just noted the tendency of investors to sell winners faster than losers. When they coined the term disposition effect in 1985, SS cite SLL's findings and also add evidence of their own from the mutual funds industry to support their theory. Odean (1998) performed a largescale study based on individual trades to confirm the DE hypothesis. He also used an innovative methodology that differed from the methodology used by SS and SLL and performed many robustness checks to verify that his findings could not be attributed to some other confounding factors. Below, we focus on his research.

Odean's Methodology

> ➤ All transactions were classified into realized losses and realized winners (ties were discarded). The following variables were then calculated:
> ➤ PGR = ratio of realized gains to total gains (realized and paper) for the day.
> ➤ PLR = ratio of realized losses to total losses (realized and paper) for the day.
> ➤ If the inequality PGR > PLR holds significantly, this indicates that investors have a higher propensity to sell winners than losers.

In this course, we will not generally walk through the methodology of the research in all the topics we discuss. It is, however, informative to discuss methodology at least once during the course to give students a glimpse into the work that the researcher performs "behind the scenes" to arrive at his conclusions. I chose this lecture as one of these times because this topic was one of the first in behavioral finance that used observations of a large-scale sample of real investors' decisions rather than controlled classroom experiments. Moreover, the methodology Odean used is innovative and different from the methodology of the researchers preceding him. This fact contributes to the robustness of the conclusions if supporting evidence comes from different angles.

Furthermore, the robustness checks Odean performed to verify his hypotheses are an excellent example of the obstacles that researchers must overcome to empirically support their theories.

PGR and PLR were calculated daily as follows: After classifying all transactions as winners or losers, Odean restricted his sample to consider only days when a transaction was made in portfolios comprising two or more shares. Every sale (every stock that is sold) is labeled a gain or a loss depending on whether its selling price was higher or lower than its average purchase price. A stock that is not sold is declared a paper gain or loss, depending on whether its price is higher or lower than its average purchase price. End-of-day prices were used to calculate paper losses and gains. A paper gain or loss is what would have been gained or lost if the stock had been sold that day. The proportion of realized gains (PGR) is the ratio of the number of realized gains to total realized and paper gains for the day. The PLR is defined similarly for losses.

There are subtleties as to how to calculate PGR and PLR: either calculate these propensities for each investor for each day and then aggregate over all investors in the sample or calculate them over all investors each day. Odean used the second methodology. These subtleties are not that crucial and the same qualitative results are reached regardless of the way the variables are calculated.

Note that in Odean's study, stocks that are neither losses nor gains do not enter into the calculations.

More on the Methodology

This study actually tests a joint hypothesis:

1. Traders are more eager to sell winners than losers, and
2. Traders use the purchase price as their point of reference.

We conclude that the disposition effect exists if the averages of PGR and PLR (APGR and APLR, respectively) significantly satisfy

APGR/APLR > 1, or equivalently,
APGR — APLR > 0

Odean found that APGR is statistically significantly larger than APLR and concluded that the effect exists for the population he studied.

Some Alternative Explanations that Need to be Ruled Out

➤ Taxes
➤ Rebalancing of portfolio
➤ Personal information
➤ Trading costs
➤ Belief in negative correlation in stock returns

Although we have seen that the average PGR is larger than the PLR, Odean's work was not over. He had to explore what drives the results and confirm that indeed they indicate a psychological bias rather than being an artifact of other factors. All the issues noted above could have potentially driven the results and therefore had to be ruled out.

Taxes: Taxes are important in discussions of the DE in the US because of differences between capital gains taxes and personal income taxes. One issue to explore is what portion of sales are tax-driven. Sales in December would be indicative of awareness of tax considerations. Odean found that if whole year samples are considered then APGR = 0.148, APLR = 0.098, and the difference between them is Dif = 0.050. If the samples are restricted to December only, then APGR = 0.108, APLR = 0.128 and Dif = − 0.020. In months other than December, APGR = 0.152, APLR = 0.094 and Dif = 0.058. We see that there is in fact an increased propensity to sell losers in December. Taxes affect the realization of losers and profits, but the difference between the propensity to sell winners and losers remains even in months when tax motivations are not that strong.

Rebalancing the portfolio: When the price of a stock goes up, its relative weight in the total portfolio increases. The investor may then wish to sell part of his/her holdings of this stock to restore the previous weights. Odean looked at the trades in which investors liquidated all their holdings in a stock — these are trades that were not likely to be driven by the rebalancing motive. The DE prevailed in this sub-sample as well.

Personal information: If the price of a stock falls, investors that purchased this stock might think that markets do not reflect their personal information (since they purchased the stock presumably they thought its price will rise), and that they should therefore wait until the market reflect their "correct" information, and therefore they do not rush to sell. If the price rises, investors might think that this confirmed their private knowledge and hence there is no reason to wait for further rises and they should sell. The DE could therefore be driven by this kind of thinking among investors.

Trading costs: The smaller the stock the higher the trading costs, but losers are smaller (because of the loss), so investors may be more reluctant to sell them.

Belief in negative correlation in stock returns: There is no evidence for a negative correlation. In fact, market efficiency (weak form) implies that no such correlation exists. Nonetheless, some investors might believe in this.

Issues that Odean's Study did not Address

➤ Are professionals also susceptible to the disposition effect?
➤ Is the disposition effect universal or merely an American syndrome?
➤ Is this effect particular to stocks or is it observed in decision making involving investments in other assets?

These questions were later explored in studies by Shapira and Venezia (SV) (2001) and Genesove and Mayer (2001). Ben David and Doukas (2006) also explored the question of the difference in the DE of individuals and professionals and raised the possibility that some traders would have the DE with respect to a reference point other than the purchase price.

SV (2001) examined the DE for Israeli investors, and in contrast to Odean who researched only clients of a discount brokerage house, SV sought to determine whether professionals are also susceptible to this bias, and they also compared the severity of the bias in amateur and professional investors.

In times where financial investments are being increasingly managed by large institutions such as mutual funds, pension funds, and other professional money managers, decisions are made by professionals. Therefore, the question of whether professional investors are also susceptible to psychological biases is of utmost importance as well as the question of how do they differ from the lay investor.

The question whether the disposition effect prevails only in the US or is found in other countries as well is important for two reasons:

First, the more countries (markets) exhibit a phenomenon, the more robust it is.

Second, the disposition effect is considered a bias because it leads to loss of tax benefits. Although Odean (1998) controlled for tax considerations, these considerations were not completely eliminated. Studying the disposition effect in a market with a difference tax code would be beneficial in analyzing the extent to which selling decisions are influenced by tax considerations, and hence the extent to which taxes affect the disposition effect. Shapira and Vanezia (2001) address this issue. By today, the DE has been found in almost all countries.

SV Study's Contributions

➤ It generalized the DE across country borders.
➤ It employed a different method for calculating the DE.
➤ Its analysis of the DE was made at a time when profits from the stock market were essentially tax free in Israel.

Data for the Study by Shapira and Vanezia (2001)

The dataset comprises all transactions and durations of "round trips" of 1,642 independent and 2,688 managed investors in a large bank in Israel (which also functions as a brokerage house) in 1994. A "round trip" is a sequence of transactions in which an investor buys and then sells a stock. The managed investors have their transactions decided by professional investors who are bank employees. In addition to all transactions, SV also had the opening balances of all investors as of January 1, 1994.

Hypotheses and Methodology — Shapira and Vanezia (2001)

Longer duration of round trips for losers than for winners would indicate the existence of the disposition effect.

The hypotheses tested:

(1) Does the disposition effect exist for the investors in the sample?
(2) Is there a difference in the extent of the effect between amateurs and professionals?

SV's methodology differs from Odean's, but has been used by SS and SLL. According to SV, a longer duration of round trips for losers than for winners would confirm the disposition effect in their sample. They also tested for a difference in the extent of the effect between amateurs and professionals.

The extent of the DE is measured by "Dif" (the difference between the length of the round trips of losers and winners). Longer durations of round trips for losing stocks would indicate that more time elapsed before investors let go of losing stocks than winning stocks. The difference between the Dif of amateurs and professionals indicates if, and to what extent, the two groups are affected by the bias.

Most of the round trips are what SV call "simple round trips" as each purchase and sale comprised a single transaction. Some fraction of the round trips (around 20%, depending on the group) were "sequential" (involving more than one purchase or sale). In such cases, the definition of a round trip may be ambiguous (see note below). SV then tested the adequacy of this procedure by comparing the behavior of simple and sequential round trips.

Note: For example, assume that there are two buy orders of 100 shares of some stock at different prices ($50 and $60) and one sell order of 200 shares. While this might be considered two round trips of 100 shares each, SV considered this a single round trip, where the price of the purchase is the weighted average (according to value) of the two prices. The duration of the round trip is the weighted average of the time from the first buy to the sale and the time from the second buy to the sale. The reason for this method is that the investor, who considers whether the deal was successful or not, may view it as a single deal involving a specific security.

For all deals, the average durations of the round trips of managed investors (professionals) were found to be 55.42 for losers and 24.84 for winners and those of independent investors (amateurs) were found to be 63.27 for losers and 20.18 for winners. You can see that for both types of investors, the average duration of the round trips is longer for losers than for winners. The difference between the round trip duration of losers and winners (Dif), which is a measure of the DE, is smaller for the professionals than for the amateurs (30.58 for professionals vs. 43.03 for amateurs). The difference between the Dif measures of the two groups is 12.45, which indicates that amateurs' investment decisions are more strongly affected by the DE.

Note: The number of observations is 29,962 and 21,670 for losing and winning round trips, respectively, for the managed group, and 6,640 and 3,884 for losing and winning round trips, respectively, for the amateur group. All differences are significant at $p < 0.01$.

A similar conclusion we get also for simple deals. For both types of investors, the average duration of the round trips is longer for losers than for winners; the difference between the round trip duration of losers and winners is smaller for the professionals than for the amateurs (30.25 for professionals vs. 46.37 for amateurs). The difference between the Dif measures of the two groups is 16.12, which indicates that amateurs' investment decisions are more strongly affected by the DE.

We see that the qualitative results for the simple deals are similar to those obtained for all deals. SV's results for sequential deals (not shown here) are also qualitatively similar.

Note: The number of observations is 22,150 and 17,208 for losing and winning simple round trips, respectively, for the managed group, and 4,594 and 2,859 for losing and winning simple round trips, respectively, for the amateur group. All differences are significant at $p > 0.01$.

More Conclusions for the Israeli Study

➢ All investors — amateurs and professionals alike — exhibit the disposition effect.
➢ The investment decisions of professionals are less affected by the disposition effect.
➢ Former findings are generalized to countries other than the US, other tax systems and other methods for calculating the disposition effect.

Does the DE Exist for Other Assets?

Generalizing the DE beyond the stock market is of course an important issue, since as finance professionals, we are interested in all types of assets (stocks, bonds, derivatives and real estate). Today, it is well established that the DE affects decision making involving many other types of assets in most countries. A study by Genesove and Mayer (GM) (2001) was the first to address this issue by exploring the evidence for DE in real estate markets. Below, we expand on their study.

The DE in the Real Estate Market

➢ Casual empiricism indicates the existence of a DE in real estate.
➢ The purchase price is often the reference point in real estate deals.
➢ Regret occurs when losses occur (both in real and nominal terms), and pride in winning is felt when prices rise.

The analysis of assets traded in organized markets such as options and bonds is quite similar to that of stocks, but the examination of the disposition effect in real estate deserves special attention not only because of the importance of this asset but also because confirming the DE in this market is a daunting task for several reasons: First, unlike stocks, houses are unique assets and hence they carry no well-accepted market value. The price obtained for a house is not only a function of the asset's quality and features, but often also a function of the buyer's idiosyncrasies. Second, there is typically a long lag between the time an owner puts his/her asset for sale until the sale occurs (if any). Third, price data for houses are not as easily accessible as stock market data. Given these obstacles, Genesove and Mayer (2001) pioneering research in exploring the DE in the Boston housing market is particularly laudable.

Findings from the Boston Housing Market

Owners that are subject to nominal loss:

1. Set asking prices higher than non-losers do by 25–35% of the difference between the expected selling price of the property and the original purchase price.
2. Achieve 3–18% of this difference.
3. Wait longer until the occurrence of the sale.

GM's research was based on the Boston housing market (condominiums) in the 1990s and was based on data on condominium owners.

You can see that owners who suffered nominal losses waited more for a proper buyer, thus exhibiting the DE.

One wonders if the losers' wait was worthwhile. According to GM, when the asking price is set between 25% and 35% of the difference between the expected selling price of the property and the original purchase price they achieve 3–18% of this difference. Suppose an owner is in the mid-range of these values. Setting the price higher by

30% (mid-range between 25% and 35%) gets the seller an increase in price of 10.5% (mid-range between 3 and 18%). This raises the expected price the loser receives by 3.15% (30% × 10.5%).

The higher asking price will probably entail a longer wait until the sale, and hence the question arises if setting a higher asking price and accepting a longer wait are worthwhile. GM estimate that a 10% increase in asking price commands additional several weeks of wait at most. If this is extrapolated to the average figures above, the higher asking price and the wait it implies are quite profitable, as the alternative potential interest that could be earned by delaying the payment by a few weeks was much lower than 3.15% (this issue still requires further investigation).

Note: The research was conducted by estimating the following regression:

$$L = \alpha_0 + \alpha_1 \text{ (Expected sell price)}$$

$$+ m \text{ (expected paper loss) } + \text{random errors}$$

In the above equation, the expected sales price was separately estimated by GM, and the expected paper loss is a truncated value that assumes a zero value if no loss is expected and the difference between the expected sales price and the purchase price if a loss is expected. The crux of the research is that it shows that the parameter m is positive, or, in other words: Facing a loss, the property owner will ask for a higher price and hence wait longer for a sale. GM established that indeed $m > 0$.

Additional Results of GM's Study

➤ Losses are not calculated in real terms (they are "nominal"). Repeating the study in real terms yielded similar qualitative results.

➤ Both investors and occupant owners are affected by the disposition effect, but it is stronger for occupant owners.

Conclusions

➤ The disposition effect (DE) exists and is quite evident across investors, countries and assets: Investors sell winners too fast and hang on to losers for too long.

➤ The DE exists for amateurs and professionals, but is less pronounced for professionals.

➤ The DE has implications for capital asset prices.

➤ Although the DE is a bias with potential harmful consequences in taxes and timing of investments, it may be beneficial in some instances.

OVERCONFIDENCE

Agenda

➤ Describe Overconfidence

➤ Discuss the Origins of this Bias

➤ Study the Effects of Overconfidence on Investments

➤ Explore the Effects of Overconfidence on Corporate Decisions

What is Overconfidence?

Two major schools of thought concerning overconfidence:

✓ Overestimating the precision of our own estimates (miscalibration): The mean estimate is correct, but its dispersion is too narrow.

✓ Overconfidence in the sense of optimism, or a belief that we are better than the average.

The first type of overconfidence (miscalibration) occurs if people have too precise an idea about things they know little about. For example, people might say they are certain something will happen when there is only an 80% chance for it, or they say some things can never happen, when they actually occur 20% of the time (see Alpert *et al.* 1982). To measure people's confidence in their knowledge, they were asked to give confidence intervals for some unknowns (a 95% confidence interval is the range of values that you are 95% sure the true value lies within). Say, they were asked to give a 95% interval to the length of the Nile, the weight of a Jumbo jet, and other similar questions. If you are giving a 95% confidence interval, you must be correct 95% of the time. Based on many experiments, it turns out that people were correct much less than 95% of the time. In one experiment, when the task was to estimate the length of the Nile (4,135 miles), participants supplied confidence intervals that covered the correct length only 20% of the time. This implies that the confidence intervals they provided were too narrow, possibly because participants were too confident in their knowledge.

Note: Participants might have misunderstood the meaning of a confidence interval. The above experiments were conducted decades ago, today, they would consult Wikipedia before providing an estimate.

The second definition is related to optimism: In many cases, people underestimate how long it takes to complete a task and overestimate how profitable a project will turn out to be, how long their new restaurant will stay open, and other similar issues related to their own performance. In the same vein, people also think they are better than the average in almost everything: better than average drivers, better looking than the average, better business people, etc. Of course, only 50% of the people are better than average (assuming symmetry)! When people were asked about the chances that a business like their own (say, a restaurant) will succeed, they replied that the chances are quite slim, yet they estimated their own chances to succeed in the same line of business as quite high.

These two types of overconfidence were found in all cultures and in almost all aspects of life. For a review, see Lichtenstein *et al.* (1982).

Overconfidence was observed in practically all occupations, including:

➤ Physicians and nurses (Christensen-Szalanski and Bushyhead, 1981; Baumann *et al.*, 1991)
➤ Lawyers (Wagenaar and Keren, 1986)
➤ Engineers (Kidd, 1970)
➤ Negotiators (Neale and Bazerman, 1990)

➤ Entrepreneurs (Cooper *et al.*, 1988)
➤ Investment bankers (Staël von Holstein, 1972)
➤ Accountants (Bar-Yosef and Venezia, 2008)
➤ Managers (Russo and Schoemaker, 1992)

The Origins of Overconfidence: Why are People Overconfident?

➤ Evolutionary biology (men are more overconfident than women).
➤ Self-attribution.
➤ Confirmation bias.

Evolutionary biology is the most common explanation for over-confidence. In order to overcome the tough challenges of the past, people had to be overconfident. Specifically, men who had to hunt and fight wild animals for food needed some degree of overconfidence, otherwise they would not dare to undertake such dangerous ventures. For them, overconfidence was necessary for their survival and for their potential to mate, as women needed mates who would be good providers. This argument may also explain why men are more overconfident than women.

Another explanation is biased self-attribution: Suppose you do not initially know or are sure of your skills. If you proceed to perform some task, and succeed, you will probably attribute the success to your superior skills, yet you will blame any failure on luck or on the inadequacy of your teammates. If you revise your beliefs about your abilities according to Bayes rule (rationally), your estimates will eventually exceed their true values. Daniel *et al.* (1998) and Gervais and Odean (2001) expand on how self-attribution contributes to investors' overconfidence.

In the life of academics, we can find the following example of self-attribution: Authors were asked to assess their percentage contribution to the papers they co-authored. The average answer was around 70% even though the actual average contribution across all contributors is 50% (or less, when there are more than two co-authors). Even academics, known for their rationality, believe that they are better than the average.

Yet, another explanation for overconfidence is the confirmation bias. According to the confirmation bias, people seek out evidence that confirms what they already believe and interpret new information in a confirmatory manner. Assuming people want to believe they are good and assuming they are rational and hence Bayesian learners, the confirmation bias will strengthen their beliefs making them overconfident both in the terms of miscalibration and in terms of believing they are better than average.

Managers are More Overconfident than the General Population

Why?

➤ Complex capital budgeting decisions can be quite daunting; addressing them requires one to be very confident.
➤ Little learning from mistakes.
➤ Self-attribution by successful managers.
➤ Selection bias.

There are several reasons why we might expect managers to be more overconfident than the general population. First, people are typically most overconfident involving difficult problems, and capital budgeting decisions can be quite complex. Second, because of the very infrequent nature of major decisions, managers are confronted with few confidence-reducing mistakes they made. Third, managers may be more overconfident than the general population because of selection bias. Those who are overconfident and optimistic about their prospects as managers are more likely to apply for these jobs. Firms, too, may select on the basis of apparent confidence and optimism because, as shown in Palmon and Veneza (2012), it is beneficial for shareholders to hire optimistic managers who are willing to exert more effort for less pay because enthusiastic executives overestimate the effects of their efforts on share prices and consequently on the value of the options and other performance-sensitive compensation they receive.

Explanations of Overconfidence — Evolution Theory in Business

➤ The benefits of innovations resulting from overconfidence balances the costs of errors they entail.
➤ Winning in tournaments.
➤ Performance-sensitive compensation.

Some of the more general explanations for overconfidence were adapted also for the special cases of managers. These explanations stress that there are advantages to managers from being overconfident or that there are some other factors which prevent this bias from being eliminated by market forces. Here are some examples:

Bernardo and Welch (2001) explain why seemingly overconfident, irrational behavior persists over time. They argue that information aggregation in most groups is poor; overconfident managers ignore the herd and come up with nice, innovative ideas and act as "entrepreneurs" whose actions convey their private information and reward society. Nonetheless, these bold acts lead entrepreneurs to make mistakes and thus "die out" more frequently than the general public. The socially optimal proportion of entrepreneurs trades off the positive information externality of their innovations against entrepreneurs' high attrition rates.

Goel and Thakor (2008) and Kräahmer (2003) suggest that overconfidence enhances managers' chances of success in tournaments and contests. Overconfident managers are more willing to take risks and therefore are more likely to end up winning tournament-like contests.

Gervais and Odean (2001) use the attribution effect to provide an elegant model explaining managers' overconfidence and why it persists. Heaton (2002) claims that the bias persists because in corporate environments, optimistic managers are not likely to be "arbitraged away" (that is replaced by more efficient ones). Palmon and Venezia (2013) explain the persistence of overconfidence among managers in the effects of this trait on managers' willingness to invest effort to improve firms' productivity.

The theories of managerial overconfidence have been even more specialized to deal with overconfidence among traders.

Theories that Explain Why Traders' Overconfidence Persists

➤ Overconfident investors take more risks and, in the long run, earn higher returns.
➤ Overconfident investors have an advantage over rational rivals in trading competitions.

De Long *et al.* (1991), Hirshleifer and Luo (2001), Kyle and Wang (1997), and Wang (2001) show that some overconfident traders may survive and some may even thrive in the stock market. They allow for overconfidence both in the optimism and the narrow estimates sense.

Based on their findings, De Long *et al.* argue that overconfident individuals under-estimate risk and compose their portfolios with greater emphasis on stocks rather than on fixed income, which requires a high risk/high return strategy and hence earns higher returns over time. Hirshleifer and Luo make a similar argument that the high profits of overconfident traders stem from their overreactions to their assessments of mean returns. Overconfident traders exploit their information more aggressively, in either a long or a short direction. Eventually, they take more risks and hence also generate greater returns.

Kyle and Wang (1997) and Wang (2001) base their conclusions on a model of imperfect competition in securities markets where traders compete against each other in a trading game (contest) to secure assets/trades at better prices. According to their theory, rational traders who know they are trading against informed overconfident opponents become intimidated and might back out of some of the trades, to the benefit of their overconfident competitors.

There actually is a common thread to these theories that explain the persistence of overconfidence among traders, and the persistence of overconfidence in general, and that is the assumption that overconfident people take more risks. This is true for the prehistoric male who hunts to provide food, thereby increasing his chances to attract and keep a female mate with whom he can procreate, as well as for the trader who seeks higher profits in order to buy a yacht. Overconfidence persists because risk generates higher returns.

Evidence for the Overconfidence Effect in Investors

➤ Overconfidence and excess trading by clients of discount brokers.
➤ Overconfidence and excess trading by Finnish investors.
➤ Evidence from internet surveys.

Barber and Odean (BO) (1999, 2001) and Odean (1999) show that investors trade excessively: They replace their portfolios with inferior portfolios and, on top of that, pay high transactions fees. BO claim that it is investors' overconfidence that causes excessive trading. Using the same data set Odean used in his study of the disposition effect, BO show that men trade more frequently than women, and spend more on fees and transaction costs and consequently earn lower returns. They conclude that since men are more overconfident than women, overconfidence is to blame for men's excessive trading. This conclusion should be qualified because BO did not rule out the many other traits that separate men from women as explanatory variables for the differences in men's and women's trading patterns. In addition, not all investors' trades are based on speculative motives. Investors also trade for liquidity demands, taxes and portfolio rebalancing, and therefore one cannot argue that the returns on portfolios do not justify the trading fees when the trading is performed for other motives. On the other hand, BO show that these other motivations are not sufficient to rule out the conclusion that investors trade excessively and that overconfidence plays a major role in this behavior.

Grinblatt and Keloharju (GK) (2009) find evidence for overconfidence and its effects on trading, using a large data set from Finland. Their data set has a great advantage over BO's data set since the latter aggregated all the overconfidence data they had into two groups: men and women. This aggregation does not allow the researchers to disentangle the effects of other factors that potentially separate men from women (such as wealth, income, age, and occupation) from the effects of overconfidence on trading. GK's extensive data set, which was similar to the extensive trading data used by BO, additionally contained detailed data on the personal profiles of Finnish traders, such as information on men's psychological profiles. These data were collected by the Finnish army, which administers personality tests to all army recruits upon induction into mandatory military service. GK had access to this data set and were able to create an individual overconfidence score for each male trader. Supplementing the trading data with individual measures of overconfidence allowed GK to conduct a more reliable test of the effect of overconfidence on trading. GK found a positive correlation between overconfidence and trading and showed that this correlation is obtained even after controlling for potentially confounding variables. GK's results provide important support to BO's findings and bolster the theory that overconfidence is partially responsible for excessive trading. In their study, GK also expand on sensation seeking and show that this psychological trait has a major influence in elevating trading frequency.

Glaser and Weber (GW) (2007) used a large-scale Internet questionnaire to explore the effect of overconfidence on trading. They correlate individual overconfidence scores with several measures of individual investors' trading volumes. In their Internet survey, investors completed a questionnaire designed to measure their overconfidence in the sense of miscalibration and sense of being better than average. GW were able to create such measures for 215 individual investors. GW found that investors with higher overconfidence scores (in the above the average sense) also traded more frequently. Measures of overconfidence in the miscalibration sense, on the other hand, were not found to affect trading.

GW's results are important because many theoretical models of the effects of overconfidence are based on the definition of overconfidence in the miscalibration sense. If this type of overconfidence has a limited effect on actual behavior, then these studies lose some of their significance. Does GW's study conflict with the evidence of correlations between excessive trading and overconfidence presented by BO and GK? Apparently not. The hypothesis that BO use in their study (that men are more overconfident than women) has been supported for overconfidence both in the calibration and in the optimism sense. GK's measures of overconfidence were also of the optimism sense, and hence their result that this type of overconfidence matters is consistent with GW's findings.

GW's findings notwithstanding, there might be a connection between overconfidence in the miscalibration sense, self-attribution, and the disposition effect. Statman *et al.* (2006) explain this theory as follows: Overconfident investors overestimate the precision of their own valuation abilities, and consequently, they make investment decisions by relying on their own private signals while basically ignoring public signals. That is, they buy (sell) stocks that they believe to be undervalued (overvalued). In addition, they update their beliefs asymmetrically between favorable and unfavorable signals. While favorable signals (recent price increases) are interpreted as confirmation of their prior beliefs and actions, unfavorable signals (recent price declines) are discounted. As a result, investors are inclined to sell their shares following price increases because they believe that their valuation assessment has been fully revealed to the market; In contrast, they hold on to their shares following a drop in prices, believing that other market participants have not yet realized their true valuation. Investor overconfidence therefore generates asymmetrical trading volumes between gains and losses. (We discussed this point in Lecture 6 on the disposition effect; but here, we emphasize the role of overconfidence in this argument).

In what follows, we will discuss some of the effects of overconfidence on corporate decisions. We'll start with their negative effects and continue with their positive ones.

The Effect of Overconfidence in Corporate Finance: Value-destroying Effects of Overconfidence

---

The Effect of Overconfidence on Mergers and Acquisitions (M&As)

➤ The hubris hypothesis.
➤ Exaggerated self-confidence.
➤ Empirical tests of the effect of overconfidence on mergers and acquisitions.

One of the more puzzling phenomena in corporate finance is the ubiquity of mergers and acquisitions where the stockholders of the acquiring firm lose from these transactions.

Roll (1986) was one of the first to use overconfidence and irrationality to explain this phenomenon (although he used the term hubris rather than overconfidence). He argued that the bidding firms exhibited hubris in their bids for the acquired firms and contended that bidders overestimate their power to make a better evaluation of the target firms than the market.

Hayward and Hambrick (HH) (1997) provided evidence that reinforces Roll's conclusions in attributing the popularity of mergers and acquisitions to the hubris argument. They suggested that hubris (which they interpret as exaggerated self-confidence) can explain the large size of premiums paid for acquisitions and hence the losses they entail. In a sample of 106 large acquisitions, they find significant correlations between their proxies for the CEOs' hubris and the size of the premiums paid. They also found that this correlation was strengthened when the board's control was weaker, which strengthens the suspicion that CEOs' idiosyncrasies might lead to mergers and acquisitions that have adverse consequences for stockholders.

In a series of studies, Malmendier and Tate (MT) (2005a, 2005b, 2008) and Malmendier *et al.* (2007), (Malmendier Tate and Yan, MTY) empirically examined the correlation between CEOs overconfidence and several corporate practices. Here, we focus on MT's 2008 findings concerning the effect of CEOs' overconfidence on the chance that their firms will be involved in a merger or acquisition. The study used lists of mergers and acquisitions and their financial outcomes, which are public knowledge and relatively easy to obtain, but MT's main challenge was to find good measures of managers' overconfidence. Fortunately, they developed the clever measures of overconfidence described below and were able to find interesting results.

One of the measures of overconfidence they developed (the "Longholder") identifies CEOs who systematically maintain high exposure to company-specific risks in their personal portfolios, despite a strong incentive to diversify their holdings. Not only is this a bad practice from a portfolio perspective, but in the CEOs' case, diversifying away from their own employer's stock is imperative because their human capital is also tied to their employer's fortune. A plausible motive for this practice is that these CEOs overestimate their firms' expected future cash flows. MT address and rule out the importance of several alternative explanations, including signaling and risk tolerance. Their choice of this measure of overconfidence thus has compelling support. A "Longholder" CEO is probably overconfident.

As a robustness check, however, they devised a second scale to measure CEOs' overconfidence based on their portrayal in the business press as "confident" or "optimistic" (a measure also used by HH).

Based on these two measures of overconfidence, MT find that there is a positive correlation between CEOs' overconfidence and the incidence of acquisitions. The fact that this correlation was obtained for two independent scales of overconfidence enhances the validity of their findings.

In the sequel, we present more evidence on the effect of overconfidence on corporate decisions.

Other Effects of Overconfidence on Corporate Financial Decision Making

➤ Overconfidence affects usage of debt, dividends, and investments.

➤ Overconfidence and short term vs. long term debt.

Ben-David *et al.* (2007) (Ben-David, Graham and Harvey, BGH) conducted a large-scale study of the effect of overconfidence on the financial decisions of firms. They surveyed hundreds of CFOs in the US over several years (from March 2001 to June 2007) and proposed proxies for CFOs' overconfidence profiles based on these surveys. Proxies for overconfidence of the miscalibration type were constructed as follows: BGH asked the CFOs to predict market returns and provide an 80% confidence interval for their prediction. The proxies were defined as the narrowness of the confidence intervals (the narrower the interval, the more overconfident the CFO). In their research, GBH obtained almost 7,000 observations of CFOs' probability distributions.

They then measured the extent of the CFOs' miscalibration and whether the miscalibrations were correlated with the actual financial decisions of the firms. They found that the executives in their sample are indeed overconfident (they miscalibrated): The realized market returns that they were asked to predict were within the executives' 80% confidence intervals only 38% of the time.

GBH also found that their overconfidence proxies were positively correlated with:

1. lower discount rates used in the evaluation of cash flows,
2. higher investment rates,
3. higher rates of debt usage,
4. lower dividend payment and higher share repurchase rates,
5. preference of proportionally more long-term, as opposed to short-term, debt.

It remains to be further investigated to what extent CFOs (and their overconfidence) influence these decisions, since some of them are not in their hands.

There are some other findings on the effects of overconfidence on corporate decisions, which are descriptive in nature and do not negatively reflect on the effect of overconfidence on corporate decisions. For example, Landier and Thessmar (2008) show that optimism causes managers to prefer short-term over long-term financing. MT (2005) found that investments of overconfident CEOs are significantly more responsive to cash flows, particularly in equity-dependent firms. MTY found that, given firms' access to capital markets, overconfident CEOs are more likely to raise capital by debt than by equity. Such CEOs, MTY argue, are more likely to underutilize debt and forgo some of the tax benefits that come with the debt.

Above, we emphasized the negative effects of overconfidence. However, for overconfidence to persist, a balance must exist between its positive and negative effects since if all effects were negative, market forces would have eliminated it. Below, we expand on the positives of overconfidence.

Positive Effects of Overconfidence in Finance

The positive effects of overconfidence in corporate finance include:

➤ Positively affects the initiation of startups.
➤ Expedites undertaking of new valuable investments.
➤ Enhances team productivity.

Cassar and Friedman (2007) demonstrated that individual overconfidence is associated with more aggressive entrepreneurial investment decisions and with the propensity to begin startup activities. Furthermore, for individuals who initiated startup activities, overconfidence increases the likelihood that this activity will develop into an operating business.

Gervais *et al.* (2011) demonstrated that overconfident managers are less likely to postpone decisions to undertake new valuable investments and therefore, overconfidence improves welfare.

Overconfidence also affects team productivity. Gervais and Goldstein (2007) studied firms in which the marginal productivity of team members depends on that of their coworkers. They show that the presence of an overconfident team member who overestimates her marginal productivity may make all team members better off, including herself. This conclusion holds even when compensation is endogenously determined.

Effects of Overconfidence on Executive Compensation

➤ Effects of optimism on the use of options in executive pay.
➤ Overconfidence impact on managers' investments in information.
➤ The effects of overconfidence on the form (strike prices) of executive options plans.

Bergman and Jenter (BJ) (2007) analyzed the effect of optimism (and other sentiments) on compensation. They specifically explore why firms use equity-based compensation for rank-and-file employees who see only a very weak connection between their actions and firm's performance. Firms as well as the low-ranking employees are also aware of this weak connection and therefore, it is unlikely that providing options affect these workers actions. BJ suggested that the popularity of option compensation is driven by employee optimism. According to their theory, employee overconfidence (optimism) cannot explain the popularity of option compensation in full, yet they suggest that employees' optimism increases the subjective value that the employees attach to the options they receive as compensation, thus contributing to the popularity of this form of pay. BJ presented empirical evidence that supports firms' use of broad-based option compensation when employees are likely to be excessively optimistic about company stock.

Oyer and Schaefer (OS) (2005) discuss the role of optimism in sorting employees according to their optimism about the firms prospects. OS do not believe that incentives can explain the popularity of incentive-based compensation for lower echelon employees. They suggest that these forms of compensation are more likely used for employee sorting and retention. They claim that paying employees with stock options is an efficient way of compensation since such employees overvalue the options they get. For example, OS argue that because of their optimism, risk-averse employees who expect their employer's stock to increase by about 25% annually prefer option-plus-salary packages over a cash-only compensation plan that costs the employer the same amount.

Palmon and Venezia (PV) (2013) show that overconfidence helps mitigate the agency problem caused by sub-optimal investments of effort by managers, who do so because their effort is not observable and can be compensated only through its impact on firm value. Stockholders therefore offer managers compensation contracts that includes bonus stocks and/or options to enhance managers' motivation. By simulating the compensation contracts that stockholders offer, and the corresponding effort choices of overconfident managers, PV demonstrate that overconfident managers exert more effort than realistic managers, which partially mitigates the agency problem described above. PV also constructed a measure of the total welfare of a firm's stakeholders (managers and stockholders), taking into account managers' efforts and risk choices, and show that this total welfare measure increases with managerial overconfidence. Their work illustrates that some aspects of managerial overconfidence may be socially beneficial and may offset their other value-destroying effects. These favorable impacts on firm value and total welfare may help explain the persistence of this bias, as evolution prefers socially enhancing phenomena.

Gervais *et al.* (2011) consider the effect of overconfidence on compensation, but they define overconfidence in the sense of overly precise estimates. In their theory, managers exert effort to obtain better estimates of the investment parameters rather than to increase production. This study provides important insights on the effects of overconfidence on information gathering.

Palmon *et al.* (2008) and Dittmann and Yu (2008) also show that overconfidence may explain the pervasive habit of firms to determine the strike prices of managerial options in the money (firms could provide more options out of the money or fewer options deep in the money).

Conclusions

✓ Overconfidence is defined in terms of "optimism", "better than average assumption" or "miscalibration."

✓ Overconfidence has evolutionary origins and can result from self-attribution and the confirmation effects. These reasons may lead men to be more overconfident than women.

✓ Overconfidence can lead to excessive trading and hence such trading is more prevalent among men.

✓ Overconfidence can be instrumental for innovations, startup initiation and entrepreneurship.

✓ Overconfidence has important implications in corporate finance through its impact on managerial compensation, M&As, and other financial decisions.

LECTURE 8

HERDING

Agenda

➤ Define Herding
➤ The Causes of Herding
➤ Rational and Irrational Herding
➤ Herding Measures Around the World
➤ The Effects of Herding on Capital Markets
➤ Cascades and Rational Herding of Investors
➤ Rational Herding by Analysts

What is Herding?

➤ Herding occurs when the decision maker (investor) undertakes or refrains from undertaking an action just because other decision makers (investors) have undertaken it or refrained from undertaking it.
➤ It is not merely the act of behaving like others!
➤ Genuine herding occurs when investors base their decision only on observed behaviors of others and disregard their own information.

Herding has received a bad reputation in the last few years as it was blamed for bubbles and market crashes and for destabilizing markets and increasing volatility.

Lecture Notes in Behavioral Finance

Note: According to other definitions investors herd if they alter their decision when they observe the decisions of other investors (see Bikhchandani and Sharma, 2000). Our definition does not require that investors alter their decisions. An investor will be considered to be engaged in herding if he makes up his mind after observing others and decides not to seek further information.

What Causes Herding?

➤ Informational motives: Investors think that others know something they do not.
➤ Due to people's inherent need of conformity and social validation, they try not to deviate from the norms.

In many cases, herding is a byproduct of information availability or the lack thereof. Different groups of investors receive information of varying types and quality. Differences between group characteristics and available information may cause investor groups to behave differently from one another while concurrently exhibiting herding within each group.

Types of Herding

➤ Intentional
➤ Spurious

Intentional herding occurs when investors consciously imitate others. Spurious herding occurs when investors merely act in a similar manner, which might happen for a variety of reasons. In finance, the most obvious causes of spurious herding is that many groups of investors face similar information and goals and share other relevant characteristics (e.g., wealth and education) and therefore can be expected to behave similarly. One of the greatest challenges of researchers in this field is to determine if similar behaviors are the result of intentional decisions or merely represent correlations due to the various factors mentioned above. As we see below, herding may be rational.

Who Herds?

➤ Almost everyone.
➤ Herding has been found in all fields of business and finance, among investors (in all types of assets: stocks, options, real estate, etc.), traders, analysts, institutional investors, bankers, bank depositors (e.g., bank runs).
➤ Evidence for herding comes from all countries.

Comparing Herding Measures (HM) Around the World

➤ In the US, Grinblatt *et al.* (1995), HM around 2.5%.
➤ In the UK, Wylie (2005), HM = 2.6% for entire sample, 9% when the number of traders is 25 more.
➤ In Israel, Venezia *et al.* (2011), (HM = 6.5%, for amateurs, 5.8% for professionals.
➤ In Korea, Choe *et al.* (1999), HM > 16%.
➤ In Portugal, Lobao and Serra (2002), HM > 10%.
➤ In Poland, Voronkova and Bohl (2005), HM > 10%.

The absolute values of the numbers are not that informative, but the ordinal measures shed light on the relative intensity of herding in different countries. At a glance, herding appears to be more intense in less developed markets.

The Effects of Herding

➤ Herding reduces market efficiency by restricting information dissemination.
➤ Herding can increase market volatility and therefore may have a destabilizing effect.
➤ Herding can cause contagion of crises from one country to the next.

(Continued)

(Continued)

➤ But, the effects of herding are not necessarily all negative; herding saves information costs and some investment mutual funds may benefit from it.

Herding reduces market efficiency by restricting information gathering and dissemination. If people stop seeking information after observing others and ignore their own information, this implies that potentially important information does not reach the market. But, less information gathering can save costs.

Herding can increase the volatility of markets and hence has destabilizing effects. If all investors act in unison (let's say, all buy) and all imitate few leaders, then the effect on market prices could be strong; If the leaders are wrong, this could be disastrous. If, on the other hand, investors do not imitate a small group of leaders and each investors makes decisions based on their own information, there is a smaller probability that everyone will follow a wrong signal. Venezia *et al.* (VNS) (2011) offer evidence from the Israeli stock market that herding has destabilizing effects on stock prices.

Calvo and Mendoza (2000) show that rational herding can cause contagion in international markets when a crisis in one country "infects" and spreads to other countries. They suggest that the spread of several international crises may have been exacerbated by herding. They offer numerous examples, such as the Mexican crash of 1994, which they argue might have led to the fall of the stock markets of Argentina, Brazil, Chile, and Singapore as a result of herding. Calvo and Mendoza similarly claim that herding may have been the cause of the spread of the financial crisis that originated in Thailand across several countries in East Asia. Chiang and Zheng (CZ) (2010) also offer evidence to support these claims. They show that crises trigger herding activity in the country of origin and then produce a contagion effect that spreads the crisis to neighboring countries.

The effects of herding are not necessarily negative. Wermers (1999) finds that stocks that are purchased in herds have higher subsequent quarterly returns.

Factors that Affect Herding

➤ Type of traders (e.g., individuals vs. professionals).
➤ Market characteristics (e.g., emerging vs. developed markets).
➤ Type of assets (e.g., small vs. big, volatile vs. tranquil).
➤ Period (regular vs. volatile, boom vs. crisis).
➤ Volume (number of trades).

Type of traders

One would be tempted to think that all individuals in similar situations would be as prone to herding, but there are some factors that affect the disposition to herd. When individuals have less information, it might be natural for them to assume that others know more. In fact, there is some evidence that professionals herd less and also offer evidence supporting the theory that herding is driven by a lack of information (e.g., VNS). Institutions have been found to herd less than individuals (e.g., Nofsinger and Sias, 1999), and residents in some emerging markets were found to herd less than non-residents (Kim and Wei, 2002). All these studies, however, found evidence that lay investors, professional investors, and institutions all engage in herding to some extent.

Market characteristics

In this case too, it seems that herding is less likely to occur in developed markets. In these markets, information is more readily available to investors, which reduces the need to imitate others. Investors in developed countries are also more sophisticated, which might make them more confident about their own information.

Type of assets

VNS find evidence that herding is inversely related to the target firm's systematic risk and size. They find significant evidence that the investors in their sample herd less on large stocks, which is consistent with evidence offered by Grinblatt, Titman and Wermers (GTW) (1995) that mutual funds tend to herd into small, but not large stocks.

Period

Regular vs. volatile, boom vs. crisis: CZ showed that crises trigger herding. Herding may be the cause of contagion, or the transmission of crises from one country to another, where there are no apparent reasons for such transmission (several competing theories, however, posit that all the affected countries share the "blame"). Calvo and Mendoza (2000) and Rigobon (2002) offer support for these ideas. The 2008 US sub-prime crisis illustrates the potential of global contagion of a financial crisis.

Volume

Both VNS and GTW show that larger trading volumes are positively correlated with higher herding measures.

In what follows, we study how herding may result from the rational behavior of investors and analysts. Two theories will be presented: Investors cascades theory — Banerjee (1992), Bickchandani *et al.* (1992), (Bickchandani, Hirshleifer and Welch, BHW), Welch (2000), and analysts herding behavior — Scharfstein and Stein (1990).

Cascades Theory of Rational Herding (BHW)

Setup

➤ Investors consider the purchase of an asset (an investment).
➤ Investors sequentially observe the binary decisions (buy or not buy) of the investors before them and then decide whether or not to invest.
➤ Investors receive an informative (but non-perfect) signal about the quality of the asset.
➤ The signals that different investors receive are not correlated.
➤ Investors will buy the asset if its expected value exceeds its price.
➤ All investors are similar (have similar initial information and preferences, and all are risk averse).

After observing the decisions of several investors preceding them, rational investors (who update their probability assessments according to Bayes rule) may make their decisions based on the decisions of the preceding investors and will ignore their own signals and will not seek new signals since such signals cannot change their probabilities enough to change their mind.

Model's Parameters

➤ The asset's value, V, is unknown and could be either $0 or $1.
➤ Initially, the probability that the value, V, is $0 or $1 is 50% to 50%.
➤ The price of the asset is $0.50.
➤ Each investor receives an informative signal in turn, that could either be B (bad) or G (good), and updates the probability that $V = \$1$ according to Bayes rule.

The signals

The signals are not perfect, but they are informative: There is a higher probability of obtaining a G signal when $V = 1$ and a higher probability of obtaining a B signal when the value of V is 0.

For ease of exposition, assume that when $V = 1$, the probability of obtaining a G signal is 0.6, and when $V = 0$ the probability of obtaining a B signal is 0.6.

The signals that different investors receive are independent of each other.

The first investor

Assume that the first investor received a G signal. According to Bayes rule, the posterior probability (the probability after the signal is received) that the $V = 1$ is now 0.6 (see formula below), and the expected value of the asset becomes $0.6 ($0.6 \times 1$). Since its cost is $0.5, the investor will make a decision to buy the asset.

If the investor receives a B signal, the posterior probability that $V = 1$ becomes 0.4 and since $0.4 < \$0.5$, the investor will not buy the asset.

The calculation needed to reach the probability that $V = 1$ given that a G signal was received, $\text{Prob}(V = 1/G)$, is

$$\text{Prob}(V = 1/G) = \frac{\text{Prob}(G/V = 1)\,\text{Prob}(V = 1)}{\begin{array}{l}\text{Prob}(G/V = 1)\,\text{Prob}(V = 1)\\+\,\text{Prob}(G/V = 0)\,\text{Prob}(V = 0)\end{array}}$$

$$= \frac{0.6 \times 0.5}{0.6 \times 0.5 + 0.4 \times 0.5} = 0.6$$

Similarly, $\text{Prob}(V = 1/B) = 0.4$

The second investor

Assume that the second investor observes that the first investor purchased the asset. She can justifiably assume that the first investor received a G signal.

She then obtains a signal of her own. If she receives a G signal, she infers that the asset received two G signals (her own and that of the first investor). In that case, her assessment of the probability that $V = 1$ is even higher than the probability calculated by the first investor, and hence she will buy the asset.

If the second investor's signal is a B signal, she infers that the asset received one G signal and one B signal, which cancel each other out. As a result, the asset's expected value remains 0.5 and she will not purchase the asset.

We see that the first investor will buy the asset only if he receives a G signal (in which case, the probability that $V = 1$ is 0.6). If the next investor also receives G signals, the probability that $V = 1$ increases and the second investor will also purchase the asset.

Note: BHW assumed that when the expected value is exactly the same as the price, there is an even chance (50%–50%) that the investor will buy or refrain from buying. We assume that the expected value of the asset must strictly exceed the price to induce an investor's purchase decision. Our assumption simplifies matters considerably without impairing the integrity of the theory.

The third investor

Suppose the first two investors in line purchased the asset. The third investor can justifiably infer that they both received G signals.

Should the 3rd investor look at his own signal?

If his signal turns out to be a G signal, he will certainly purchase the asset. But even if his signal turns out to be a B signal, he will purchase the asset.

According to Bayes rule, the posterior probability that $V = 1$ after observing two G signals and 1 B signal is 0.6, and the expected value of the asset is \$0.6 (see calculation below).

We see that the third investor's signal is meaningless if the two preceding investors purchased the asset; he will purchase the asset in this case regardless of his own signal.

Calculation of the posterior probability that $V = 1$:

$$\mathrm{Prob}(V = 1/GGB)$$

$$= \frac{\mathrm{Prob}(GGB/V = 1)\,\mathrm{Prob}(V = 1)}{\begin{array}{l}\mathrm{Prob}(GGB/V = 1)\,\mathrm{Prob}(V = 1)\\ + \mathrm{Prob}(GGB/V = 0)\,\mathrm{Prob}(V = 0)\end{array}}$$

$$= \frac{0.6 \times 0.6 \times 0.4 \times 0.5}{0.6 \times 0.6 \times 0.4 \times 0.5 + 0.4 \times 0.4 \times 0.6 \times 0.5} = 0.6$$

A similar herding (cascade) phenomenon of non-buys (down cascade) will emerge if the first two investors receive a B signal. The 3rd potential investor in line will not invest regardless of his signal.

For an up cascade to occur after two investors, we need that that the two investors will buy the asset; for a down cascade, they should refrain from buying the asset. No cascade will occur if one buys and the other does not.

The Chances of a Cascade After Two Observations

Assume that the probability for a G signal is p.

The probability for an up cascade after the decisions of two investors is p^2 (since this will occur if they both buy), and the

(*Continued*)

(Continued)

probability for a down cascade after two investors have traded is $(1-p)^2$ (as the two of them should not buy).

The chances for no cascade (either up or down) after two investors is therefore $1 - p^2 - (1-p)^2$.

For example, if $p = 0.5$, the probability of an up cascade is 0.25, the probability of a down cascade is 0.25, and the probability of no cascade in 0.5.

The Chances of a Cascade after more than Two Observations (Investors)

If a cascade does not occur after two observations, it will occur only after an even number of observations (including two identical signals in succession).

The chances that a cascade will eventually occur approach 1 if the number of potential investors is sufficiently high.

The chances for an up cascade if the line is infinite are given by $P_b = \frac{p^2}{1-2p(1-p)}$.

The chance for a down cascade is the complementary probability.

The chances of no cascade are close to 0.

The formulas for any number of investors, n, are complicated and beyond the scope of this book.

Adverse Effects of Cascades

- Cascades may be misleading. If the first two investors receive wrong signals, many investors will make the wrong decision.
- Information is not collected or wasted. A huge amount of information goes to waste since many investors ignore their own signals (on the other hand, if signals are costly, investment in meaningless information is saved).
- There is no way to reverse a cascade based on incorrect decisions.

Strengths of Cascades Theory

- Cascades theory captures the point that once investors have observed a large enough number of other presumably rational and independent investors behave in a certain way, it makes sense to assume they are right.
- This is some version (or explanation) of the wisdom of the crowds.
- The model was experimentally tested and supported.
- For empirical support of the theory, see Cipriani and Guarino (2005, 2008).

Critique of Cascades Theory

Strong assumptions:

1. Sequential decisions.
2. Investors know others investors' decisions.
3. Investors do not communicate; they merely observe other investors' decisions.
4. The price of the asset remains the same, even after investors observe the action of others and their own observations.

The final point (that the price remains the same even after investors obtain additional information) was made by Avery and Zemsky (1998). They showed that in BHW's model, cascades will not occur if the prices are updated rationally after each observation, but cascades will occur if there is uncertainty not only about the asset's mean value but also about its variance.

Herding by Financial Analysts

Extensive literature shows that financial analysts engage in herding behavior. One of the popular axioms used by investments managers is: *No one ever got fired for buying IBM.*

It is safe for analysts to follow the herd, since if they fail, they have an excuse that they are not alone. In contrast, if they fail when they act outside the mainstream, their decisions are much more difficult to defend.

A Theory of Rational Herding by Analysts

This theory was introduced by Scharfstein and Stein (1990). In their paper, they classify analysts into "smart" and "dumb", but I prefer "good analysts" and "charlatans."

Main assumptions:

✓ Analysts' investments are a signal of their quality (skills and ability).
✓ There is a large number of analysts in the market, some are good and some are charlatans.
✓ *A priori*, no one, including the analysts, knows who is good and who is not.
✓ All analysts try to signal that they are good.
✓ All good analysts obtain their information from the same, reliable, sources.
✓ All charlatans receive their information from a variety of (uncorrelated) sources that are less reliable than the sources used by the good analysts.

The Significance of Correlated Signals

➤ Because the signals used by the good analysts are correlated, we would expect their recommendations to be correlated as well.
➤ We have no such expectations about the charlatans' recommendations.
➤ This reasoning motivates good analysts to invest/recommend like other analysts, since such decisions will increase their chances of being considered good.

Model Setup

✓ The market consists of 50% good analysts and 50% charlatans. The analysts receive their information in the form of a good signal (G) or a bad signal (B).

✓ All good analysts receive the same signal.

✓ The chances that two charlatans receive the same signal is only 50%.

✓ The analysts provide, sequentially, a buy or not buy recommendation.

Conclusion: Suppose two analysts make their decisions sequentially. It is optimal for the second analyst to make the same decision as the first because otherwise she risks being considered a charlatan (together with the first analyst).

This model resembles BHW's cascades theory in its construction and methods. It is a game theoretic model however. The above equilibrium that the players reach is not unique, but it makes the most sense of all potential equilibria.

Whereas this theory is reminiscent of BHW's cascades theory in the sequential nature of the decisions and in their binary nature, the driving force of the two theories is, however, different. The crux of the Scharfstein and Stein's rational herding by analysts theory is that a similarity of opinions signals the high quality of information sources.

Benchmarking-induced Rational Herding

When fund managers' compensation depends not only on their absolute performance but also on their performance relative to others (e.g., because of benchmarking), herding may be rational.

In such conditions, fund managers deviate from return-maximizing portfolio allocations and herd after their benchmark. In some situations, fund managers ignore their own superior information and "go with the flow" in order to reduce deviations from their benchmark.

Assuming that analysts are risk averse, they will invest close to the benchmark because this investment strategy will bring their performance (and their compensation) close to the mean.

Conclusions

➢ Herding is universal. Contrary to popular belief, it is not necessarily an irrational phenomenon.

➢ In the popular press, herding is considered a harmful phenomenon, and there is empirical evidence to support these beliefs.

➢ Herding plays a role in destabilizing markets and in the transmission of crises across borders.

➢ Information gathering is hampered by herding, and thus, herding reduces market efficiency.

➢ Investors, analysts, and portfolio manager may herd rationally.

LECTURE 9

OVERREACTION AND UNDERREACTION

Agenda

➤ Definitions of Underreaction and Overreaction
➤ Empirical Evidence of Overreaction and its Critique
➤ Casual Evidence of Overreaction: The Subprime Crisis of 2008 and Brexit 2016
➤ Empirical Evidence of Underreaction
➤ How can Overreaction and Underreaction be Reconciled?

Overreaction occurs when decision makers respond disproportionately to new information. Underreaction means that investors do not react enough to information. If investors do not adequately react to information, this poses a challenge to the efficient market hypothesis.

If investors sometimes overreact and sometimes underreact, then it might seem that the two effects could just cancel each other and therefore, such behavior will not affect the efficient market hypothesis. However, as we shall see, underreaction and overreaction do not randomly occur and there are several systematic factors that affect the occurrence of underreaction and others that lead to overreaction. We will start with overreaction.

Overreaction may occur as a result of an excessive adjustment of the probability of an event, or from a gut reaction without a deliberate consideration of probabilities.

Assume that a firm fails to meet its expected profit. If investors estimate that this will cause a 50% drop in its P/E ratios even though the new information only implies a 10% drop in profitability, the investors are overreacting.

According to the overreaction hypothesis, investors may give unduly more weight to the new information than to the base information.

Kahneman (2011) says that overreaction in the stock market is an emotional phenomenon that is so strongly embedded in investors' psyche that even professional investors are unable to overcome this bias. If this is the case, Bayes' rule may not be relevant for predicting investors' reactions.

Undervaluing the Base Rate

See the following example (we used it in Lecture 4, but we repeat it here to make this lecture more self-contained). A car was involved in a hit-and-run incident. Two taxi companies operate in this town: green and blue. Of all the taxis in the town, 85% are green and 15% are blue. A witness identified the offending vehicle as a Blue taxi, but it is well known that witnesses make correct identifications only 80% of the time.

What is the probability that the offending vehicle is a blue taxi?

On average, people said 65%, although the correct probability according to Bayes rule is about 41%.

The reason for the participants' excessively high estimates is probably that the participants disregarded the low base of blue taxis, which is 15%.

Overreaction's Reflection in the Evolution of a Stock Price

Assume that a favorable and unexpected event occurs to a firm. Also, assume that the market is efficient and investors do not overreact. The graphs in Figures 9.1 and 9.2 illustrate the evolution of stock returns when investors overreact with and without overreaction.

Figure 9.1 presents the returns on the stock in the days surrounding the arrival of a new favorable information (an event). The event

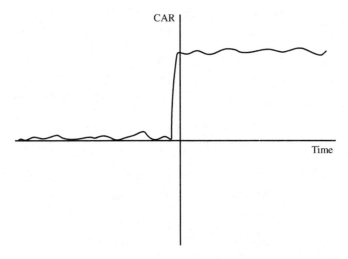

Figure 9.1. Stock returns around a positive news event with no overreaction.

day is time 0. Until the event day, above-normal returns are quite stable with small "normal" fluctuations due to noise and hence the CARs (cumulative abnormal returns; at any point t, CAR_t is the sum of the abnormal returns from the time analysis has begun to this point) also fluctuate around zero. Then, on the day of the event, returns rise to above-normal rates because of the favorable news, yet immediately come back to normal (zero). The CARs therefore remain at about the same level they reached on the day of the event.

Figure 9.2 presents the returns on the stock in the days surrounding the arrival of a new favorable information (an event) assuming overreaction. Until the event day, returns are quite stable with small "normal" fluctuations due to noise and hence the CARs fluctuate around zero. Then, on the day of the event, returns rise to above-normal rates because of the favorable news and the CARs turn positive. However, since the investors overreact the prices rise "too much" on the event day. In the following periods, investors realize their mistakes, prices fall and the CARs decline until they reach the correct level appropriate to the news.

If the news is unfavorable to the firm, then on the event day, the CARs will disproportionally fall, and then, after a non-trivial period, come back to the appropriate level.

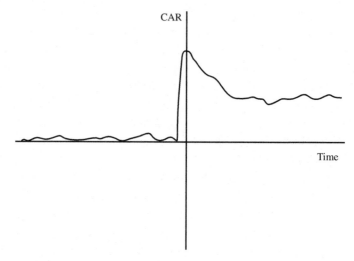

Figure 9.2. Stock returns around a positive news event with overreaction.

Do markets overreact?

In a seminal study, De Bondt and Thaler (DBT) (1985) studied stocks that performed very well and stocks that performed very poorly at some point in time to examine whether they exhibited overreaction.

DBT assumed that the extraordinary performance of these stocks was probably due to some unexpected favorable or unfavorable information. In the absence of overreaction, the effect of extreme information should immediately be reflected in the stock prices, and abnormal returns should subsequently fluctuate around zero. Therefore, the pattern of the excess returns following the extreme rise or fall in prices may indicate to what extent the markets did or did not overreact.

DBT's methodology

DBT collected returns on all stocks for the years 1930–1980, and they created portfolios of 35 of the highest-gaining and 35 of the lowest-gaining stocks (high performers and low performers, respectively) for each three-year interval. Then, they tracked their performance over the next 36 months. The high and low performers are suspected of overreaction. To prevent overlapping portfolios, the data allowed them 16 repetitions of the experiment (dividing the 50 years sample period into three years intervals; $50/3 \sim 16$).

On the vertical axis of the graph in Figure 9.3, which is loosely based on DBT, we see the average cumulative abnormal returns (CARs) of the portfolios. The horizontal axis in Figure 9.3 shows the number of months that elapsed since the portfolio was constructed. The upper graph depicts the CARs of the losing stocks, and the lower graph depicts the CARs of the winning stocks.

One notes in Figure 9.3 that over the three years period, the returns of the losing stocks exceeded those of the stock market (normal returns) by about 19.6% whereas the CARs of the winning stocks fell short of the market by about 5%, thus representing a 24.6% difference between the two portfolios. Note also the asymmetry in the overreaction of the winning stocks and the losing stocks: The overreaction was stronger for the losing stocks than for the winning stocks.

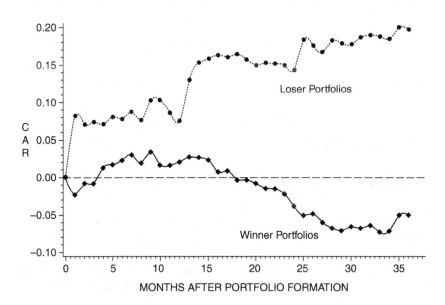

Figure 9.3. Performance of the winning and the losing stocks.
Source: De Bondt and Thaler (1985).

DBT performed robustness checks on their results. They altered the number of stocks in the portfolios from the original 35 and studied different evaluation periods (in contrast to the original 36 months) and found results that are qualitatively similar to the results of the parameters of their original study. But they were not yet satisfied. They also studied whether seasonal effects (specifically, the January effect) contributed to these patterns. In Figure 9.3, seasonal effects are difficult to detect, but these effects are more marked in Figure 9.4, which is similar to Figure 9.3 (and is also loosely drawn according to DBT), yet presents the results for a longer period.

In Figure 9.4, we can see a distinct increase in the losing stocks every January (actually, what we see is a decline in November–December and then a rise in January). This is the January effect (that we mentioned in Lecture 1 and we will discuss in more depth in Lecture 17). You may wonder what would happen to the results if we eliminate these months, and this is exactly what the authors examined. They found that overreaction prevails even after controlling for the January effect.

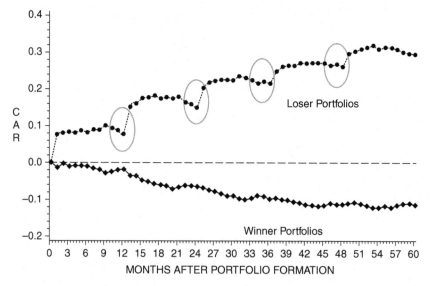

Figure 9.4. Seasonal effects.

Source: De Bondt and Thaler (1985).

Does DBT's Study Provide Slam-dunk Evidence of Investors' Overreaction?

Not so fast!

➤ The winning-most (losing-most) firms might have become large (small) because of their performance, and hence the pattern of returns DBT found might have been due to the size effect.
➤ The beta of the winning-most (losing-most) firms might have decreased (increased) because of their performance.
➤ Much of the effects, but not all of them, are due to the January effect.

May the results be due to size and beta effects and not to overreaction?

Winning firms become larger as their profits add to their assets and their market value (equity) increases. As the winning firms' equity increases, their leverage declines, as a result of which their betas decrease as well. Since lower beta firms require lower rates of return, the drop in the winning firms' returns can be explained by their lower betas.

DBT's overreaction theory has come under attack by some scholars using the above arguments, although they could explain how their data can meet these critiques in their 1987 paper. Their study however received support from Zarowin, 1989.

Vermalean and Verstringe (1998) and Jegadeesh and Titman (1993, 2001a, 2001b and 2002), in separate studies, found results opposite to those of DBT. We will later analyze if these differences could be reconciled. However, in recent years, some major events occurred in the financial markets which may provide support for the overreaction theory: the subprime crisis of 2007–2009 and Brexit in 2016. Below, we'll briefly discuss these events.

The sub-prime crisis — An example of overreaction?

The stock market fell sharply in 2007–2008 due to the subprime crisis and the failure of several investment houses, but has rebounded

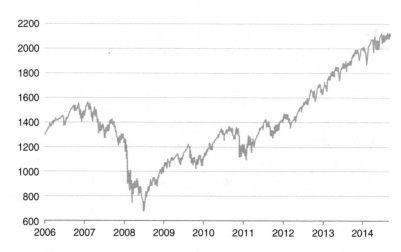

Figure 9.5. The subprime crisis: An example for overreaction?
Source: Yahoo finance.

since (see Figure 9.5 that was drawn using data from Yahoo Finance), prompting the question of whether the decline in 2007–2008 represents a major overreaction.

Brexit — An example of overreaction?

In June 2016, a referendum at the UK determined that the country will leave the European Union. This was a surprise, as most polls predicted that British voters would vote to remain in the EU. Remaining a member of the EU was considered a good decision for the British economy and for the global economy. In the few days preceding the referendum, as markets predicted a stay, market returns were slightly positive in almost all markets, see, for example, in Figure 9.6 (drawn based on data from Bloomberg), the DAX (Germany) and the FTSE indices. Once the results of the vote became public, the markets dropped sharply only to rebound to their pre-Brexit level a few weeks later. In contrast, on news of the Brexit, the British pound dropped and by February 2017 had not returned to its pre-Brexit level.

Underreaction

Underreaction occurs in markets when prices do not immediately adjust to reflect new information as assumed by the efficient market

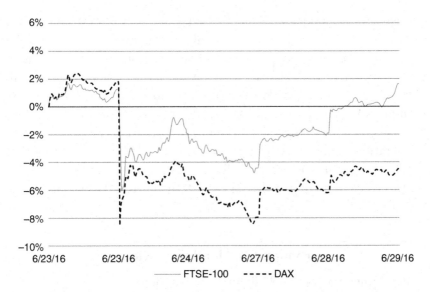

Figure 9.6. Brexit as an overreaction.

Source: Bloomberg.

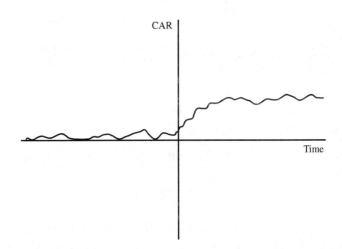

Figure 9.7. Stock returns around a positive news event with underreaction.

hypothesis. Rather, prices adjust slowly to the new information and a significant time elapses between the arrival of a new information and its full reflection in prices.

Figure 9.7 presents the returns on the stock in the days surrounding the arrival of a new favorable information in a manner consistent with underreaction. In Figure 9.7, the event day is time 0. Until the event day, above-normal returns are quite stable with small "normal" fluctuations due to noise and hence the CARs fluctuate around zero. Then, on the day of the event, returns rise to above-normal rates because of the favorable news and the CARs turn positive. However, since the investors underreact, the prices do not rise enough to fully reflect the new information. Rather, the new information is only slowly digested and the CARs continue to rise. It takes some time before the full significance of the news is reflected by the price and the CARs plateau at the correct level justified by the news.

Evidence of Underreaction

Major phenomena which signify overreaction:

Momentum in stock prices
Post-earning announcement drift

Other examples

Stock splits and stock dividends
Tender offers
Open market repurchases
Dividend initiations and omissions
Seasoned issues of common stocks

For a more extensive list of examples of underreaction, see Daniel *et al.* (1998).

Momentum in stock prices exist if returns of stocks that have risen (fallen) in the past continue to do so. Actually, momentum means that there is a positive correlation in stock returns. We have seen above that such correlation would arise from underreaction and hence evidence of positive correlation in returns or investment strategies that are based on such correlations (buying when stocks go up believing they would continue to climb) would be indicative of underreaction.

Traders and Momentum Strategies

➤ Relative strength is a popular momentum investing technique (this is a strategy that involves buying stocks when their current price is substantially higher than their average price over, say, the preceding 27 weeks, or variations of this rule).

➤ The popularity and success of the relative strength strategy and other momentum strategies point to a ubiquitous belief in momentum and hence probably indicates underreaction.

➤ Mutual funds are frequent users of momentum strategies.

➤ Can this be reconciled with DBT's claims of investors' inherent overreaction?

Some academics questioned the profitability of momentum strategies since they contradicted the EMH. Yet, Grinblatt *et al.* 1995) investigated the profitability of momentum strategies. They sampled a large number of mutual funds and found that the majority of them tended to buy stocks whose price increased over the preceding quarter. Jegadeesh and Titman (JT) (1993) review the literature that supports relative strength strategies. The literature they review suggests that these strategies largely realize significant abnormal returns. An additional support for momentum strategies is that relative strength is one of the components of Value Line rankings (which measure the total risk of a stock relative to approximately 1,750 other stocks), so it thus seems that relative strength strategies (and thus momentum) probably has some merit.

The above findings still needed more scrutiny and statistical rigor. JT (2001a, 2001b and 2002) picked up the gauntlet and further explored the profitability of momentum strategies. If momentum strategies are profitable, this implies that some kind of underreaction is probable.

Momentum Strategies — Evidence of Short-term Underreaction

➤ JT (1993, 2001a, 2001b and 2002) explore the profitability of relative strength strategies over 3–12 months horizons.

(Continued)

(*Continued*)

> ➤ Their evidence is consistent with underreaction to firm-specific information.

JT explored the profitability of relative strength strategies over 3–12 months horizons. After controlling for systematic risk and ruling out that their strategy's success results from delayed stock price reactions to information about some common factor, they show that these strategies generated significant profits in the period of their sample (1965–1989).

Compared with DBT's study, JT's study uses more strategies and more sophisticated statistical methods and they control for size and beta (which DBT did not). However, JT did not control for momentum, but showed that momentum definitely affects returns.

Note: One can then speculate that the addition of the momentum factor to Fama and French's (1996) pricing model could be partially attributed to the findings of JT in 1993.

We note that JT's results do not necessarily contradict those of DBT. JT's underreaction refer to the shorter term (returns for holding periods of up to 12 months), whereas DBT refer to holding periods of 3–5 years.

How Can We Reconcile between the Findings of Overreaction and Underreaction?

Henceforth, we will present two theories, which rely on two different behavioral biases that attempt to reconcile between overreaction in the long run and underreaction in the short run:

- A theory based on representativeness and conservativism — Barberis, Shleifer and Vishny (BSV)(1998).
- A theory invoking overconfidence and self-attribution — Daniel, Hirshleifer and Subrahmanyam (DHS) (1998).

In order to better understand these theories, it will be helpful to review the concepts of representativeness and conservatism, and emphasize the differences between them.

The Representativeness Heuristics vs. the Conservatism Bias

Representativeness, as we defined it in Lecture 3 (we briefly repeat this material here to make this lecture more self-contained), is one's tendency to view extreme events as typical or representative of a specific class and consequently err in their probability assessments by giving them too much weight relative to the prior information. Conservativeness is one's tendency to give too little weight to new information. Representativeness and conservatism therefore seem to be contradictory: The first implies overreaction and the second implies underreaction.

Griffin and Tversky (1992) argue that decisions makers will overreact to some types of information and underreact to other types. They contend that when people make forecasts, they pay too much attention to the strength of the news and underestimate the statistical significance of their prior information and hence overreact. When the information is of "low strength", the decision makers underweight the new information and underreact. Representativeness occurs in response to salient (striking and extremely noticeable) information. Conservatism occurs in response to "low-strength" information.

BSV offer the following example from the stock market to show how investors may be affected by representativeness. They say that investors might classify some stocks as growth stocks based on their history of consistent earnings growth. By classifying stocks in this way, these investors focus on a firm's string of successes and ignore the prior information that very few companies maintain sustained growth over time and hence they may overreact.

BSV propose that corporate announcements such as earnings announcements that are not too salient represent low-strength information, even though they may have considerable statistical weight. This assumption led them to posit that stock prices would underreact to low-strength information, leading to underreaction (momentum) in the short term, while a long series of above-normal financial successes would constitute high-strength information that induces investors to overreact in the long term.

DHS propose an alternative theory whereby the coexistence of overreaction and underreaction can be explained by over-confidence and self-attribution (see also Hong and Stein, 1999). In their theory, DHS consider investors who receive both private and public signals about the quality of firms. Overconfident investors grant greater accuracy to their private information than to the public information they receive. The overconfidence of these investors is due to self- attribution (defined in Lecture 7). DHS provide an additional explanation for self-attribution in the context of how people react to confirming and disconfirming signals. A confirming signal accords with the investor's view; for example, good news about a firm after the investor made a buy based on his private signal. The opposite holds for disconfirming signals.

DHS assume that if investors receive confirming public signals, they self-attribute and hence such signals increase their confidence. However, their treatment of disconfirming signals is asymmetric; such signals have little or no effect on the investors. This asymmetry leads DHS to the conclusion that on average public signals increase investors' confidence and leads them to overconfidence.

Accordingly, investors who receive public information will repeat their actions (if the information is confirming) and will do nothing if it is disconfirming, causing on average momentum-like increases in prices (underreaction) in the short term. In the long run, reality will eventually catch up with them, and prices will revert to their normal levels, creating long-term price reversals (overreaction).

In the discussions above, we considered overreaction and under-reaction in the context of investments. Such phenomena (especially underreaction) however can also be witnessed in the reaction of stock price to corporate events. Underreaction has been observed after many types of corporate announcements: Earnings announcements (we will discuss the post-earnings announcement drift at length in

Lecture 16), stock splits and stock dividends, tender offers, open market repurchases, dividend initiations and omissions, and seasoned issues of common stock. Because of the similar nature of the pattern of returns following corporate announcements, we only list some of the more prominent examples and limit our discussion to the case of the behavior of returns following stock splits and dividends.

Underreaction to Corporate Announcements

Figure 9.8 (loosely redrawn according to Grinblatt *et al.* 1984) shows the behavior of returns around the event day. You can see that stock prices rise on the announcement date, since the stock splits and stock dividends are considered good news. The underreaction is inferred from the fact that the stock prices continue to rise without any apparent news to justify these rises. It therefore seems that the full extent of the good news was not realized on the announcement date and that the market requires some time to "digest" the information.

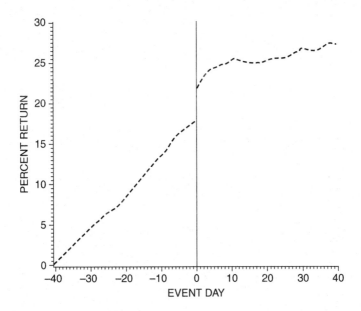

Figure 9.8. Returns around announcement of stock splits or stock dividends. *Source*: Grinblatt *et al.* (1984).

Incidentally (to underreaction), stock prices rose before the announcement. This could be interpreted as a sign of inefficiency (investors expected the good news) or as the underlying cause of the dividend distribution and the stock split (the firm was doing well).

Conclusion

- There is evidence of underreaction in stock prices in the short term and for overreaction in the long term.
- These biases might stem from overconfidence, conservatism, representativeness and self-attribution.

THE EQUITY PREMIUM PUZZLE AND MYOPIC LOSS AVERSION

Agenda

➤ The Equity Premium Puzzle (EPP): Definition and Scope
➤ Traditional Explanations for the EPP
➤ Myopic Loss Aversion Rationale for the EPP
➤ Implications of the EPP for Investors

The Equity Premium Puzzle (EPP)

Equity risk premium, or equity premium, is the excess return that investing in the stock market provides over a risk-free rate such as the return from government treasury bonds.

This excess return compensates investors for taking on the relatively higher risk of equity investing. Stocks have outperformed bonds on average, and this is not surprising. The puzzle is in the degree that stocks outperformed bonds. Over the years, this premium has been 8% on average, too high to be explained by mainstream financial as a "proper" level of compensation that would occur as a result of investor risk aversion. According to theory, the premium should actually be much lower than the historic average.

The puzzle was framed by some researchers as why are the returns on equity so high as to allow a high spread between stocks and bonds,

Lecture Notes in Behavioral Finance

but others framed it as the question of why are the returns on bonds so low. Today, when the returns on risk-free assets are close to zero in nominal terms and might even be negative in real terms, the second question has become increasingly more relevant.

High equity premiums in real terms have been demonstrated for many periods in four different studies detailed in Mehra and Prescott (2008). These studies spanned quite extensive periods although they overlapped somewhat.

The risk premiums however within shorter sub-periods (say yearly) of these long periods were fairly volatile. Thus, the existence of large risk premiums for long stretches of time would provide cold comfort to investors with short investment horizons. The possibility of losses for such investors was not negligible.

More convincing evidence of the EPP is the following statistic: Equities have outperformed bonds for most 20-year intervals that have been studied. Although the length of the intervals in which one class of assets outperforms the other sheds important light on the relative desirability of the two classes, one wonders what well-founded theories such as utility theory or prospect theory would recommend to decision makers choosing between these classes of assets.

EPP is not limited to the US

Mehra and Prescott (1985, 2008) show that high equity premia prevailed for almost all countries, and that a high equity premium is not only a US phenomenon. During the period between 1900 and 2005 the lowest premium was recorded in the UK (6.1%) and the highest in France (9.3%). These data reinforce the idea that some general forces induce the high equity premium.

Mehra and Prescott's Original Formulation of the EPP

Mehra and Prescott (MP) (1985, 2008) presented a general equilibrium model where consumers determine how much to consume, how much to invest and how much of their investments to allocate to bonds and to stocks. They assume that consumers make their choices so as to maximize their lifetime expected utility:

$$E\left[\sum_{t=0}^{t=\infty} \beta^t u(c_t)\right]$$

They assume a utility function of the form:

$$u(c) = \frac{c^{1-\gamma} - 1}{1 - \gamma}$$

Then, they asked the following question: What parameters of this function would best fit (explain) the actual consumption, wealth and returns of bonds and stocks patterns that prevailed historically in the US economy?

In the formulas above, c_t denotes consumption at time t, and $u(c)$ is the individual's utility function. MP assume a utility function that belongs to the class of constant relative risk aversion (CRRA) functions, where γ denotes risk aversion (a higher γ reflects greater risk aversion). This type of utility function has been widely used in finance and seems to represent decision makers' preferences quite well. With a CRRA utility function, the consumer's aversion to gambles that are small and proportionate to her wealth is constant regardless of her wealth. We mentioned this when first we introduced prospect theory. The parameter $\beta(0 < \beta < 1)$ denotes a time discount factor which describes the preference of the consumer between current and future consumption. The lower the β, the less the consumer likes future consumption relative to current consumption.

MP showed that in order to explain the equity premium — the returns on bonds and stocks, and especially the difference between them — the risk aversion parameter γ must be of an order of magnitude of 30. This is an unreasonably high rate of risk aversion. Mankiw and Zeldes (1991) offer the following example that illustrates how unrealistic this level of risk aversion is: An individual with a risk aversion parameter of 30, who is offered a 50–50 gamble of winning $50,000 or $100,000 will be indifferent between this gamble and a certain amount of $51,209. The more common risk aversion measure γ used in finance is around two. Using this rate of risk aversion in Mankiw and Zeldes' example, the individual would be indifferent between the gamble and $66,667.

The prevailing high premium thus implies that individuals are extraordinarily risk averse, much higher than we generally assume. The observed risk premiums therefore seem paradoxical (for a thorough review of the puzzle see Ewijk *et al.*).

Resolutions of the EPP

➤ Alternative assumptions about preferences (say, habit formation).

➤ Modified probability distributions to admit rare but disastrous events.

➤ Limited participation of consumers in the stock market.

The EPP hypothesis is actually a joint hypothesis which postulates that both the equity premium is too high and that MP's model is solid. Most of the explanations argue that the puzzle largely hinges on the utility function used by MP (for an extensive evaluation of the explanations see Siegel and Thaler, 1997). Although MP have gone to great lengths to defend their economic model and the usage of the above-mentioned utility function, some researchers have shown that the EPP can be resolved by introducing some modifications to MP's model.

The habit formation approach advanced by Constantinides (1990) maintains that consumers are averse to reductions in their levels of consumption, a feature not captured by MP's utility function. According to Constantinides, consumers are more willing than ordinary utility-maximizers to forgo returns in order to avoid reductions in their consumption levels. Consequently, they will be more willing to invest in riskless securities than the consumers represented by MP's utility function, and therefore, their behavior is not so puzzling.

A similar approach is to define utility of consumption relative to average per capita consumption. This is an external habit model where preferences are defined on the ratio of consumption to average per capita consumption. This type of preferences, also known as "Catching up with the Joneses," redefines the individual's reference point (see Zapatero, 2016). As in the case of habit formation, this perspective on utility makes the consumer more sensitive and averse to consumption reductions.

The distribution functions of returns used by MP are quite smooth, even though they are based on historical returns. If their model is revised to admit rare events of catastrophic nature, then as in the arguments above, consumers will be more tolerant to the low returns provided by riskless assets (e.g., Rietz, 1988).

Finally, MP's approach postulates the existence of individual investors only and does not consider financial intermediaries, financial institutions and other organizations. MP's representative economic agent that maximizes his lifetime expected utility of consumption does not fit well these organizations. Also, in MP's model, all individuals participate in the stock market whereas in fact, this is not so.

Explaining the EPP Using a Myopic Loss Aversion Approach

According to Benartzi and Thaler (BT) (1995), the key to explaining the EPP is to replace MP's utility function with a prospect theory utility function that incorporates loss aversion.

If investors review their portfolios often and if they are loss averse (BT call this combination myopic loss aversion), they may become very risk averse and will refrain from investing in stocks.

Using an example provided by Samuelson (1963) and analyzed by many others (see for example, Lopes, 1981 and Tversky and Bar Hillel, 1983), we show how frequent reviewing of investors' portfolios may lead them to increased risk aversion.

The Betting Game

A decision maker is offered the following bet: Flip a fair coin. Get $200 if it comes up head or lose $100 if it comes up tail.

➢ Suppose you are offered to play it once, would you take the offer?

➢ Suppose you are offered to play this game 100 times, would you take the offer?

Samuelson offered this bet to his friend, who said he is not willing to take the single bet, but would be happy to take 100 such independent bets. Samuelson argued that this is irrational: If the individual does not like one bet, he should not take 100 bets. Samuelson proves his point by dynamic programming: Assume that you already took 99 bets and now you are offered the 100th bet, would you take it? The answer is no. Samuelson moved back recursively to show that you would not take the 100 bets if you refuse the one bet.

Samuelson's recursive argument however assumes that his friend cannot commit himself to take 100 bets (the recursion starts with the friend having made 99 bets and needing to decide on the 100th bet), so Samuelson's argument cannot be used against his friend's logic since the latter was willing to commit.

The explanation for the friend's willingness to take the 100 bets while refusing the single bet hinges on the possibility to commit. Taking 100 bets and reviewing only the result of the 100 bets and none of the interim results would provide a totally different distribution function of returns to the bettor. To see how the number of bets affects the distribution of receipts in these bets, we observe that if you play the betting game once, you have a 50% chance of losing. If you play twice, the chances fall to 25% (if the coin comes up tails twice). If you play the betting game 100 times, the probability of losing is very slim since, in order to lose in a game of 100 bets you need to lose in 33 or more of the coin tosses, and the chances of this are merely 0.089%.

The point is that if the expected value of every single bet is positive, the more independent bets you play, the greater your chances of winning. If you commit to take the 100 bets and you do not peek in the middle to see how you are doing, then you will be more likely to take the whole bet. Investing in stocks is similar. Each coin toss can be considered as investing in the stock for a specific period. If you check your returns more frequently, say weekly, you will be more risk averse than if you review your portfolio less frequently, say once a month.

In what follows, we will analyze how the expected prospective value of the bettor varies with the number of bets

---

Suppose the decision maker's value function is the following variation of KT's value function:

$$V(x) = x \qquad \text{if } x > 0$$
$$= 2.25x \quad \text{if } x < 0$$

For this function and one bet, the expected prospective value of the hypothesized value function is

$$E[V(x)] = 200 \times 0.5 - 2.25 \times 100 \times 0.5 = -12.5$$

The expected value of the prospective value function is negative, and the bet therefore should not be taken even though it has a positive monetary expected value.

What happens if the bet is taken twice?

Let's see what our decision maker does if the bet is played twice, the second bet is independent of the first, and the player commits to two coin tosses.

The distribution function of winnings is

➤ Win 400 with probability 0.25
➤ Win 100 with probability 0.50
➤ Lose 200 with probability 0.25

The expected value of the bets in this case is therefore:

$$E[V(x)] = 400 \times 0.25 + 100 \times 0.5 - 2.25 \times 200 \times 0.25 = 37.5$$

In this case, the individual will take the two bets when he observes just the results of the two of them combined.

We note that with one bet, the probability of losing is 0.5, but with two bets, when we observe just the end result (and are not allowed to see the result of the first bet before making the second bet), the probability of losing is only 0.25. Although taking two bets is riskier than taking one bet (it has a larger variance), taking the two bets yields a higher prospective expected value because of the different distribution and since according to prospect theory decision makers are risk lovers in the losses domain.

The lesson from this example is: The lower the frequency of viewing the results (viewing the results only after two bets), the more desirable the bets become.

How does this resolve the EPP?

The above betting game is analogous to investments in the risky stock market where each investment period is parallel to the above one bet. The expected returns on stocks are positive as they must earn some risk premium (although not necessarily as high as the prevailing risk premium). If you evaluate the results of the investment frequently, you become more risk averse and are more likely to choose the risk-free asset over an investment in the stock market. As a result of your increased risk aversion, you make choices that will hurt your returns. The less frequently you review your investment, the more desirable stocks become. Thus, according to BT, the high returns that equities earn are due to excessive evaluations of investors' portfolios which in turn result from their short investment horizons which lead to excessive risk aversion.

The Behavioral Finance Foundation for the Explanation

BT base their argument on two concepts: Loss aversion and mental accounting.

➢ Loss aversion is a property of the utility function that is consistent with the puzzle.
➢ Mental accounting allows for a separate evaluation in each period.

BT's research methodology (we review this study's methodology since it is quite unique).

> ➤ Investors' investment horizon is broken into n sub-periods (months) in which investors divide their portfolios between stocks and bonds.
> ➤ The expected value of an investor's utility is calculated as a function of n for two types of portfolios: all stock and all bonds.
> ➤ BT used a prospect theory utility function and a distribution of returns based on actual stocks and bonds returns to evaluate the expected prospective value of investments in bonds and stocks.

Having calculated the expected value of the investor's utility as a function of the number of evaluations periods, n, for bonds and stocks, BT explore at what point (in which evaluation period, n, measured in months) will the expected prospective value of investing in stocks equal that of investing in riskless assets. They believed that for very short evaluation periods, investors will be extremely risk averse and therefore prefer a fixed income, but as the evaluation period increases, the expected value of investment in stock increases. The point at which the two values are equal is an equilibrium point.

BT argue that if the theoretical n coincides with the n observed in the market, then this is the explanation for the current equity premium.

From the expected utility functions that are depicted in Figure 10.1, loosely based on Benartzi and Thaler (1995), and which are plotted as a function of n, we can see that the equilibrium is reached at $n = 12$ (one year). This, BT claim, coincides with the common review period for individual investors. Therefore, BT conclude that the observed equilibrium returns (and equity premium) is consistent with KT's utility function and frequent evaluations.

However, the assumption that investors choose between bonds-only and stocks-only portfolios is a simplification. BT therefore also

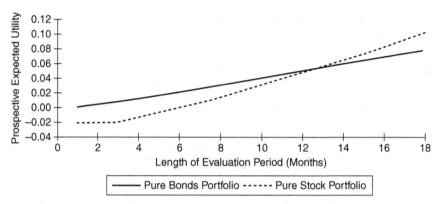

Figure 10.1. Prospective utility as a function of the number of evaluation periods.

use the current evaluation period ($n = 12$), KT's value function and the historical distribution of returns to explore an investor's (prospective) expected value as a function of the percentage of her portfolio invested in stocks.

The optimal allocation of an investor's portfolio, given all the data above, is about 50% stocks and 50% fixed income, an allocation that is consistent with the allocation prevailing at the market at the time of their research. BT therefore conclude that KT's utility function, together with mental accounting and loss aversion, explain the observed equity premium.

Experimental support for BT's results

Gneezy and Potters (1997) offer experimental support for BT's model (see also Amar and Kroll for support for this theory). In their simulated market game, they find clear evidence that participants took higher risks in a market with less frequent evaluations. However, their experiment is stylized and does not fully reflect reality: the experiment took 1 hour, while in reality investors face much longer evaluation periods, and participants received much more precise information than is typically available to investors. Finally, as in many experiments, the stakes were much lower than in the case of real-life investment decisions.

More insights from BT's theory

BT's results point to the advantages of passive investment strategies and the dangers of too active strategies (beyond the obvious high transaction costs which excessive transactions entail). Their results clearly indicate that individuals are too risk averse and should invest more in equity.

One may also wonder to what extent are BT's results relevant today since nowadays data are more readily available than in the past and hence the assumption that the evaluation period is 1 year may not hold. On the face of it, the more readily available data may increase the incidence of reevaluation and exacerbate the myopic risk aversion.

Whereas individuals inherently have short planning horizons, institutions, foundations and university endowments have a longer life span (which in principle is infinite), so why are their evaluation periods so frequent and planning horizons short? BT suggest that this may be due to agency issues where the manager mainly considers the profitability of the investments in their own short planning horizon rather than the long-run profitability of their institutions. This implies that clients and directors of such institutions should monitor more closely how often the managers reevaluate their portfolios and examine their risk taking levels. The analysis also indicates that age-dependent savings plans (e.g., the Chilean model) that are sensitive to planning horizons could be instrumental in avoiding unnecessary reevaluation of portfolios.

Conclusions

- We reviewed the equity premium puzzle and showed how behavioral finance contributes in explaining it.

(*Continued*)

(*Continued*)

- Investors tendency to reevaluate their portfolios too often may lead them to invest too timidly.
- The dangers in too frequent evaluation of portfolios point to the advantages of passive investment strategies and long planning horizons.

THE HOME BIAS

Agenda

➤ Definition of the Home Bias
➤ Is the Home Bias Really a Bias?
➤ The Effects of the Home Bias on Investors
➤ Local Home Bias
➤ Investing in the Employer's Firm

The Home Bias

Home bias is the empirical phenomenon that when composing their portfolio, investors tend to put too great a weight on stocks from their own county. This has puzzled academics since portfolio theory recommends diversification, including internationally. For any given expected return, international diversification can lead to a substantial reduction in risk. Over the last few decades globalization has increased international investments, but even today many researchers think that investors have not taken entirely the advantage of international diversification, and that the bias still exists. If there is no economic justification for this underdiversification, then behavioral considerations may play a role in this phenomenon. In this lecture, we review several explanations and explore several facets of the phenomenon' although there is no single explanation that solves the puzzle completely.

In general, people root for the home team and feel more comfortable investing in familiar firms and firms from their own country and they are more optimistic about such firms. For example, *in an experimental study German (business) students were more optimistic about German stocks relative to American stocks, but the opposite was true for American students.*

Heath and Tversky (1991) claim that investors prefer investing in the known. They call this the "authority" hypothesis. They also suggest the competence hypothesis, according to which when people feel skillful or knowledgeable in a specific area, they are more willing to bet on their own judgments, and vice versa. As people believe themselves more knowledgeable on stocks from their own country, their willingness to trade on such stocks is higher. Graham, *et al.* (2005) argue that this mental tendency bias can explain the home bias.

Variations on the International Home Bias

The "original" home bias has been extended to include the following phenomena:

➤ *Local home bias*: preferring to invest in close firms within the same country.
➤ *Regional home bias*: investments of European countries in countries of the Eurozone.
➤ Investing in the employers' firms.
➤ International capital immobility (countries invest most of their savings locally rather than in other countries).

Early evidence of the home bias

The first academic article on the home bias I found (in a Google search) is a paper by Feldstein and Horioka, published in 1980, which shows a strong positive correlation between countries savings and local investments, though this paper refers to international capital immobility and not to the home bias *per se*. The issue of the paucity of international diversification was first documented by French and Poterba in 1991, but they did not refer to it as the home bias. In the same Google search stated above, I found the earliest mentions of the term "home bias" in a title of a published paper in Cooper and Kaplanis, (1994), and Tesar and Werner (1995) (Apologies if there were prior such mentions).

According to Poterba (1991), in the late 1980s, US investors held almost 94% of their equity portfolios in domestic equity. The home bias was even stronger for Japanese investors, but not so strong for UK investors, who held "only" 82% of their portfolio in UK stocks.

Tesar and Werner present the evolution of the percentage of international investments out of the total portfolio for several countries between 1970 and 1990. They demonstrate a very slight trend of increased diversification, discernible mainly between 1985 and 1990. They also show a remarkably higher international investment (weaker home bias) than the other countries in the UK, and that the US and Canada exhibited the lowest levels of international diversification as well as the lowest rates of growth of these levels over time.

Is the home bias really a bias?

The empirical fact is that investors hold few international assets, but it remains to be seen whether portfolios like this can be justified on rational economic grounds.

There are several potential financial justifications for preferring home stocks:

✓ Informational and communication disadvantages.
✓ Lower liquidity of foreign stocks.
✓ Exchange rate risks, transaction costs.
✓ Differences in trading times.
✓ Regulatory constraints on trading.
✓ Taxation.

As some of these factors change over time, we might expect the home bias to change over time. Should we expect the home bias to diminish?

✓ Yes — because globalization reduces transaction costs of international trade.

✓ Yes — because people have easy access to information through the Internet and other inexpensive modes of communication.

✓ Yes — because restrictions on investors in other countries are more relaxed.

✓ Yes — because accounting standards have been unified (IFRS).

✓ No — because globalization might have increased the co-movements (correlation) between markets and therefore lowered the benefits from diversification.

Figure 11.1, loosely based on Levy and Levy (2014), presents the evolution of the home bias in US equity over time, where the home bias is defined as the difference between the proportion of US investments in US portfolios and the weight of US equity in the world equity market. You can see that although the home bias diminished

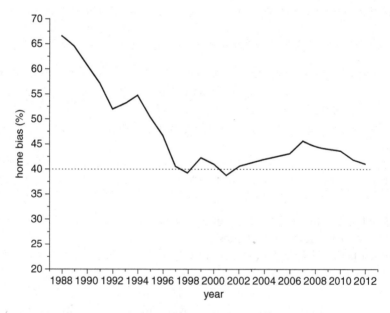

Figure 11.1. The home bias — recent evidence.

Source: Levy and Levy, (2014).

considerably from the 1980s to the beginning of the new millennium, it has basically plateaued since.

Levy and Levy (2014) predict that the home bias is a fixture of financial markets that will not go away any time soon, despite the fact that the costs of foreign investments have fallen steadily over the last two decades (and might drop further), because the correlation between countries has increased from around 0.4 to around 0.9. In other words, they suggest that the positive effects of the diminishing costs of foreign investments were offset by the increasing correlations between countries. They predict that these two opposing factors will continue to offset each other.

The home bias is not limited to the United States. It appears in almost all countries, although to varying degrees. Schoenmaker and Soeter (2014) report the prevalence of the home bias in many regions (US, Euro, EU-14, non-Euro). They also report that its extent in European countries fell in the Euro era partly because of the decline in the exchange rate risk. They find however that the regional home bias in European countries increased over time, and that the extent of the home bias differed in crisis and non-crisis periods.

Do all investors exhibit the same degree of home bias? One would expect that investors exhibit different degrees of home bias since barriers to foreign investments may vary considerably between investors. Kyrychenko and Shum (2009) found differences between professional and non-professional investors' tendency to invest in US stocks.

Local home bias

Local home bias, interesting in its own right, could shed some light also on the reasons for the international home bias. Most of the economic reasons for the existence of international home bias do not exist when firms in the same country are considered: Factors such as differences in language, exchange rates, culture, taxes, etc. are irrelevant when considering investments within the same country. Therefore, evidence of a local home bias also bolsters the case for behavioral explanations for the home bias both locally and internationally. To explore this question, Coval and Moskowitz (1999) studied the weight of stocks in the portfolio of managers and the distance between the firm's headquarters and the manager's address. They found a significant correlation between the weight of the stocks and the distance to the manager's address. This supports the theory that investors show preference to local firms, even if this proximity is just geographic.

In 2001, Coval and Moskowitz revisited mutual funds' propensity to invest locally. Their 1999 paper was based on Nelson's Directory of Investment Managers, which contains a cross-section of the 1995 holdings of largest money managers in the US. Their 2001 study is based on Investment Company Common Stock Holdings and Transactions tapes, obtained from CDA Investment Technologies. They reach different conclusions in the two papers, and the difference in the data sets may be one of the reasons for the different conclusions.

In the 2001 study, mutual funds earned higher returns when investing in local stocks. The reason why funds earn more from nearby firms may be related to mutual fund managers' ability to obtain more information on local firms due to the ease of interactions they enjoy with these firms. In light of these findings, Coval and Moskowitz themselves were wondering why such funds refrain from holding an even greater proportion of local stocks, suggesting that a reverse home bias may be in play. In addition to the insights obtained from such reversal of opinions on the local home bias, this tells us about pervasiveness of disagreement about financial theories.

Is the local home bias a behavioral phenomenon?

Huberman (2001) studied this question using a very unique data set.

In 1984, AT&T (Bell Co.) was ordered by the courts to restructure its activities into seven regional firms ("Baby Bells"), or Regional Bell Operating Companies RBOCs.

Huberman looked at investors' propensity to put their money in the Baby Bell operating in their own state compared to investing in other Baby Bells. There are no good economic reasons for an investor to prefer his local Baby Bell over the other Bells: these firms are almost perfect substitutes; the residents of any given state usually do not have more information on their local operator than on the other Bells; there are no higher obstacles to trade in non-local Baby Bells compared to trading in a local Baby Bell; and finally, a good diversification strategy calls for holding less of their own state RBOC because the values of many of their other assets (such as their home and salary) are more strongly correlated with their own RBOC than with other states' Baby Bells. If nevertheless, residents of a state prefer to invest in their local RBOC instead of other Baby Bells, this would indicate that their investment decisions are driven by behavioral rather than economic motives.

Huberman showed that the residents of any state hold a larger fraction of their portfolios in their local RBOC than in other Bells. For example, Arizona residents' holdings of their local RBOC (2.04%) is significantly (t-statistic of 21.20) higher than their holdings of out-of-state RBOCs (1.22%). The situation is similar for residents of all states.

Huberman performed analyses of other potential indicators of local home bias before he reached his conclusions. He found, for example, that every regional Baby Bell has more stockholders in its own region than in other regions, and that a larger proportion of the net income of all households in each state is invested in a local than in a non-local Baby Bell.

All of these findings led Huberman to conclude that residents of any state prefer to invest in their local RBOC, even though all RBOCs are almost perfect substitutes. Given that no financial reasons exist for this preference, we conclude that sentiments or other behavioral factors are responsible for this bias.

Investing in employer's stock — An example of local home bias

Investing in employer's stock is an extreme version of local bias. Investments in employer's stock are very popular although they are inefficient from a portfolio perspective: First, workers investing in their employer's stock usually invest too much in it. If the employer constitutes a tiny fraction of the stock market, a rule of thumb would suggest that the workers invest the same proportion of the employer's stock in her portfolio, but in many cases, workers invest more than that. Second, workers should invest an even smaller proportion of their portfolio in their employer's stock than the above rule of thumb recommends. Employees are already highly invested in their employer's future: A worker's human capital is highly correlated with his employer's stock. Should the employer go under, the employee would not only lose his investment but also his job. This makes investing in the employer's stock even less desirable. The fate of Enron and Worldcom workers who were encouraged to invest in their firms and ended up without jobs or savings is a poignant example.

Evaluating losses from investing in employer's stock

The losses due to investment in the employer's stock are significant. Meulbroek (2005) simulated the welfare of a worker who invests in her company's stock to the welfare of a similar (same utility function and wealth) worker who holds a well-diversified portfolio. She made standard assumptions about the shape of the worker's utility function (similar to those we made when we discussed the Equity Premium Puzzle) and wealth. Based on these assumptions, she compared the wealth of the employees under several scenarios. She found that the value of investments in employer's stock is inversely related to:

✓ The percentage of the employee's total wealth invested in the employer's stock;
✓ The variability of the stock;
✓ The length of time the employee holds the stock.

Meulbroek showed that a worker who holds 25% of his portfolio in his employer's stock (assuming the stock represents an average risk rate) for 10 years, loses 42 cents for every $1 held in that stock. That is, the value of the employee's investment in his workplace stock is worth 58% of the value of a similar investment in a well-diversified portfolio. Although the losses would decline to 33 cents per dollar if the stock is held for 15 years, even these losses are considerable.

Why do Employees' Invest in their Employer's Stock?

➤ Coercion
➤ Loyalty
➤ Biased perspective
➤ Mental accounting

In addition to the reasons for the home bias discussed above, employees' have several specific reasons for investing in their employer's stock.

Employees might wish to demonstrate their loyalty to their employer by investing in the employer's stock (see e.g., Cohen, 2009). They might believe that the employer expects them to make such investments, and that they might be rewarded for doing so and penalized if they do not. Sometimes, employers encourage their workers to invest in company stock (as in the infamous Enron case), in which case employees might feel uneasy if they refuse.

There are also some other reasons. Driscoll *et al.* (1995) claims that many workers believe that investing in their workplace is less risky than investing in a well-diversified portfolio. Benartzi and Thaler (2007) use mental accounting to explain this paradox: They claim that employees do not consider the employer's stock as part of the portfolio, but as a separate and distinct account to which the diversification rule does not apply.

Conclusions

➤ Investors tend to underdiversify internationally.
➤ Investors tend to overinvest in stocks close to home and in employer's stocks.

(*Continued*)

(*Continued*)

> Whereas the costs of international diversification have diminished over time, their benefits also declined because of increased global correlation.
> While there are some justifiable economic reasons for the home bias, the bias is also driven by behavioral considerations.

LIMITS TO ARBITRAGE

Agenda

➤ What is Arbitrage?

➤ Risks and Costs of Arbitrage

➤ Examples of Limits to Arbitrage

➤ Performance-based Arbitrage

Arbitrage is "the simultaneous purchase and sale of the same, or essentially similar, security in two different markets for advantageously different prices" (Sharpe and Alexander, 1990).

Will anomalies and biases persist over time in the presence of arbitrage opportunities?

If the arbitrage opportunities are genuine, then anomalies should not persist over time since arbitrageurs will exploit these opportunities to make above-normal profits and their endeavors will change prices until the opportunities are eliminated. The absence of arbitrage possibilities is often considered as the basis for the theoretical pricing of all financial assets (see e.g., Berk and DeMarzo, 2007): prices are determined so as not to allow arbitrage opportunities. No arbitrage is also the basis for option pricing formulas. But mispricing may persist when the arbitrage opportunities cannot be exploited (for various reasons discussed below). Strategies that are designed to correct the mispricing can be costly and risky and in such cases, the arbitrage opportunities are spurious. Likewise, if behavioral biases

are costly to economic agents, then the laws of evolution and competition should get in motion to eliminate them. The economic agents
exhibiting these biases should learn from mistakes, and markets will
eliminate the agents subject to biases as they will not be able to
compete with the rational ones.

Although traditional theory predicts that arbitrage opportunities would not persist, many examples have been provided in the
literature that document such opportunities. Controversy however
surrounds these examples concerning whether or not these arbitrage opportunities are exploitable or unexploitable (or not worthy
of exploiting) and hence spurious.

Examples of Persistent Arbitrage Opportunities

➤ Siamese twin shares Royal Dutch/Shell Transport
➤ ADRs
➤ 3Com spinoff of its Palm division
➤ "On the run" vs. "off the run" bonds

Siamese twins are firms that have two types of shares with fixed
claims on the firm's cash flows and assets. The classic example is
the Royal Dutch/Shell Group, the parent company of Royal Dutch
and of Shell Transport. These firms are entitled to receive 60%
and 40% of the parent's cash flows, respectively. The ratio of their
prices should therefore be 1.5, but history shows they were not (see
Lecture 4).

American Depositary Receipts (ADRs) are shares of foreign countries trading in the US, which are held, in trust by US financial
institutions for regulatory reasons. In principle, they should trade at
exactly the same price as their underlying assets, yet slight deviations
from these prices occur every now and again.

In March 2000, in an IPO, 3Com spun off part of its subsidiary,
Palm Inc., and promised to spin off its remaining shares within 9
months. Shareholders of 3Com were promised 1.5 shares of Palm for
each share of 3Com they own. At the close of trading on the first day
after the IPO, Palm shares traded at $95, implying that the value of

a 3Com share should be at least \$142.5 (95 × 1.5), yet 3Com traded at only \$81. This gross mispricing persisted for few weeks.

"On the run" long-term Treasury bonds (the most recent bonds) are traded at higher prices than equivalent "off the run" bonds (that were issued earlier). Persistence of this seeming arbitrage opportunity was explained by Amihud *et al.* (2001), who attributed this to the former's higher liquidity. Pasquariello and Vega (PV) (2009), however, show that the differences in liquidity are insufficient to justify the significant difference in prices between the two types of bonds. PV also ruled out other factors such as duration, convexity, repo rates, and term premiums as potential explanatory factors for the differentials. It therefore seems that the mispricing is genuine and persists.

While not entirely related to this topic but worthwhile mentioning is the ostrich effect, another oddity of bond rates related to liquidity. Using data from Israel, Galai and Sade (2006) showed that investors sometimes prefer to hold illiquid assets over more liquid ones with similar returns and are willing to pay a premium for them. The researchers attribute this seemingly anomalous behavior to investors' aversion to receiving information on potential interim losses.

Risks and Costs of Arbitrage

➢ Noise trader risk
➢ Fundamental risk
➢ Implementation costs

Noise traders risk

Noise traders are investors who make their trading decisions without using fundamental data. They trade for a variety of reasons, some rational and some irrational. Rational reasons might include liquidity (they would sell assets if they need to purchase a house or pay taxes), a desire to alter their portfolio's composition to increase or reduce diversification, sell or buy securities for tax considerations (to capitalize on tax losses), etc. When trading for such reasons, investors are less attentive to fundamental trading considerations. The above describes one type of noise traders who are mainly driven by some exogenous factors unrelated to the quality of the firms they trade in. Another type of noise traders might buy and sell securities for purely speculative reasons based on unfounded beliefs about the quality of the assets they buy or sell. Noise investors are likely to exhibit some of the cognitive biases we covered in class: overreaction to good and bad news, following trends, underreaction and so on (see De Long *et al.* 1990a, 1990b and 1991).

Noise trader risk is the risk that noise traders will push the price of a stock away from the fundamental value of an already mispriced asset.

Are noise traders important for pricing? If noise traders were completely uncorrelated, one would expect them to be irrelevant for pricing since the effects of buyers will be counteracted by those of sellers. However, if noise traders' activities are correlated (for example, if they all buy or all sell at the same time), then their trades will affect market prices. In fact, there are reasons to believe that the trades of noise traders are correlated because these types of investors are driven by market sentiment, which affects them all in the same direction.

Fundamental risk

> Consider the following example (Barberis and Thaler, 2003):
> Assume that the fundamental value of a share of Citigroup is \$50. Some (irrational?) traders become pessimistic about Citigroup and its price falls to \$40. Could this price persist?

Fundamental risk in this context is not the risk that the fundamental value will change. It is the risk that the price of a firm (Citigroup in the above example) will be pushed away from the "correct" fundamental value because of the behavior of noise traders (there is therefore some overlap between noise traders risk and fundamental risk). In a completely efficient market with no limits to arbitrage, the mispricing will not persist. Rational investors (arbitrageurs) will buy the stock that becomes a bargain and wait for its price to rise to its "true" value. Arbitrageurs who might be wary of investing in Citigroup as this will expose them to banking industry risk might finance the purchase of Citigroup by shorting JP Morgan. These actions will cause the price of Citigroup to rise and the arbitrage opportunity to vanish.

There are however many obstacles in the way of the arbitrageurs before they can realize their gains. First, rational investors cannot be 100% sure about their valuation. Second, even if they are correct, it could take the market a long time to realize the mispricing, and as a result, shorting costs may not be trivial. Third, things might even become worse if Citigroup's stock drops even further before it bounces back. Finally, JP Morgan is not a perfect substitute to Citigroup and the arbitrageurs would be exposed to the banking industry risk. Therefore, an arbitrage opportunity is far from being a guarantee of above-normal profits.

Mispricing does not need to be always downward. If trend chasers — investors who buy the stock after it has risen for a while — push the price above its fundamentals, arbitrageurs might assume that these noise traders will continue to push up the stock's price even further in the short run. Under such assumptions, the arbitrageurs will buy the stock themselves and try to sell it before the stock returns to its fundamental value. Such a strategy entails risks that are similar to those described above.

Implementation Risks/costs

➤ Transaction costs
  ✓ Commissions
  ✓ Bid-ask spread
➤ Implementation time effects
➤ Price impacts
➤ Different markets
➤ Costs of researching and funding arbitrage opportunities

Transaction costs: These may eliminate arbitrage opportunities as the benefits from the arbitrage must be large enough to offset them. These costs, especially of shorts, might be high. For example, D'Avolio (2002) finds that the costs of borrowing stocks, needed for shorting, are typically between 15 and 20 basis points, but can be much higher. Moreover, sometimes, no assets are available for borrowing, which are an essential part of shorting, and a short "squeeze" might occur. This is a situation where the price of a heavily shorted stock moves sharply higher, forcing short sellers to close out their short positions (they are "squeezed out) usually at a loss.

Other transaction costs are commissions and bid-ask spreads. Bid-ask spreads are also essentially commissions since investors pay the higher ask prices when they buy and receive the lower bid price when they sell.

Implementation time: Actions to realize an arbitrage opportunity are not implemented instantaneously. As a result, the prices that arbitrageurs face when they determine their strategy may differ from the prices they encounter when they close it. Such changes might occur for a variety of reasons as many factors might change in this interval.

Price impacts: Arbitrageurs' actions can affect prices, and as a result, the prices they envision when they initiate their strategy to exploit the arbitrage opportunity may differ from the prices they actually receive and pay. This is similar to the implementation time risk, but in this case, it is the actions of the arbitrageurs that cause the risk. This risk is actually more ominous because price impacts will more often go against the arbitrageur (if the arbitrageur buys an underpriced asset, his action will raise the price; implementation time risk is more neutral).

Different markets: When the arbitrage calls for the purchase of one asset in one market and the sale of the same or a similar asset in another market, the prices may not be the same in the two markets. Even a tiny difference in the timing of the purchase and the sale might make a difference.

Funding and research costs: If investors need to borrow to finance their trades or forgo an alternative investment, the explicit or implicit costs of such financing might be non-trivial. In addition, the arbitrage profits should cover costs of looking for and finding such opportunities.

Limits/obstacles to Arbitrage Example

Below, we present Shleifer and Vishny's (1997) example of the obstacles for arbitrage. It is presented here as it appears in their seminal paper because it is a classic. Today, DMs are no longer used for trading, but owners of DM can exchange them for Euros at the Deutsche Bundesbank Eurosystem. Whereas the currencies and assets used in the example are old, the economic principles of the example are as relevant today as they were 20 years ago.

Example

➤ Consider two Bund (such securities once existed) futures contracts to deliver DM 250,000 face value of German bonds at time T; One is traded in London on LIFFE and the second is traded in Frankfurt on DTB.

➤ Assume that at some point in time, $t < T$, the first contract sells for DM 240,000 and the second sells for DM 245,000.

➤ How certain are we that a genuine arbitrage opportunity exists?

Assume further that the contracts are exactly the same. In theory, this is an example of a surefire arbitrage opportunity. In this situation, an arbitrageur would sell a futures contract in Frankfurt for DM 245,000 and buy one in London for DM 240,000 and guarantee a DM 5,000 profit. But as we see below, the profits are not that easy to arrive.

Note that the arbitrageur will not realize the DM 5,000 profit until the future contracts close. At initiation, the arbitrageur must put up DM 6,500 as good faith money (DM 3,000 in London and DM

3,500 in Frankfurt). Now, assume that the price in Frankfurt moves farther away from the price in London, and reaches DM 250,000. Although a good change in principle, the arbitrageur now must put an additional DM 5,000, otherwise she is forced to liquidate her position prematurely and lose.

Additional obstacles might arise before she is able to realize her profit:

➤ The contracts may trade at different hours.
➤ Settlements dates may slightly differ.
➤ Delivery terms may differ.

As a result of all these factors, the opportunity becomes a risk arbitrage and there is no certainty that the arbitrageur will realize any profits.

Another type of obstacle to arbitrage is that of Performance-based arbitrage (PBA) which we'll discuss below.

Performance-based Arbitrage (PBA)

PBA occurs when funds under management are responsive to past returns rather than future expected returns. PBA may fail because of agency considerations. An agency problem or "the principal–agent" problem arises when one person (the agent) makes decisions on behalf of, or that impact, another person (the principal). In such cases, the agent is motivated to act in his own best interests, which may differ from the principals' best interests.

Arbitrageurs may trade on behalf of investors who fund them. These investors, who are not familiar with the arbitrageur's strategies, may misinterpret poor short-term performance as an indication of arbitrage transaction's failure and consequently withdraw their funding, endangering the implementation of the arbitrage strategy. As a result, arbitrage transactions are risky.

In the above Bund example, the arbitrageur can maintain her positions as long as she has enough funds, regardless of how far apart prices are. She is certain that they will converge on the expiration date. However, if she were to conduct the above strategy to some clients who do not know or precisely understand her strategy, they may think she is losing money and consider her to be less competent than originally believed. The clients will be tempted to cut their funding. Caught midway in the arbitrage operation, the arbitrageur might incur a loss.

Conclusions

➤ Arbitrage opportunities often entail risks.

➤ We review the many reasons seeming arbitrage opportunities may fail.

➤ An example is given of the risks inherent in a "perfect" arbitrage opportunity.

➤ Agency costs create obstacles for arbitrage when arbitrageurs act on behalf of investors who are not familiar with arbitrage idiosyncrasies.

MARKET SENTIMENT

Agenda

➤ Market (Investor) Sentiment: Definition and Scope
➤ Measurements of Sentiment
  ✓ Market Based
  ✓ Non-market Based
➤ The closed-end Fund Puzzle as an Example for the Effects of Market Sentiment
➤ Does Sentiment have Predictive Abilities?

Market sentiment — Definition and scope

➤ Market sentiment: The value of a firm's future cash flows and risk that cannot be explained by economic factors.
➤ What are the features that make firms more prone to market sentiment?
➤ Does market sentiment carry informative or predictive value?

In 1996, Alan Greenspan, then chair of the US Federal Reserve Bank, described stock market sentiment as "irrational exuberance." Shiller used the phrase as the title of his book published in 2000. In this lecture we give some structure to the popular concept of market sentiment and analyze the role that market sentiment plays in capital markets.

Due to their sheer magnitude, impact or inexplicability and influence, many events have been attributed to market sentiment: These include the Dutch Tulip mania (aka "Tulipomania") of 1634–1637, the crash of 1929, the Black Monday crash of 1987, the Asian flu of 1997, the dot-com bubble of the late 1990s, the Brazilian fever of 1999, the Argentine monetary crisis of 2000, and the sub-prime crisis of 2007–2009, to name just a few.

There are quite a few measures that have been used to assess market sentiment. In what follows, we review these measures and discuss their properties.

Market-based Measures of Sentiment

- Trading volume
- Dividend premium
- Closed-end fund discount
- The "fear" index (VIX)
- IPO (Initial price offering) mispricing
- The share of equity issues
- Retail investors purchases
- Mutual fund flows
- Surveys

Trading volume: It might be cheaper, especially for individual investors, to trade on their sentiment when this feeling is bullish than when it is bearish, since buying and then selling (which is recommended when prices are expected to rise) entails lower transaction costs than short sales (which are more appropriate when sentiment is bearish). Individual investors are therefore more likely to trade when they are optimistic than when they are pessimistic. Since individuals are also more likely to be noise traders, higher trading volume may indicate higher participation of noise traders in the market. Some researchers therefore use market turnover, defined as the ratio of trading volume to the number of shares listed on the New York Stock Exchange, as a proxy to market sentiment.

Dividend premium: The dividend premium is defined as the difference between the average market-to-book-value ratios of dividend-paying firms and non-payers. When investors become more risk averse, they may prefer dividend-paying stocks because they (perhaps erroneously, based on "the bird in hand" fallacy) believe that such firms are less risky, and hence drive the prices of such firms relatively higher than the prices of non-dividend paying firms.

Closed-end fund discount. (we have a special section on this later)

The "fear" index (VIX): This is a measure of implied (or inferred) volatility of the S&P 500 stock index based on option prices. Since option prices are positive functions of volatility, volatility can be inferred from their prices by inverting the Black–Scholes formula. VIX captures the extent to which investors feel uncertain about future prices, and thus, to some extent, it is an indication of investors' anxieties. It has been shown that spikes in VIX are concomitant to crises.

IPO mispricing: High first-day returns on IPOs potentially serve as a measure of market sentiment because they may be indicative of investors' enthusiasm as they are optimistic regarding the success of the new issues.

The share of equity issues: Another potential indicator of market sentiment is the proportion of equity of the sum of equity and debt financing. Higher proportions of equity issuance may indicate pessimism, as current stockholders who predict lower returns will be less resistant to sharing them with new stockholders.

Retail investors' purchases: Kumar and Lee (2006) proposed to develop sentiment measures for retail investors based on whether such investors are buying or selling. They base their suggestion on Barber, et al. (2009a, 2009b) findings that retail investors' trading patterns are consistent with a systematic sentiment.

Mutual fund flows: Brown, et al. (2003) propose an overall market sentiment measure based on how fund investors are moving into and out of various investment vehicles such as a move from "safe" government bond funds to "risky" growth stocks funds. Frazzini and Lamont (2008) suggest using fund flows to proxy for sentiment for individual investors. They claim that "individual investors have a striking ability to do the wrong thing" (*ibid*, p. 319) and hence at any given time, they invest in funds that do poorly in subsequent years. One can then predict which funds will do poorly in the future by looking at which funds get higher flows of money from individuals. The stocks held by such funds are also destined to underperform. Fund flows which indicate individuals' investment choices can then be used to measure market sentiment.

The Closed-end Puzzle The Puzzle: Price < NAV

- Traditional explanations:
  - ✓ Agency costs
  - ✓ Tax liabilities
  - ✓ Illiquidity of asset
- A behavioral explanation: Investor sentiment/noise trader risk

---

A closed-end fund is a mutual fund that holds publicly traded securities. Unlike an open-end fund, a closed-end fund sells a fixed amount of its shares and these shares are traded on the stock market. Investors who wish to liquidate their holdings must sell them on the market rather than redeem them with the fund for their net asset value (NAV). It has been documented that the shares of closed-end funds typically trade at a non-trivial discount from their NAV. This is puzzling because arbitrageurs could buy the closed-end fund for the current price and then sell its assets for their higher NAV, and pocket arbitrage profits.

Although various theories attempt to explain this puzzle, we will direct special attention to the theory that uses market sentiment. Not only is it the more convincing explanation and most appropriate for this course in behavioral finance, but this explanation has also been instrumental in highlighting the importance of sentiment in mispricing.

This puzzle has been studied by many researchers, who have offered both behavioral and non-behavioral explanations. The non-behavioral explanations include (a) agency cost theory, according to which, the discount in the prices of the funds stems from high management costs or below par management performance (this does not explain why the arbitrageurs are unable to exploit the discount), (b) the funds sell below par because some of the assets carry tax liabilities that are not taken into account in the NAV calculations, and hence arbitrageurs will receive less than the NAV if they try the above arbitrage strategy; and (c) Some of the assets held by closed-end funds are restricted securities that cannot be traded if the fund is liquidated.

The above arguments are compelling, but according to Lee, *et al.* (1991), (Lee, Shleifer and Thaler, LSF) they are insufficient. LSF offer market sentiment as a better explanation for the puzzle. They suggest that the closed-end fund puzzle can be explained by the existence of noise traders (who are not fully rational, as defined by De Long, *et al.* 1990a, 1990b) (De Long, Shleifer, Summers and Waldman, DSSW), who misestimate the value of assets, and are influenced by sentiments or non-informative factors for the evaluation of stocks. DSSW assume that the arbitrageurs (rational investors) have short horizons and although they know the correct value of the asset, i.e., the discounted present value of the dividends they yield, they are aware that they might not be able to sell the stocks for their "correct" value in the short run, because of noise traders' idiosyncrasies, which by definition are unpredictable. Furthermore, the arbitrageurs cannot diversify these risks as they simultaneously affect many assets (the idiosyncrasy is attributed to investors and not to the assets). As a result, similar to other non-diversifiable risks, noise traders risk carries a risk premium.

LSF adopt the above concepts and also assume that noise traders are more likely to hold and trade in closed-end funds than in their underlying assets. This assumption is crucial as it implies that changes in sentiment affect the price of the closed-end fund and the NAV differently: NAV is less affected by the sentiment since the underlying assets held by the closed-end fund are more likely to be traded by rational investors. Market sentiment thus inserts a wedge between the price of the closed-end fund and that of the underlying assets. Indeed, LSF introduce evidence that closed-end funds are mainly traded by individuals. LSF then conclude that the closed-end fund discount reflects market sentiment and hence can serve as a good measure for it.

Non-market Sentiments and Their Measures

Mood and factors that affect mood

✓ Weather, seasonal effects and atmospheric factors that might affect mood
✓ Sports results
✓ Disasters
✓ Surveys' measures of mood

There are several non-market sentiment-related factors that might affect stock prices. Psychologists suggest that mood may affect behavior (see, e.g., Isen, 2011), but the effect of non-market-related factors on asset prices seems puzzling because these factors do not affect the cash flows from the assets. They argue that mood may affect the way investors perceive firms' specific events and hence prices.

Weather, seasonal and other atmospheric factors that may affect mood: Kamstra *et al.* (2003, 2012) find that market returns are on average lower through the fall and winter periods which they attribute to diminished light hours daylight which induces lower spirits and increased inclination for depression. Seasonal and weather effects were also found by Cao and Wei (2005), Dolvin and Pyles (2007), Goetzmann and Zhu (2005), Hirshleifer and Shumway (2003), Kaplansky *et al.* (2015), and Kliger and Kudryavtsev (2016), and others. Weekends and Mondays could also affect mood and hence returns (beyond the well-known economic reasons for the weekend effect). Are investors happier during the weekend and do they feel Monday blues? And could these feelings affect stock prices? Helliwell and Wang (2014) find evidence to support such effects.

Sports results: International sports results, victories or defeats in important games, winning medals in the Olympics can boost national morale and mood, which in turn can affect stock prices. Indeed, many researchers have shown that such effects exist. Edmans *et al.* (2007) use international soccer results as a mood variable and find that losses in major games predict poor returns in the losing country the following day, particularly in small stocks. Kaplanski and Levy (2010a) find similar results using FIFA matches.

Disasters: Kaplanski and Levy (2010b) find that aviation disasters could also affect prices.

Surveys: Conducting a survey is a straightforward means to measure mood. Surveys used to measure sentiments include Shiller's investors' attitude surveys, UBS/Gallup surveys of randomly selected investor households, and investors' intelligence surveys conducted by financial newsletter writers.

Which firms are more Affected by Market Sentiment and Does Market Sentiment have a Predictive Power?

- Do speculative stocks and those hard to arbitrage suffer from more sentiment?
- Can the strength of the sentiment predict the returns on the stock once the sentiment's effect is dissipated?
- Since difficulties to arbitrage will cause more overvaluation in high sentiment firms, will they also cause lower returns in such firms after the sentiment vanishes?

Baker and Wurgler (BW) (2007) provide answers to the questions posed in the previous slide. Figure 13.1, loosely based on BW, depicts the theoretical relationship between sentiment, valuation and firm type and their findings on the actual relationship between valuation predictability and difficulty to arbitrage are given in Figure 13.2.

On the horizontal axis of Figure 13.1, we find firms sorted according to how difficult it is to exploit arbitrage opportunities that involve them. On the vertical axis, the relative (to true) valuations of the firms are presented. Being difficult to arbitrage will positively affect the valuation of high sentiment stocks, which explains the positive slope of the high sentiment line and the negative slope of the low sentiment line.

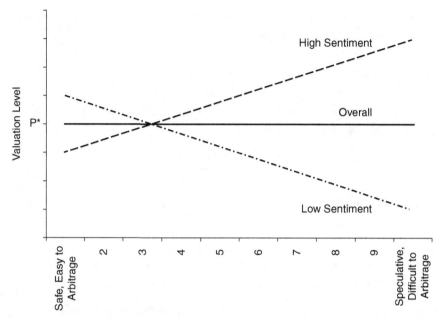

Figure 13.1. Theoretical relationship between sentiment, valuation and type of firms.

Source: Baker, and Wurgler, (2007).

In Figure 13.2, loosely based on BW, we see how well the data match the theoretical predictions about the relationship between overvaluation and firm type. This figure, presented by BW, uses a composite sentiment measure constructed of five sentiment measures: trading volume, dividend premium, closed-end fund discount, VIX ("fear" index), and IPO mispricing.

On the x-axis, firms are sorted according to difficulty to arbitrage. The y-axis represents the firms' average monthly returns 1 month after their sentiment index was recorded. The solid line represents the returns of all firms (both high sentiment and low sentiment) as a function of difficulty to arbitrage. The heavier (lighter) dotted line represents the returns of low (high) sentiment firms as a function of difficulty to arbitrage.

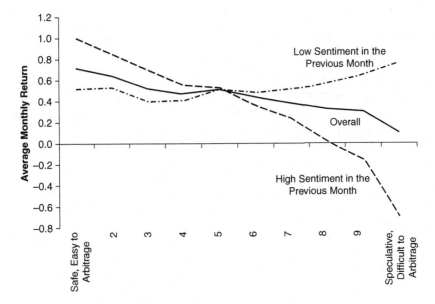

Figure 13.2.   Predictive power of market sentiment.
Source: Baker, and Wurgler (2007).

From this figure, you can see that the theoretical prediction of
the relationship between difficulty to arbitrage and sentiment agree
with the empirical results. We see a distinct negative correlation
between difficulty to arbitrage and future returns for high sentiment
firms, which indicates that difficulty to arbitrage causes significant
mispricing when sentiment is high. On the other hand, for low sentiment firms, there is only a slight difference in the mispricing of
difficult to arbitrage and easy to arbitrage firms.

Conclusions

➤ We showed how market sentiment can be measured either by
  market factors or by non-market factors.
➤ We expanded on the closed-end fund discount as a measure for
  market sentiment.

(continued)

(continued)

> ➤ We showed that market sentiment has important effects on capital asset pricing.
> ➤ Sentiment also has predictive power.
> ➤ We reviewed which firms are more prone to market sentiment and showed that the current performance of such firms has more predictive power.

BIASES IN SAVINGS AND INSURANCE

Agenda

Biases in Savings

➤ Do people behave rationally in their savings decisions?

➤ Do people save enough?

➤ How can we induce people to save enough?

➤ Do people invest wisely their savings?

Biases in Insurance: The Full-Coverage Puzzle

➤ Popular explanations for the full-coverage puzzle

➤ An anchoring explanation for the full-coverage puzzle

➤ How to avoid buying unworthy warrantees

Why are Households Prone to Biases when Making Savings Decisions?

For optimal savings, households need to devise a plan of accumulating then de-cumulating assets to maximize their expected lifetime utility function.

For this they need:

1. The cognitive capacity to design such a complicated problem.
2. The ability to avoid the temptation to deviate from the plan.
3. The ability to avoid other cognitive biases that may reduce savings.

One of the more common beliefs among academics, policy makers and practitioners is that people often do not behave rationally in their savings decisions. Another strong belief is that individuals do not save enough. For example, Skinner (2007) shows that "most households with post-graduate degrees fall short of the wealth needed to smooth spending through retirement." Benartzi and Thaler (BT) (2007) argue that "for workers who do not have other significant sources of retirement income, the savings rates typically observed in 401(k) plans are unlikely to provide anything close to complete income replacement in retirement," and Choi *et al.* (2002) (Choi, Laibson, Madrian, and Metrick, CLMM) report that most participants in their survey feel their savings are inappropriately low, and that they should have saved more.

Why don't people save enough? If not due to mistaken calculations, individuals may undersave for a variety of reasons, most of which are related to their unwillingness to sacrifice satisfaction now for the sake of a better future.

The optimal savings decision is a cognitively challenging task. Even theoretically, it is difficult for professional economists to devise an optimal savings plan because of its dynamic nature that requires households to accumulate and then decumulate assets. The task is all the more difficult for ordinary individuals. Solving such a complicated optimization problem is well beyond the cognitive abilities of most savers. Furthermore, even if such a plan is devised, savers also need to have the will power to give up current consumption for the sake of uncertain consumption in the future, which is no mean feat.

Given that the savings decision is so difficult, is it surprising that people deviate from rationality? And since the theory of savings is quite complicated, how can we tell if someone acts rationally when theory is not conclusive about what constitutes a rational decision? It appears that we can state with certainty that savers are behaving irrationally only when the deviations from rationality are egregious.

Extreme Cognitive Biases in Savings

➤ Employers would match contributions and workers could withdraw funds any time, yet only 50% exploit this opportunity.

➤ In some plans in the UK, workers merely need to join a savings plan to which it is possible that only the employer contributes. Yet, not all employees exploited this bonanza.

Unexploited arbitrage opportunities. According to Choi *et al.* (2005a) (Choi, Laibson and Madrian, CLMM), many employees who receive employer matching contributions in their 401(k) plan and are allowed to make discretionary, penalty-free, in-service withdrawals contribute below the matching threshold. They are making a huge mistake since if they increase their contributions to the allowed limit, their employer will match their contribution, and the employee can then withdraw her contribution thus recovering it without having to increase savings. This arbitrage opportunity is not exploited by about 50% of the employers who are entitled to it. According to CLMM, what is even more surprising is that workers don't take advantage of this opportunity even after being told about it.

Benartzi and Thaler (2007) report that some defined benefit plans in the UK do not require any employee contributions at all and are fully funded by the employer. Although all employees have to do in order to benefit from this "free lunch" is to join the program, it turns out, from data on 25 such plans that almost 50% of the workers did not sign up for it.

Beyond these extreme cases of decision errors, what can we say about savers' decision making?

How Savers Make Their Decisions

• Savers are mostly passive.
• They invest very little time or effort in their savings decision.
• They leave most of the decisions to their employers.
• They use heuristics and rules of thumb.

Savers are mostly passive

Savers' passivity is reflected in many of their (in)actions. They would gladly enroll in a savings plan if the enrollment were automatic, but express less enthusiasm when they are required to perform a deliberate action to enroll. CLMM reject the argument that automatic enrollment may force savings on employees. They show that this is not the case. They compared the percentage of workers who dropped out of automatic plans to the percentage that dropped from non-automatic plans, and found that if any, the percentage of the latter was lower. Another facet of savers' passivity is savers choice of the amounts to save. Most savers prefer to make easy decisions, and therefore choose the default alternative (this is true for many other decisions such as donations and is not unique to savings decisions).

Given that a worker is already enrolled in a plan, the amount she saves is also largely determined by the default offered by the employer. Not only are employees passive about the amounts they save, they are also quite passive in allocating assets to savings: They make an allocation early on when they enter the program and continue to maintain the same allocation for years (see, e.g., Agnew *et al.* 2003; Samuelson and Zeckhauser, 1988; Thaler and Sunstein, 2009).

Savers invest very little time and effort in the savings decision

Beartzi and Thaler (1999) report that 58% of the savers in their survey spend less than 1 hour before deciding how much and in what to invest. Individuals leave a lot of the decision to the employers. Given that savers cannot come up with the optimal savings amount for them, they turn to the employer to make the decision for them, and they in turn leave it to the government to determine the default savings rates. Savers are so passive and so dependent on their employers that their decisions are affected by even small details, such as the physical layout of the forms they are required to sign.

Savers use heuristics and rules of thumb

The little deliberate decisions employees make in the little time they invest in making these decisions are based on heuristics and rules of thumb. However, you cannot really blame them for behaving that way since the cost of an analytic optimal decision-making process is too prohibitive.

How Can Savers be Induced to Save More?

➤ Education for savings
➤ Automatic enrollment
➤ Simplification of the process
➤ Menu of defaults
➤ "Save more tomorrow" plans

Education for savings

We intuitively expect savers to "repent" and save more once they are shown how little they save and they become aware of their errors. Education for savings therefore seems a surefire way to increase savings. However, CLMM show that most attempts at educating households to save more were effective only in the short run. In the long run, they made little or no difference.

Automatic enrollment

One strategy that has been shown to be effective is automatic enrollment in savings plans, where all employees must enroll in a savings plans by their employers. This practice is almost universal and helped to increase savings. But this practice does not guarantee that people will save enough. The more relevant question is how to induce individuals already enrolled to increase savings.

Simplification of the process

It has been shown that the savers are passive. The less effort required to enroll or to change plans or allocations, the higher the chances that the individual will take action.

Menu of defaults

Not all defaults and employer matching plans are the same; some matching structures are more effective in inducing savings than others. For example, BT argue that an employer matching 30% of the first 10% of pay may induce higher savings than matching 50% on the first 6%. Furthermore, using workers' preference for round number matching would also help encourage savings.

Save more tomorrow

Thaler and Benartzi (2004) and Thaler and Sunstein (2009) propose a plan that has been shown to be quite effective in increasing savings. The plan asks workers to agree in advance to increase their savings every time they receive a pay raise. The idea behind this plan is that individuals will be more willing to agree to increase their contributions because the increase will take place in the future and also because the increase in savings will not entail a reduction in their take-home pay (since the increased contributions will come out of a pay rise).

Cognitive Biases in Savings: Mental Accounting and Myopic Loss Aversion

➤ Mental accounting

   ✓ "Old Money" vs. "New Money"

   ✓ Company stock: neither stocks nor bonds (Benartzi and Thaler, 2001)

➤ Myopic loss aversion

"Old Money" vs. "New Money"

There is a difference between the way individuals allocate "old" and "new" money. This indicates a bias since there is no reason to treat current savings differently from former savings. Whenever new savings are made, they should be added to the existing portfolio and a new optimal portfolio should be constructed based on the old portfolio and the new savings. The separate treatment savers give to "old" and "new" money is a manifestation of the mental accounting bias. Savers consider the new money and the old money as separate accounts.

Company stock

This error was discussed in the home bias lecture (see also Benartzi, 2001 and Cohen, 2009). Investing in employer's stock is a bad decision from a portfolio/diversification perspective, yet, this practice is quite common. It can be explained by mental accounting: Savers regard company stock as a separate account from their total savings portfolio.

Myopic loss aversion

Providing participants with information on short-term rates of return on the different investment funds induces "myopic loss aversion", as discussed in Lecture 10. The behavior of savers provides additional support for the portfolio reviewing effect on risk taking. Benartzi and Thaler (1999) show that funds are allocated differently by savers who view one-year returns and savers who view long-term returns. The latter group allocated, on average, more of their portfolio to stocks than the former group (82% vs. 41%).

The $1/n$ Heuristic

Given n venues for savings, investors will allocate $1/n$ of their investment into each of the venues regardless of the nature of the venues (stocks vs. fixed income).
This rule applies as long as $n < 10$.

This is just one of the many examples that show how individuals (in this case, savers) use heuristics rather than serious thinking in their decision making. The $1/n$ heuristic, which was discovered by Benartzi and Thaler (BT) (2001), is an extreme example of framing and/or an extreme violation of the independence of irrelevant alternatives axiom. The availability of additional stock funds should not increase the weight of stocks in the portfolio (unless the added funds have some special feature that is missing in the original funds).

This heuristic implies that a savings plan can manipulate savers' risk taking by simply adding or subtracting mutual funds of different degrees of risk. For example, if investors are offered four stock funds and one fixed income fund, they will adopt a risky portfolio by allocating 80% of their savings to stocks, but if the same investors are offered four fixed income funds and one stock fund, their allocation to stocks will drop to 20%, which implies a much less risky portfolio.

This heuristic is important not only for understanding how people invest their savings, but also for demonstrating how fickle investors can be.

BT sampled a large group of UCLA employees and surveyed their preferences. BT divided the participants into two groups. The first group was presented with four equity funds and one fixed-income securities, and the second was presented with one equity fund and four fixed-income securities. It turns out that an average of 68% of the first group invested in equity funds, while only 43% of the second group on average invested in equity. This allocation is not strictly according to the $1/n$ rule, but it clearly shows that the more stock funds are offered, the greater the share of savings that will be invested in stocks.

The $1/n$ theory was examined by other researchers including Huberman and Jiang (2006), who found it to hold by with one important caveat: the number of funds offered must be fewer than 10 for the rule to apply.

Insurance Puzzles: The Full-Coverage Puzzle

Contrary to the predictions of utility theory, consumers frequently prefer full coverage or low deductibles even when deductibles or higher deductibles are available. This is called "the Full-Coverage Puzzle." Choosing full coverage when deductibles are available is tantamount to buying a policy with a deductible and an additional policy to insure the deductible. However, when the premium is not fair, that is, when its expected value is less than its price, insuring against small risks conflicts with maximization of expected utility. Mossin (1968) demonstrated that if the price of an insurance policy is proportional to, but higher than, the expected payments made by the insurer and if the insured is risk averse, then full coverage is suboptimal for the insured. He also showed that under these conditions, there always exists a policy with a strictly positive deductible, which dominates the full-coverage policy. Mossin's normative logic stands in contrast to the high demand for full-coverage policies and policies with very low deductibles.

It is hard to defend the purchase of a full-coverage policy under the utility theory framework. Researchers have shown that the purchase of full-coverage policies can only be explained by extraordinarily high risk aversion (see, e.g., Pashigian *et al.* 1966; Shapira and Venezia, 2008a, 2008b). As in the case of the equity premium puzzle, this seemingly irrational behavior could only be justified using explanations outside traditional utility theory framework, including the behavioral explications presented below.

Why is the Purchase of Full-Coverage Insurance Policies Puzzling?

When considering a full-coverage policy costing P_f against a policy with a deductible D whose cost is P_d, we are actually considering paying an extra $(P_f - P_d)$ to insure a loss of D.

When the expected payments that the insured will collect from the insurance company are considerably lower than the price she paid, "insuring the deductible" is not worthwhile for reasonably risk averse individuals.

Assume that a collector of fine arts has a painting valued at L. The collector can buy full-coverage insurance against theft of the painting for the price of P_f or a policy with a deductible of D for P_d. This choice can be framed as follows: If the full-coverage policy is purchased, then the owner is sure to pay P_f and she is protected against the painting's theft. If she buys the policy with the deductible she saves $(P_f - P_d)$ and loses the deductible in the event of a theft. It hence follows that if she buys the full-coverage policy, she is paying $(P_f - P_d)$ to insure a loss of D. Is it worthwhile to purchase this extra insurance? That, of course, depends on the chances of theft and on the value of the deductible. But insurance premiums are usually not fair: their actuarial value is typically greater than the expected losses, and the value of the deductible is usually small. It is not recommended to buy insurance against small losses when the price is higher than the expected loss. For small losses, the owner cannot be so risk averse as to pay prices that are considerably higher than the actuarial value, which is the case in most insurance policies.

Example: Suppose the value of the painting is $25,000, the deductible is $500 and the price for a full-coverage policy and a policy with a deductible are $1,875 and $1,837, respectively. The buyer of the full-coverage policy pays an additional $38 for insuring $500. Is this worthwhile? The answer depends on the chances of theft and on buyer's risk aversion. If the buyer's wealth is $200,000 and the probability of theft is 5%, then for any reasonable risk aversion parameter (when discussing the equity premium puzzle, we saw that a reasonable risk aversion parameter for the CRRA utility function is around 2 and certainly less than 30), the insured will rationally prefer the policy with the deductible.

For example, Sydnor (2010) reports that according to a large sample of homeowners' insurance policies of a specific insurance company, more than 80% of homeowners choose a deductible of $500 for an additional premium of $100 rather than that a deductible of $1,000. Since the probability of damage or need for home repairs is less than 5%, the average value of reducing the deductible from $1,000 to $500 is only $25 (5% × $500), but consumers actually pay an additional $100 for this.

Anecdotal Evidence for "too Much Insurance"

➢ Collision Damage Waiver costs around $20 a day.
➢ Homeowners pay an additional $100 for a deductible of $500 rather than of $1,000 in home insurance.

(Continued)

(Continued)

> ➤ State of Pennsylvania outcry when Insurance Commissioner tried to raise the minimum deductible for automobile policies from $50 to $100 and had to withdraw it because of a major public outcry.
> ➤ Appliances and electrical products insurance.
> ➤ Many insureds buy full medical insurance.
> ➤ Large corporations buy insurance with deductibles as low as $10,000.
> ➤ Almost all liability insurance is full coverage.

Consider also collision damage insurance for car rentals. While specific rates vary by location, a typical collision damage waiver (CDW) policy for a rental car costs on average $25 per day, which is equal to $9,000 on an annual basis. In stark contrast, comprehensive automobile insurance for one's own car costs no more than $1,000 per year in most locations in the US. The difference in price is clearly non-trivial. Why are people willing to pay such high premiums rates for CDW when renting a car?

Another example is related to the deductibles on automobile insurance policies. The deductible on automobile insurance is often as low as $100 and almost always below $500, in which case they are exposed to risk of losses of no more than $500. Cummins and Weisbart (1978) report that when Herbert Denenberg, Pennsylvania's Insurance Commissioner tried to raise the minimum auto insurance deductible from $50 to $100 during the 1970s, he was forced to withdraw this idea due to the massive consumer outcry. People apparently feel quite strong about risks that in fact are minimal.

Merchants who sell various electrical products such as cell phones that cost $200 or less also offer insurance against loss, for a non-trivial additional cost. Buying such insurance does not seem to be rational even when those policies include a service component.

Companies offering such a warranty in their service policies stand to make a considerable profit from consumers' irrational preferences. According to a Harvard Business School case (see Burns, 2004,

Shapira and Venezia, 2008b), Circuit City sold electronics at cost and made its profits on extended warranties. It seems that buyers did not appreciate the true cost-benefit considerations of the warranties.

The preference for full insurance is salient also in medical insurance. For example, the US Bureau of Labor Statistics reports that during the years 1994–1997, 34% of full-time private sector employees enrolled in non-HMO medical care organizations had no deductibles in their medical plans. This percentage rose to 42% for "Preferred provider organizations" (U.S. Department of Labor, 1999).

Large corporations buy insurance with deductibles as low as $10,000 (see Shapira and Venezia, 2008b). Losses of $10,000 are trivial for such firms and hence the rationale for such insurance purchases is not clear.

Popular Explanations for the FC Puzzle

➤ Deductibles are inconvenient
➤ Bargain insurance (pessimism)
➤ Risk aversion
➤ Indivisibilities

Deductibles are inconvenient: While utility theory clearly refutes the desirability of full coverage and recommends purchasing insurance with deductibles, such policies may be cumbersome or inconvenient. Individuals may wish to buy peace of mind and the knowledge that no losses will occur to them. Also, as we have seen from the insurance of the painting example above, the difference in prices between the full coverage and the policy with a deductible could be sometimes small in absolute value ($38 in that example). You do not expect people to care too much about such sums of money.

Bargain insurance: The case against full-coverage rests on the assumption that the expected insurance benefits will be lower than their price (the policy premium). But what if the insurance is a bargain and the chances for a claim against the insurance company are larger than what the insurer thinks? In such situations, full coverage is recommended. However, since insurance companies make profits on their operations, this situation applies to only a small fraction of the policies sold and to a small segment of the population. Those consumers who choose small or no deductibles are likely to be pessimistic, and assume that the insured event will occur at an unrealistically high probability. For such clients, the full coverage might seem a bargain although realistically it is not.

Risk Aversion: The purchase of full-coverage insurance is rational only for extreme risk averse cases and hence also this argument has limited applicability.

Indivisibilities: While some deductible is usually recommended, not all deductible levels are available. In such cases, the insured might find full coverage preferable to the deductible levels available to him.

Academic Explanations for the FC Puzzle

➤ Multi-period habit formation utility
➤ Prospect theory
➤ Regret
➤ Framing
➤ Anchoring
➤ Self-selection

In light of standard utility theory's difficulty to explain the demand for low deductibles, many alternative theories have been offered for this puzzle. We discuss several of these theories below.

Multi-period habit formation utility: Ben-Arab *et al.* (1996) try to explain why people buy "excessive" insurance by assuming a multi-period habit-formation utility function. This type of utility function introduces a greater desire to smooth consumption over time than a "usual" single-period utility function. As a result, it implies a stronger incentive to purchase insurance and a greater tolerance of lower deductibles.

Prospect theory: Prospect theory and the assumption that decision makers overweigh small probabilities can explain why people prefer full-coverage insurance to probabilistic insurance (Kahneman and Tversky, 1979, Wakker *et al.*, 1997).

Regret: When an insured buys insurance with a deductible and the insurance event occurs, the insured may feel regret that he did not choose full coverage. This sense of remorse may be exacerbated if he has to justify his decision, which may be interpreted as stinginess (by people who are unfamiliar with utility theory). Of course, the insured may also experience regret if the insured event does not occur. Thus, the insurer has to weigh these two types of regret against each other. Braun and Muermann (2004) use aversion to regret to explain the purchase of full-coverage insurance.

Framing: How the deductibles are framed can also affect the decision to buy full-coverage insurance or insurance with a deductible. Schoemaker (1976) demonstrates that when faced with decisions described as insurance against hypothetical losses, individuals chose full-coverage alternatives over those with deductibles, but when the same choices were framed as lotteries, their choice pattern was reversed. Similarly, in an elaborate experimental design, Johnson *et al.* (1993) found that students preferred insurance alternatives framed as "rebates" rather than as policies with a deductible.

Also, recall our discussion in Lecture 4: Participants preferred a full-coverage policy to a policy with a deductible, but reversed their preferences when the same problem was presented to them as an ordinary decision under uncertainty.

Anchoring: Shapira and Venezia (SV) (2008a, 2008b) conjectured that the tendency to buy too much insurance is caused by an initial and erroneous assumption (based on the anchoring heuristic) that people make about how a policy should be priced with and without a deductible and the methodology people use to calculate and judge the fairness of the policy's price. SV theorized that the specific anchoring heuristic works as follows:

People first consider the price of a full-coverage policy, and anchor on it their estimate of the value of the policy with the deductible by subtracting the amount of the deductible from the price of the full-coverage policy. By doing so they fail to take into account that there is only a small probability that they will be involved in an accident and will have to pay the deductible. A policy with a deductible priced according to the true expected payments may therefore seem overpriced to the insured, and because consumers do not tend to think that full-coverage policies are overpriced, they may consider them to be relatively better "deals." For example (see Statman, 2017): Consider a full-coverage policy for your car costing $2,500 per year. A policy with a $500 deductible costing $2,300 might seem overpriced if we anchor our estimate of the value of this policy to $2,500 and expect it to cost $2,000 ($2,500–$500).

In a set of experiments, SV found support for the above hypotheses. SV also compared the decision-making processes of insurance professionals to those of the general public and found that professionals are less prone to the above biases.

How to Avoid Buying too Much Insurance? Insights from Warranties

- Mood affects purchase decisions
- Emotions need to be ignored
- Imagine yourself a wholesaler

Purchasing extended warranties is a striking example of buying too much insurance as these warranties represent insurance that covers small losses, and usually cost much more than their actuarial value (see Chen *et al.* 2009, and Darlin, 2009). Why then do customers buy these warranty contracts? The above-mentioned biases and individuals' tendency to insure against small losses probably apply to these warranties, too. Extended warranties can also be considered as service contracts rather than insurance and hence some of the arguments above, based on risk aversion and risk-cost-benefit analysis, maybe are not applicable here. However, the risk minimization aspect of the warranties makes them to a large degree an insurance product which justifies our skepticism about their worthiness.

Is there a way clients can avoid falling into the warranty trap? In a sample of customers of a major department store, Chen *et al.* found that customers have a higher tendency to purchase extended warranties for products that bring them pleasure. Chen *et al.* argue that one of the reasons for this phenomenon is that the purchase of such products induces a positive mood in the purchasers, which makes them more willing to buy the extended warranties. They also contend that consumers tend to overestimate the odds of a loss when they really like a product, and consequently, they wish to further protect it.

The implications for smart shopping are to strip away the emotions from the purchase decision. Goldin (cited in Darlin, 2009) presents an argument how customers can avoid the purchase of extended warranties by removing emotions from the purchase. The key is to imagine yourself a wholesaler. Assume the price of insurance for a Wii is $300 and the price of an extended warranty is $30. The customer will most likely buy this warranty. However, if we pose the following question to the customer: Would you spend $300,000 to protect 10,000 Wiis? her answer will most likely be no.

Conclusions

➤ Decision-making behaviors of savers and insurers are rife with cognitive biases, as a result of which they reach mistaken conclusions about how much to save and how to allocate their savings.

➤ Savers are passive and therefore the task of inducing workers to save more falls on the employers.

➤ Several suggestions for increasing savings were made.

➤ Individuals buy too much insurance because of behavioral biases.

➤ People should be more open to the idea of purchasing insurance with higher deductibles.

➤ Investors should be wary of warranties of the electrical gadgets they buy.

LECTURE 15

THE HOT HAND

Agenda

➤ Definition of the Hot Hand in Basketball Theory and Its Significance
➤ A Casual Survey
➤ Evidence from the NBA and from Non-professionals
➤ Hot Hand Theory in a Dynamic Setting
➤ The Managerial Implications of the Hot Hand

The "Hot Hand" Fallacy

People tend to jump to the wrong conclusion that a player is having a winning streak, based on too few observations.

The hot hand in basketball fallacy theory is a popular example of the representativeness bias, and it underscores that people are poor in identifying whether or not a series of events is the result of chance or of systematic factors. Although the hot hand is better known as a sports phenomenon, its managerial analogy has important implications: Can we conclude that fund managers are "hot" just because they had few successes?

A player who scores in a few consecutive shots is often considered "hot." Gilovich *et al.* (1985) (Gilovich, Vallone and Tversky, GVT) contended that people come to the conclusion that a player is hot too quickly. They claim that the fact that a player merely made few consecutive shots does not imply that his performance is better than usual. They performed a series of statistical tests on professional NBA players and laypeople, and examined the probabilities that a player will score on the next shot as a function of his history of successful (or failed) shots. GVT found, contrary to the general belief of the population at large, of basketball coaches, players and commentators, that the hot hand is a myth. The chances that a player will succeed in the next shot, given that the player succeeded in her last few attempts, are not higher than the player's normal scoring average. (There is also a cold hand theory, which is a similar theory except that it looks at a series of failures rather than successes.)

The hot hand, interesting in itself, has significant practical implications for fields beyond sports.

Psychological Explanations for the Hot Hand Fallacy

➤ The confirmation bias
➤ Difficulties in judging sequences of events
➤ Recency bias

GVT used three lines of reasoning to explain the widely accepted, and what they considered false, belief in the hot hand.

First, people look for "streaks" and they detect streaks even when no streak is present because of confirmation bias.

Second, people have a hard time recognizing chance sequences. They expect chance sequences to alternate between the options more than they actually do. For example, they might expect a chance sequence flips of a coin with H or T results to look like: HTHTHT (although such a sequence would be indicative of a non-chance sequence with a negative correlation). True chance sequences may appear to contain too many "runs" (clusters of the same result).

Third, the hot hand is one of two fallacious beliefs that affect people's detection of streaks: The first is the belief that a streak will continue. This belief — that the odds of a random event occurring are more likely after the event has recently occurred — is due to positive recency. The opposite bias — negative recency — may also affect assessments. Negative recency is the belief that a streak cannot last too long and that the odds of a random event occurring are less likely after the event has recently occurred. In other words, lightening will not strike the same spot twice, and the ball in the roulette is not likely to land on red after landing on red in the last few spins (this is also known as gambler's fallacy).

Significance of the Hot Hand Theory

➤ The basketball industry generates billions of dollars around the world and enjoys tremendous exposure and the existence (or fallacy) of the hot hand has strategic implications as to how to manage games.

➤ The hot hand conundrum also applies to money managers and analysts. Also, here if the hot hand exists, it has huge implications on where and with whom to invest.

Significance of the hot hand

Coaches who believe in the hot hand will recommend passing the ball to the player with the hot hand, but this strategy is valuable only if the hot hand prevails. If it does not, then the strategy could be harmful. The hot hand was seriously debated in the NBA (with an annual turnover of $37.5 billion) and in the professional baseball industry worldwide, which is an important industry with high exposure and influence. Professional basketball leagues operate in all developed countries. For teams playing in these leagues, making the right decisions on who should take the next shot could be a matter of winning or losing. Beyond the joy, it brings to players, managers, and fans, winning also has important financial implications. The financial success of teams heavily depends on their success on the basketball court. In addition to its economic implications for professional teams, millions of recreation players of the game are also interested in the veracity or fallacy of the hot hand syndrome. The widespread interest in this topic is therefore quite understandable.

A Casual Experiment of the Hot Hand

Students were asked:

What are the chances that a player, who normally makes 50% of his field shots, will make (miss) the next shot after making (missing) two shots in a row? Response: 61% (42%).

These results show that the students believe in the hot hand. The casual nature of this experiment and its other obvious limitations prevent us from taking its results too seriously. However, I noted from this experiment that many students were well aware of the hot hand debate and answered so as to affirm the hypothesis that there is a hot hand.

It is now more than 30 years after the hot hand controversy began and researchers are still squabbling about it. There is a huge literature both in favor and against the theory that the hot hand is a myth (e.g., Alter and Oppenheimer, 2006; Bar-Eli *et al.* 2006; Boyle *et al.* 2011), with no indication that a resolution is in sight. Daniel Kahneman, Nobel prize winner and one of the co-founders of behavioral finance, argues in his 2011 book that the hot hand is a myth, but the hot hand fallacy theory received little sympathy in the real world of basketball. When Lebron James (considered by many to be "the best basketball player in the planet") was asked why he wanted his teammate, Kevin Love, to have the ball at an important juncture of an important game, he replied: "He had the hot hand, I wanted to keep going to him" (Miller and Sanjuro, 2015). This type of view, and from such influential basketball figures, might explain Tversky's frustration in not being able to get his theory across to those for whom the truth about the hot hand matters most.

In discussions of the existence of the hot hand, Amos Tversky has been quoted as saying, "I've been in a thousand arguments over this topic [hot hand], won them all, but convinced no one" (Bar-Eli *et al.* 2006: p. 535).

The insights from the hot hand debate in basketball were not lost in the world of finance and prompted researchers to study whether parallels could be drawn between basketball players and analysts and fund managers. Is it also true for analysts and fund managers that a brief series of successes does not imply a greater probability of future successes?

The Finance Equivalent of the Hot Hand

➤ Evidence shows that there is no serial correlation between returns of money managers.
➤ Nonetheless, investors prefer to invest with managers who have a track record of superior returns.

It is well documented (e.g., Gruber, 1996) that money managers' performance is not serially correlated: superior investment results in one period are not followed by superior results in subsequent periods. Instead, superior results in a given period are followed by average investment results. Yet, analyses of money flows into and out of mutual funds suggest that investors tend to invest with money managers who showed superior performance in a preceding period (e.g., Chevalier and Ellison, 1997; Sirri and Tufano, 1998). The empirical evidence on investor money flows has been interpreted, similar to the interpretation of the not hand phenomenon, as an irrational response. Specifically, it is argued that investors see patterns — "hot hands" — in investment results where none exist. Investors transfer money to "hot hand" money managers without obtaining any superior results.

In what follows, we will study the evidence concerning the hot hand effect.

GVT sampled the shots of each of the players of the Philadelphia 76ers in its 48 home games during the 1980–1981 NBA season. First, they checked the long-term success rates of each player based on that player's track record of makes and misses. Then they checked the players' stability in each game.

Averaged over all players, the probability of success after some hits (misses) is lower (higher) than the unconditional average. For example, the unconditional probability of a hit is 0.52, whereas the conditional probability of a hit after one miss is higher (0.54) and after one hit it is lower (0.51). If anything, this indicates the opposite of the hot hand. Looking at individual players, we notice a similar pattern for almost all players, but significance tests are conclusive only for Daryl Dawkins, whose success rate is considerably better after misses than after hits. Moreover, the more misses he had, the higher his chances of making a shot (88% after missing 3 shots, 73% after missing 2 shots, and 71% after missing 1 shot). Julius Erving (the legendary Dr. J) was quite stable: Previous misses or hits had almost no effect on his shooting performance.

GVT also measured the correlation between successive shots (a hit gets 1 and a miss 0), and found a negative correlation between success rates in consecutive shots in the entire sample, and for 8 out of 9 players. Since the hot hand predicts a positive correlation between successive hits (misses), as a hit (miss) makes the player "hot" ("cold"), the negative correlation is evidence against the hot hand theory.

Alternative Explanations for GVT's Surprising Findings

➤ Game dynamics

  ✓ Overconfidence

  ✓ Stronger defense

Overconfidence: Game dynamics is complicated, and hitting or missing a shot may affect both the player and the members of the opposing team. For example, a player may become more confident and attempt more difficult shots after making some shots. This will hurt his performance and negate the effects of the hot hand.

The stronger defense explanation: Belief in the hot hand may drive the opposing team to tighten its defense on the purportedly hot player, which reduces her chances of making the next shot. If this is true, then it will be hard to detect the hot hand even if it is true.

In a foul shot, a player shoots twice. Since there is no defense in this shot (which rules out the tighter defense argument) and the player cannot become more aggressive after the first shot, tests of the hot hand using foul shots are "cleaner." They include fewer confounding variables that potentially affect the results. The same is also true for three-point contests.

GVT sampled the penalty shots of 9 of Boston Celtics players in the 1980–1981 and 1981–1982 NBA seasons. They found that the average success rate after one hit is the same as that after one miss (0.75). Moreover, GVT found a positive correlation between the success rates of four players and negative correlation for five players, but none of these correlations was statistically significant. The data therefore do not offer evidence to support the existence of a hot hand phenomenon.

On the other hand, in one of the more recent papers in this area, Miller and Sanjuro (2015) studied the hot hand by examining 29 years of shooting data from television broadcasts of the NBA Three-Point Contest (1986–2015), where the players take three-point shots (long distance) without being defended against. In such contests, as in foul shots, the tighter defense argument does not hold. They concluded, "This leaves little doubt that the hot hand not only exists, but actually occurs regularly. Thus, belief in the hot hand, in principle, is not a fallacy."

The Hot Hand and Non-professional Players

➤ 26 Cornell students
➤ Shooting from a specific distance, they would make 50%
➤ 100 shots from this distance
➤ Results: Similar to the NBA players

GVT sampled 14 men and 12 women students at Cornell. For each student, they found the range from which he or she would make on average 50% of their shots. Then the students were asked to make 100 shots from this range. GVT found results similar to those found for the NBA players: No positive correlation between consecutive successes (and failures).

How Good are People at Distinguishing between Trends and Chance Results?

The hot hand is also related to the question of how good people are at distinguishing between trends and chance results.

To answer that question, 100 fans were presented different sequences of hits (1) and misses (0). Each fan was presented with six sequences of 21 shots each. All sequences contained 10 misses and 11 hits. Fans had to decide whether the sequences came from a streak shooter, random shots, or alternate shooting (where a success is likely to be followed by a failure and vice versa). In streak shooting, we expect the length of a streak to be longer, while in random shootings, streaks are expected to be shorter, resembling the results of independent successive coin tosses. Streaks will be shortest if the shots are alternating.

GVT generated these sequences of hits and misses (1 s and 0 s) using various probabilities of alternation. If the probability of alternation is 0.5, the sequence is defined as chance shooting, if the probability of alternation is 0.4, then the sequence represents a shooting streak, and if it is 0.9, the sequence represents alternating shooting.

In Figure 15.1, loosely based on GVT, we see the correlation between the perception of streaks and the true degree of alternation. The true degree of alternation is shown on the horizontal axis of Figure 15.1 and the percentage of participants who identified the results as streaks or chance shootings are presented in the vertical axis. When the true alternation is 0.5 (chance shooting), most people regard the sequence as a streak. Only when the probability of alternation is 0.55 or higher do most people suspect that the sequence is chance. Perceptions of a chance sequence fall drastically only when the alternation is very pronounced (above 0.85). People apparently are not good judges of whether or not sequences of events are correlated and in what way. Unless the correlation or alternation are really significant, people will not detect them.

On November 5, 2016, Steph Curry, arguably one of the best three-point shooters of all times, missed 10 consecutive three-point shots. Two days later, he made 13 out of 17 three-point shots,

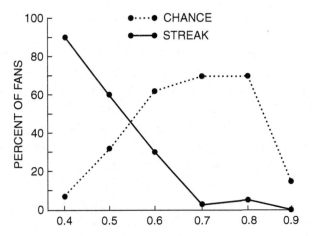

Figure 15.1. Length of streaks affects perception of a sequence as chance or streak shooting

Source: Gilovich *et al.* (1985).

breaking the record for the most three-pointers in an NBA game, with a percentage of 0.765. In one of his practice sessions, he made 77 shots in a row without a miss. I leave it to the readers to ponder if based on this information you can say he is a streak shooter, random shooter, alternate shooter or whether there is not enough information to make any conclusion on this matter.

Hot Hand and Dynamic Game Setting

Aharoni and Sarig (2012) modeled a basketball game where the defense adjusts to the success of the opposing players and reexamined the hot hand theory. They then tested their model on all 2004–2005 NBA games. The sample comprised 503 players (of the 528 signed in that period) in 30 teams that each played 82 games.

Players are classified into three categories: HH (hot hands), AH (average hand) and CH (cold hand). For maximal efficiency, the defense increases its resources allocated to guard the HHs (at the expense of the AHs) until the point where the HHs' effectiveness equals the effectiveness of the AHs. To test their theory, Aharoni and Sarig observe how success rates of HH, AH and CH change after misses or hits and explore to what extent these observations match their theory.

Aharoni and Sarig find that the FG (field goal) success rates do not depend on previous success rates, which is similar to GVT's results. However, the success rates of leading players and other players do not significantly differ. This, Aharoni and Sarig argue, suggests that the defense makes a difference, because the stars, who presumably are better players, are guarded by stronger defensive players, who reduce the stars' success rate to the average. The same logic leads us to assume that hot players will similarly be heavily guarded. Although the success rates of almost all players are the same, the stars play much more which implies their coaches consider them better players, and hence the fact that their success rates are similar to the other players indicates that they possibly are more heavily guarded. This last argument however is not conclusive, since it is also possible that the players' ranks depend on more than their offensive capabilities and are based on other parameters such as rebounds, defense, penalty shots, passing, team work, and X factors.

In the comparison between HH and CH players, Aharoni and Sarig show that HH players play longer than CH (290.95 seconds vs. 255.88 seconds), take their next shot sooner (196.12 s vs. 220.84 s), take more shots (23.5% of his team's shots vs. 16.5%), and take more difficult shots (66.95% jump shots vs. 56.46% easier layups). Accordingly, Aharoni and Sarig contend that after a HH player takes a shot, her game becomes more difficult, and therefore, it is tougher for her to excel. The "pure" quality of the player before and after becoming hot cannot be judged by comparing his performance before and after becoming hot because after becoming hot, the defense is stronger.

They conclude that it is likely that findings against the hot hand are due to the tougher defense directed against hot hand players.

Applications to the Finance Industry

- Successful managers receive more money to manage.
- The more funds the manager has to invest, the more difficult it is to find superior investment opportunities.

The notion that hot players face tougher competition than others after being identified as such (e.g., by making few consecutive shots or making a spectacular shot) also applies to hot investment managers who might face tougher competition and more difficult tasks as the funds they manage increase. Berk and Green (2004) suggest that the evidence showing that money managers receive more funds to manage after they succeed, even though they show no superior returns after that success, is consistent with superior investment ability of certain managers and with rational investors. Managers with superior investment skills receive more funds to manage. They need to invest greater efforts and devise more innovative ideas to manage the higher volume of funds. Diminishing returns to effort and limited availability of investments will undermine mangers' abilities to generate superior returns.

Conclusions

- We discussed the hot hand theory and its psychological underpinnings.
- Evidence was presented in support and against the claim that the hot hand is a myth.
- Whereas behavioral scientists believe the hot hand in basketball is a fallacy, practitioners believe the opposite.
- We saw experimental evidence showing that people are not good at identifying whether streaks are due to chance or to correlations.
- As with the hot hand in basketball (and other sports), there is extensive evidence that supports and refutes the proposition that there are hot money managers and analysts.

ACCOUNTING ANOMALIES

Agenda

➤ The Accruals Anomaly
➤ Post-earning Announcement Drift (PEAD)
➤ The Bowman Paradox

The Accruals Anomaly

➤ Accruals are the non-cash component of earnings.
➤ The accruals anomaly: the negative relation between accruals and future stock returns.
➤ The investment strategy: hold relatively large positions in low accruals companies, and low positions in high accruals companies.

The accruals anomaly is the negative relation between accruals and future stock returns.

This relationship suggests that the following investment strategy might yield above-normal profits: hold relatively large positions in low accruals companies, and low positions in high accruals companies, or equivalently, go long on low accruals companies, and short on high accruals companies.

The standard explanation for the accruals anomaly is that investors focus on bottom-line earnings and do not fully appreciate the differential reliability (or persistence) of a firm's cash flow vs.

its accruals. An alternative view is that a firm's accruals correlate with its investment decisions, which, in turn, are related to valuation errors, because investors do not understand how investments and the growth they bring affect the firm's future profitability.

The accruals anomaly was first discovered by Sloan (1996) and has persisted at least until 2005 and its magnitude has not abated over time (see for example Jiang, 2007, Lewellen, 2010, Richardson *et al.* 2010 and Wu *et al.* 2010). While investors continue to exploit the anomaly, the volume of accruals-related trading is rather small.

Since the anomaly is quite simple to identify and understand and strategies to exploit it seem relatively easy to implement, one wonders why it is not arbitraged away. The explanation lies with the type of firms that are used in accruals trading, in which the anomaly is more pronounced: These are firms with low institutional ownership; they are smaller, less profitable, and have low share turnover, and are generally the type of firms that institutional investors usually shun. Recall that in the lecture on sentiment, we saw that these are precisely the traits that prevent arbitrageurs from exploiting mispricings (Collins, *et al.* 2003).

Lev and Nissim (2006) also find that extreme accruals firms, which are the most suitable for accruals-related trading, are small, low profitability, and high risk, and command high transaction costs. They speculate that the accruals anomaly will persist since the costs involved in implementing accruals strategies are too high.

Post-earnings-announcement Drift (PEAD)

- Post-earnings-announcement drift (PEAD) — the observation that stock prices seem to underreact to quarterly earnings news.
- Stocks earn high positive (negative) abnormal returns in the three quarters following extreme positive (negative) earnings surprises.
- The effect of negative surprises on the drift is stronger.

PEAD is the tendency for stocks to earn on average high positive abnormal returns in the three quarters subsequent to an extreme positive earnings surprise (earnings that are distinctly different from the expected earnings), and, more strongly, to earn negative average abnormal returns in the three quarters subsequent to an extreme negative earnings surprise.

In one of the early studies of the PEAD, Foster, *et al.* (1984) find that a strategy of investing in the highest decile of firms with unexpectedly high earnings and shorting stocks in the lowest decile yields an annualized abnormal return of about 25% before transaction costs, over about 60 trading days. This raises a strong suspicion that the markets are not efficient, because clear evidence exists that above-normal profits can be earned.

In addition to the financial significance of the PEAD, this topic receives special attention in this course because it is a great example of an important financial phenomenon that is best explained by various concepts of behavioral finance.

Potential Explanations of PEAD

➤ Statistical issues
➤ Risk premium?
➤ Other behavioral explanations

Statistical issues: Some researchers claim that PEAD is just a statistical artifact. The statistical obstacles to prove or disprove this claim are far too many to go over here, but they are well known and have been addressed in the literature, and basically have been ruled out. One of the statistical issues that makes the statistical inference hard is that the drift refers to expected earnings, but it is not an easy task to measure expected earnings.

Can the PEAD represent a premium for risk? If the capital asset pricing model (CAPM) is an incomplete asset pricing model, as some researchers argue, then the abnormal returns calculated to claim the PEAD may not fully adjust for risk. The so-called abnormal returns therefore may be nothing more than fair compensation for risk. Firms with unexpectedly high earnings become more risky (their betas shift upward) and hence require higher returns, and the opposite occurs for firms with unexpectedly low earnings. Bernard and Thomas (1989) found that indeed there is a positive correlation between unexpected returns and betas, but it is too small to account for the magnitude of the drift.

Behavioral explanations: In their original explanation of PEAD, Bernard and Thomas do not use the word underreaction, but say that investors' response is delayed which is the same as underreaction. Bernard and Thomas however do not explain why investors underreact. They suggest that investors fail to assimilate the information because of some unexplained reason, or that because of transaction costs it is not worthwhile for many of them to immediately exploit the new information. Behavioral theory, as we have seen in Lecture 9, invokes the conservativeness bias to explain underreaction. Actually, several behavioral finance theories have been suggested to explain the PEAD. According to the behavioral theories proposed by Barberis, *et al.* (1998) and by Daniel, *et al.* (1998) (DHS), PEAD can arise as an underreaction to earnings, owing to psychological biases such as overconfidence and conservatism (see also Lecture 9). These researchers try to reconcile evidence of PEAD, which purportedly implies underreaction, to evidence presented by other researchers, which indicated overreaction in financial markets (e.g., DeBondt and Thaler, 1985, 1987). (BSV) and (DHS) suggest that markets might overreact or underreact to news depending on the length of the period considered. They suggest that markets underreact in the short term (periods between 6 and 12 months; reflecting short-term momentum) as shown by Jegadeesh and Titman (1993), but overreact for longer periods, as shown by DeBondt and Thaler (1987). PEAD, underreaction in the short term, therefore can be explained by these theories.

Note that overconfidence can lead to conservatism: When investors are overconfident, the prior distribution of events is too narrow (it is concentrated around the mean, not allowing much room for error) and hence new information receives less than its true weight, which is tantamount to saying that old information receives too much weight and decision makers do not sufficiently adjust — i.e., they are conservative.

Are individual investors responsible for PEAD?

Evidence from recent studies suggests that institutional investors are likely to be more sophisticated than individual investors. Hence, one may surmise that PEAD results from the trading activity of less sophisticated individual investors. Support for this hypothesis has been offered by Walther (1997), who found that the stock market reacts more strongly to earnings surprises when institutional shareholdings are greater. In a similar vein, Bartov *et al.* (2000) found that PEAD is more pronounced in firms with low institutional shareholdings.

As is often the case in finance, scholars disagree on this question. Hirshleifer *et al.* (2008) and Hou *et al.* (2007) found no evidence that either individuals or any sub-category of individuals in their sample cause PEAD. Individuals are significant net buyers after *both* negative and positive earnings surprises. Hirshleifer *et al.* did, however, find that individual post-announcement net buying is a significant negative predictor of stock returns over the following three quarters, but individual investor trading fails to reflect any of the extreme earnings surprises' power to predict future abnormal returns.

Accounting anomalies and market sentiment

Does investor sentiment affect the intensity of accounting anomalies? Since we have previously shown that investor sentiment affects stock prices, there is good reason to expect that price reactions to earnings surprises and accruals vary systematically with the level of investor sentiment.

Indeed, Livnat and Petrovits (2009) found support for the claim that PEAD is affected by sentiment. They show that holding extreme "good news" firms following pessimistic sentiment periods earns significantly higher abnormal returns than holding extreme "good news" firms following optimistic sentiment periods. They also documented that abnormal returns in the short window around preliminary earnings announcements for extreme "good news" firms are significantly higher during periods of low sentiment than during periods of high sentiment.

In the same vein, they found that holding low accrual firms following pessimistic sentiment periods earns significantly higher abnormal returns than holding low accrual firms following optimistic sentiment periods. These results seem to indicate that sentiment influences the source of excess returns from earnings-based trading strategies.

The Bowman Paradox

- The negative relationship between risk and return accounting measures.
- Why is it puzzling? Researchers expect a positive risk-return relationship in the accounting measures, as is common for stock returns.

The Bowman Paradox is the negative relationship between risk and return accounting measures, which was documented by Bowman (1980, 1982, 1984). Why is this relationship puzzling? Because researchers expect a positive risk-return relationship for accounting measures, as is common for stock returns. Bowman's findings raise the question of whether this negative correlation, which is the reverse of the correlation between stocks' expected returns and their volatility, indicates accounting measures' failure as representatives of financial information.

The standard explanation for the Bowman Paradox, as presented initially by Bowman, is as follows: the negative correlation between accounting mean returns and risk is consistent with losing firms that assume more risks in order to increase the chances of eventually making profits.

Fiegenbaum (1990) and Fiegenbaum and Thomas (1989) (FT) introduce the concept of target rate of return (ROE, return on equity) as reference points for firms' decisions. They argue that the Bowman Paradox is consistent with prospect theory, which posits that firms below target are risk seeking and firms above target are risk averse. FT explore the (accounting) risk-return relationship for firms below target and for firms above target. They show that the tradeoff between risk and return of the below-target firms is positive and that of the above-target is negative. They also show that the tradeoff is generally steeper for the below-target firms than for the above-target tradeoff with a median of below to above slope ratio of about 3:1.

Is the Bowman Paradox genuine?

In their 2012 paper, Brick, Palmon and Venezia (BPV) show that findings of a negative correlation between accounting risk and return could largely be attributed to the way ROEs were calculated in previous studies. In some of these studies, the ROEs were calculated by dividing net income by the firm's net equity at the end of the period (EOP). A more appropriate method, dividing net income by the equity at the beginning of the period (BOP), more closely corresponds to the practice in finance of having the initial investment in the denominator. BPV extended their criticism in a later study (2015), in which they demonstrated that findings that purportedly support the Bowman Paradox were due to missing variables in the analysis. Focusing only on the correlation between risk and return, without controlling for other variables that potentially influence the relationship, is known to introduce biased estimates. BPV presented the variables' size and leverage, and also amended ROEs to take account of additions to stockholders' capital. After these adjustments, the correlation between accounting risk and return becomes positive and refutes the existence of the paradox, which suggests that the negative correlation between measured mean returns and variances may be spurious.

Conclusions

➢ We reviewed three major accounting anomalies that seem to persist.

➢ The accruals anomaly is explained by investors' *naiveté*, as they seem not to appreciate the correlation between accruals and investments.

(Continued)

(*Continued*)

> ➤ Post earnings announcement drift is explained by investors' conservatism.
> ➤ The Bowman Paradox, receives a prospect theory based explanation.
> ➤ All these anomalies persist mainly in small stocks with high transaction costs which are held mainly by individuals.

APPEARANCE AND DISAPPEARANCE OF ANOMALIES

Agenda

➤ Overview of Some Well-known Anomalies
➤ Behavioral Explanations for the Weekend Effect
➤ Evolution of the January Effect
➤ Persistence of the Endowment Effect
➤ Behavioral Explanations for Abnormal Initial Price Offerings (IPO) Returns

---

What are Market Anomalies?

Anomalies are phenomena that suggest that above-normal profits can be made. This may either indicate inefficiency of the market or that what are considered "normal profits" are based on inadequate financial theories. Psychologists define anomalies slightly differently. For example, in Kahneman, *et al.* (1991), we find: "An empirical result qualifies as an anomaly if it is difficult to 'rationalize,' or if implausible assumptions are necessary to explain it within the paradigm" (p. 193).

We defined anomalies and discussed many of them in Lecture 1 (size, weekend effect, P/E, January, momentum), in Lecture 13 (the closed-end funds anomaly), and in Lecture 16 (post-earnings-announcement drift, the accruals anomaly and Bowman Paradox). In this Lecture, we will revisit some of our discussions and focus more on the persistence of anomalies and behavioral explanations for their existence. We will also introduce another anomaly — the underpricing of IPOs — and provide a behavioral explanation for it based on the cascades theory covered in Lecture 8.

Well-known Anomalies

➤ The January effect (the turn-of-the-year effect)
➤ The weekend (Monday) effect
➤ Underpricing of IPOs
➤ The size effect
➤ The value effect
➤ The momentum effect

The size effect, momentum and value anomalies were partly "solved" by considering these factors as risk factors. This of course did not eliminate the controversy surrounding them. Schwert (2003) offers evidence that shows that the size effect has diminished over time, if not disappeared, but in a more recent study, Asness, *et al.* (2015) claim that the evidence against the size effect is the result of disregard of several confounding factors. They find a significant size premium when controlling for firm quality. They show that the effect they find is robust to non-price-based measures of size, and is consistent across seasons and markets.

In this Lecture we will not delve into the issues of the size, momentum and value anomalies, but rather focus on a review of the January effect, the weekend effect and abnormal returns to IPOs and their behavioral explanations.

The weekend effect

The weekend effect is the tendency of average returns after the weekend to be negative (also known as the Monday effect, or the Monday seasonal effect). We highlight this effect because of the behavioral explanations offered for it and because it underscores the differences between individuals and institutional investors.

The weekend phenomenon appears in multitude of versions. Originally (e.g., French, 1980), it referred to the tendency of average returns following the weekend to be negative. This phenomenon has been observed in many countries (e.g., Gultekin and Gultekin, 1983, Solnik and Bousquet, 1990) and for various types of securities (e.g., Flannery and Protopapadakis, 1988, and Johnston-Tashijan, *et al.*, 1991).

The original and simple explanation for this anomaly has been that firms, fearing the gut reaction of investors, prefer to release bad news over the weekend. Many other alternative explanations have been proposed, including delays between trade and settlement, specialist trading behavior, and errors in measurement (for more explanations, see Kamara, 1997).

An Individual vs. Institutional Investor Explanation

➤ Individual investors tend to transact more on Mondays
➤ Small investors are more likely to sell rather than buy after the weekend

---

A popular explanation for the weekend effect (e.g., Lakonishok and Maberly, 1990, Abraham and Ikenberry, 1994, Brockman and Michayluk, 1998, Chan and Lakonishok, 1993, Chan *et al.* 2004, and Doyle and Chen, 2009) is based on the different behaviors of individuals and institutions. Individuals, according to this theory, who are more likely to trade in smaller stocks, may exert selling pressure that lead to the weekend effect. Individual investors, according to this theory, are busy at work during the week and consider trading decisions mainly during the weekend. Consequently, they are more likely to trade (either buy or sell) on Mondays. Professional and institutional investors sometimes use the beginning of the week to plan for the rest of the week, and this causes reduced activity. Amateur investors are more likely to sell rather than buy on Mondays, since even when an individual investor decides to buy, she may prefer to precede it with a sell due to liquidity considerations (e.g., Lakonishok and Maberly,

1990). This argument is not universally accepted since an investor could buy early in the day and sell later, and still have no liquidity problems if both trades are settled the same day. In any case, whether or not selling dominates buying for amateurs after the weekend and the opposite is true for institutions remains an empirical issue. This will be examined later.

Lakonishok and Maberly (1990) (LM) examined for the period 1962–1986 and for several sub-periods of this time span, the trading volume on Monday compared with the trading volume on the other four trading days of the week (and made similar comparisons for each trading day).

They found that the total volume on Mondays was significantly lower ($p < .01$ for two-tailed tests) than on the other days of the week, for all sub-periods as well as for the entire period (1962–1986). They also demonstrated that statistical tests that simultaneously examine differences between trades in various days showed significant differences when all days were considered. These tests turned out insignificant however when Mondays were not included. Taken together, these two results indicate that it is likely that the trading volume on Mondays is the cause of the difference between the days.

LM also found for all the sub-periods as well as for the entire period, that the overall volume of odd-lot trades (indicative of individual rather than institutional trades) relative to all trades, is significantly higher on Mondays than on the other days of the week. This suggests that it is likely that on Mondays individual investors' trades account for a larger proportion of total trades than on other days of the week. Put differently, individual investors' trade more intensely on Mondays than do institutional investors.

For the period between 4/23/87 and 10/3/88, LM show that the volume of block trades (indicative of institutional trades rather than individual investors' trades) on Mondays is significantly lower than on other days of the week. Their data also reveals that there are significant differences in trading volumes during the different days of the week. They conclude that it is likely that institutional investors' trades account for a lower proportion of total trades on Mondays than on other days of the week.

Summary of the Evidence for an Individual vs. Institutional Investor Explanation for the Weekend Effect

- During the period 1962–1986, transaction volumes on Mondays were lower than on the other trading days.
- There is no evidence for differences in trading volumes between non-Monday trading days.
- Mondays are the most active days of the week for individual investors, relative to institutional investors.
- There are no significant differences between individuals' trading volumes on non-Mondays.

Critique

➢ Only proxies were used for individual and institutional trades.
➢ The study did not distinguish between individual investors' sales and purchases on Mondays.
➢ The study did not correlate between returns and activity.

More Behavioral Explanations for the Weekend Effect

➢ Do professionals and amateurs differ in their propensity to buy vs. sell on the days after the weekend?
➢ Does selling dominate buying for amateurs after the weekend and is the opposite true for professionals?
➢ Are stock returns after the weekend correlated with behavioral patterns of individuals vs. professionals?

A study by Venezia and Shapira (VS) (2011) using Israeli date studied the above questions. VS examined all the daily transactions of a sample of both amateurs and professionally managed investors in a major brokerage house in Israel from 1994 to 1998. They found that weekends influence both amateurs and professional investors; however, they affect them in opposite directions. Individuals increase both their buy and sell activities, and their propensity to sell rises more than their propensity to buy. Professionals on the other hand tend to perform fewer buy as well as sell trades after the weekend, but unlike individuals, the drop in their activity is almost the same for buy trades and for sell trades. These results agree with previous hypotheses raised in the literature, but not directly tested, about the effects of the weekend on the predisposition to trade of individuals and institutions in other markets. VS also find that the returns on the days following the weekend are lower than those in other weekdays in a manner consistent with the behavioral patterns they found.

The January Effect

The January effect is the observation that the month of January appears to have systematically higher returns than other months of the year. The effect is more pronounced for the first two weeks of the month and for small stocks. The January effect is one of the most widely recognized anomalies. It was mentioned as early as 1942, but received academic attention only in the 1970s (Rozeff and Kinney, 1976).

The anomaly (also called the turn of the year effect) is not limited to the United States, and has been observed in many countries. Gultekin and Gultekin (1983) offer evidence of disproportionately large January returns in most countries around the world.

Since the effect is most pronounced for small stocks, a common zero investment strategy to exploit it is to create a "small minus big" portfolios where the purchase of small stocks is financed by the (short) sale of big stocks.

The Common Explanations for the January Effect Include:

✓ Increase in buying in January follows the drop in prices that often occurs in December due to tax loss selling (this explanation does not sit well with the prevalence of the effect in countries with different tax laws).

✓ Investors use year-end cash bonuses to purchase investments the following month.

(continued)

(continued)

✓ After mutual funds buy big stocks for "window dressing" in December to "show off" in their annual reports, they sell them in January and buy small stocks instead (this is equivalent to the strategy of going long on small stocks and short on large stocks in January).

Roll (1983) dismisses all the explanations for the January effect for lack of supporting empirical evidence. He acknowledges that the January effect indeed is an anomaly and predicts that it will persist because of trading costs.

As in other anomalies, even if the above explanations are valid, the January effect should be eliminated by investors' efforts to exploit it. Hence, its persistence is anomalous. In his popular book, "A Random Walk Down Wall Street," (1999) Burton Malkiel claims that this anomaly does not offer reliable opportunities to investors and that transaction costs are too high for most investors to be able to exploit it.

Is the January effect a persistent anomaly? The question arises every year. The answer is usually more qualified than a simple yes or no because the anomaly changes shape and form over time. Answers depend on the multiple parameters that each researcher focuses: the period examined (the years in their sample), the type of asset examined (stocks in general, different sizes of stocks, bonds, options, futures, etc.), the days in January and December (December, early January, mid-January, etc.) and the extent of volatility in the market.

Schwert, a staunch defender of market efficiency, acknowledges in his 2003 paper (p. 944) that "it does not seem that the turn-of-the-year anomaly has completely disappeared since it was originally documented," but he claims that the effect is mostly attributable to small and illiquid stock.

Moller and Zilca (2008) find higher abnormal returns in the first part of January and lower abnormal returns in the second part of January in the mid-1990s. These two changes offset each other, and consequently, the overall magnitude of the January effect appears similar to previous periods. They conclude that the basic forces that drive the January effect still persist and are as strong as they have been in the past. We should note however that finding higher returns in one period (the first part of January) and lower returns in another (the second part of January) is a mild anomaly in itself.

Ziemba (2011) argues that transactions costs, especially price pressures, make it difficult to take advantage of the January effect, and therefore, this anomaly will be easier to exploit in future markets where these costs are minimal. Ziemba examines the profitability of a Small-Minus-Big capitalized US stocks strategy since futures trading began in 1982. He finds evidence that these (futures) markets anticipate the January effect and while the anomaly still exists, it now occurs in December.

Would the Endowment Effect Disappear with Experience?

The endowment effect refers to the fact that individuals demand much more to give up a good (willingness to accept, or WTA) than they would pay to buy it (willingness to Pay, WTP).

In one of the early experiments showing this bias, Kahneman, *et al.* (1991) enrolled Cornell students in an experiment and created some frictionless exchange markets for Cornell mugs. Some participants were given Cornell mugs, and some were given items of equivalent value (pens) or money. Students were able to trade in the market created. The researchers found that participants were unwilling to pay more than $2.25–$2.75 for the mugs, but demanded $4.25–$4.75 to give them up.

Several explanations were proposed. One explanation is that the endowment effect is merely the result of loss aversion, where people have a greater disutility from losing something (giving it up) than the utility of gaining (buying) it. The endowment effect was also called the *status quo* effect by Samuelson and Zeckhauser (1988), who claimed that people simply prefer to maintain the *status quo*, and therefore, once endowed with an object, people are reluctant to relinquish it and would require more than the current price to do so.

A straightforward method to test for the endowment effect was performed by Knetch (1989). Participants are randomly allocated to two treatment conditions. In one treatment condition, participants receive good A and have the option of exchanging it for good B: In the second treatment condition, the goods are reversed (the subjects are given B and can exchange it for A). In the absence of the endowment effect, 50% of the participants should trade since they were randomly assigned to the two treatment conditions. If fewer than 50% exchange the good they were given, this would support the endowment effect. In Knetch's (1989) experiment, 90% of those endowed with a chocolate bar (good A) chose to keep it rather than exchange it for a mug (good B), but at the same time 89% of those endowed with a mug chose to keep it rather than exchange it for a chocolate bar. This is one of the early experiments supporting the endowment effect.

As in all anomalies, one wonders if the endowment effect will persist even if people have experience with this anomaly. In a series of experiments, List (2003) shows that the endowment effect disappears once participants have enough sufficient market experience.

Abnormal Returns to IPOs

Investors who purchase stocks in underwritten firm commitment of IPOs at the offering price enjoy large (abnormal) returns. This is referred to as IPO underpricing.

It is well known that investing in IPOs is a good investment strategy. Schwert (2003) argues that an investor who invests in a strategy of purchasing a random sample of IPOs each month, selling them one month later as seasoned offerings, and then reinvesting in a new set of IPOs the following month, can earn tremendous returns on her investment.

According to Schwert, this investment strategy would give an investor who started with $1,000 in 1960, hundreds of trillions of dollars by 2001, compared to $74,000 if the money were invested in the stock market. His calculations provide an excellent example of the power of compounding, but only cold comfort for individual investors. The daily first day returns on IPOs between 1980 and 2001 was 18.8% (Ritter and Welch, 2002). An investor starting with $1, who could invest daily and earn such returns for 10 years (assuming 250 days a year), would obtain $$(1.188)^{2500} = \$1.1 \times 10^{187}$$.

Schwert argues that high IPO returns are not relevant for most investors for several reasons: First, IPO stocks are allocated mainly to large institutional investors (and to "preferred individual clients such as politicians") by the underwriters of the IPO's.

Second, many investment banks prevent investors from using Schwert's strategy as they discourage the practice of buying shares in an IPO and then selling the shares shortly afterwards in the secondary market. Therefore, Schwert concludes that while IPOs seem to offer large abnormal returns to few privileged investors, it is doubtful whether this anomaly can benefit large groups of investors.

Contrary to the high one daily returns that accrue to those who can buy at the underwritten IPO price and sell within one day, the returns for those buying for the longer term were not as spectacular. Ritter and Welch (2002) report that an investor who buys shares at the first-day closing price and holds them for three years, IPOs earned 22.6%, but these returns are lower than the 23.4% that could have been achieved by investing in the market and are even lower than the returns on investments in firms of similar size (small firms).

Although the high returns calculated by Schwert for monthly investments and above for daily investments are unrealistic, it appears that IPOs might be underpriced, allowing high returns to those who purchase them for the very short term. Apparently, the issuers could have charged those buyers higher prices.

We focus on the question of how these returns can be explained. Many possible explanations for the anomaly have been proposed (see, e.g., Ritter and Welch, 2002).

Here, we present just one explanation, which is based on Bickhchandani, *et al.*'s (1992) cascades theory (which we also mentioned in the Lecture 8). According to this theory, issuers underprice in order to induce a positive informational cascade and to avoid a negative cascade. In an informational cascade, investors attempt to judge the quality of an asset by the interest other investors show in the asset. In the context of IPO's, they would request shares of the IPO when they believe the offering is "hot." If the shares are priced just a little too high, a negative cascade might develop. Investors, seeing that others are not interested in the IPO, will also shun it, believing that those investors were informed about the quality of the offering. This will trigger a non-buying cascade. On the other hand, some degree of underpricing could start a positive cascade, where investors believe that others investing in the IPO know what they are doing, and will therefore jump on the bandwagon and buy the issue, too. Issuers therefore have an incentive to underprice an IPO to trigger a positive cascade.

In support of this theory, Amihud, *et al.* (2001) found that IPOs tend to be either undersubscribed or hugely oversubscribed, with very few offerings moderately oversubscribed. This is consistent with the hypothesis that the IPO market is dominated by either positive or negative cascades.

Conclusions

- Anomalies such as the weekend effect can be explained by the different behaviors of institutions and individuals.
- Anomalies such as the January effect might persist, but their exact shape and the investment strategies needed to exploit them change over time.
- Transaction costs are a key factor in the exploitability of anomalies and in explaining their persistence.
- Experience can mitigate anomalies.
- Herding (cascades) can explain the underpricing of IPOs.

READINGS BY CHAPTERS

(The full references are listed below)

Chapters 1–5: Introduction and Prospect Theory: Allais, 1953, Ariely, 2008, 2010, Barberis and Thaler, 2003, Baker and Sesia, 2007, Berk and DeMarzo, 2007, Bodie *et al.* 2013, Breeden *et al.* 1989, Brick, 2017, Camerer and Weber, 1992, Coval and Shumway, 2005, Dunn and Norton, 2012, Edwards, 1962, Ellsberg, 1961, Fama and MacBeth, 1973, Fama and French 1992, 1993, 2014, Friedman and Savage, 1948, Griffin and Tversky, 1992, Harris and Gurel, 1986, Heath and Tversky, 1991, Jensen, 1978, Kahneman and Tversky, 1979, Kahneman *et al.* 1991, Kahneman, 2011, Levy, 1980, 2015, Mackay, 1841, Malkiel, 1999, Markowitz, 1952, 1991, Pratt, 1992, Raiffa, 1993, Ritter, 2003, Roll and Ross, 1980, Ross, 1976, Samuelson and Zeckhauser, 1988, Shefrin, 2002, Shefrin and Statman, 1984, Shiller, 1981, 2000, Thaler and Johnson, 1990, Thaler and Sunstein, 2009, The New York Times, 1987, Thompson, 2007, Tversky and Shafir, 1992, Venezia, 2016, Von Neumann and Morgenstern, 1944, 2007, Zapatero, 2016.

Chapter 6: The Disposition Effect: Baker and Sesia, 2007, Ben David and Doukas, 2006, Constantinides, 1984, Genesove and Mayers, 2001, Odean, 1998, Schlarbaum *et al.* 1978, Shapira and Venezia, 2001, Shefrin and Statman, 1985.

Chapter 7: Overconfidence: Alpert *et al.* 1982, Barber and Odean, 1999, 2000, 2001, Bar Yosef and Venezia, Baumann *et al.* 1991, Ben-David *et al.* 2007, Bergman and Jenter, 2007, Cassar and Friedman, 2007, Bernardo and Welch, 2001, Christensen-Szalanski *et al.*, 1981, Cooper *et al.*, 1988, Daniel *et al.* 1998, De Long *et al.* 1991, Gervais and Odean, 2001, Gervais, S., and Goldstein, 2007, Gervais *et al.* 2011, Glaser and Weber, 2007, Goel and Thakor, 2008, Grinblatt and Keloharju, 2009, Hayward and Hambrick, 1997, Heaton, 2002, Hirshleifer and Luo, 2001, Kidd, 1970, Kraahmer, 2003, Kyle and Wang, 1997, Landier and Tessmar, 2008, Lichtenstein *et al.* 1982, Malmendier and Tate, 2005a, 2005b, 2008, Malmendier *et al.* 2007, Neale and bazerman, 1990, Odean, 1999, Oyer and Schaefer, 2005, Palmon *et al.* 2008, Palmon and Venezia, 2012, 2013, Russo and Schoemaker, 1992, Stael von Holstein, 1972, Statman *et al.* 2006, Wagenaar and Keren, 1986, Wang, 2001.

Chapter 8: Herding: Avery and Zemsky, 1998, Banerjee, 1992, Bikhchandani and Sharma, 2000, Bickhchandani *et al.* 1992, Calvo, and Mendoza, 2000, Chiang and Zheng, 2010, Choe *et al.* 1999, Cipriani, and Guarino, 2005, 2008, Froot *et al.* 1992, Froot, O'Connell and Seasholes, 2001, Graham, 1999, Grinblatt *et al.* 1995, Kim and Wei, 2002, Lakonishok *et al.* 1992, Maug and Naik, 1995, Nofsinger and Sias, 1999, Rigobon, 2002, Scharfstein and Stein, 1990, Surowiecki, 2005, Venezia *et al.* 2011, Welch, 2000, Wermers, 1999, Wylie, 2005.

Chapter 9: Underreaction and Overreaction: Barberis *et al.* 1998, Conrad and Kaul, 1998, Daniel *et al.* 1998, De Bondt and Thaler, 1985, 1987, Fama and French, 1996, Griffin and Tversky 1992, Grinblatt *et al.* 1984, 1995, Hong and Stein, 1999, Jegadeesh and Titman, 1993, 2001a, 2001b, 2002, Kahnenan 2011, Shefrin, 1999, Vermalean and Verstringe, 1998, Zarowin, 1989.

Chapter 10: The Equity Premium Puzzle and Myopic Loss Aversion: Amar and Kroll, 2016, Benartzi and Thaler, 1995, Constantinides, 1984, 1990, Ewijk *et al.* 2010, Gneezy and Potters, 1997, Gneezy *et al.* 2003, Lopes, 1981, Mankiw and Zeldes, 1991, Mehra and Prescott, 1985, Mehra and Prescott, 2008, Pratt, 1992,

Rietz, 1988, Samuelson, 1963, Siegel and Thaler, 1997, Tversky and Bar-Hillel, 1983, Zapatero, 2016.

Chapter 11: The Home Bias: Barber and Odean, 2011, Benarlzi and Thaler 2007, Cooper and Kaplanis, 1994, Cohen, 2009, Coval and Moskowitz, 1999, 2001, Driscoll *et al.*, 1995, Feldsein and Horioka, 1980, French and Poterba, 1991, Graham *et al.* 2005, Grinblatt and Keloharju, 2001, Huberman, 2001, Heath and Tversky 1991, Kyrychenko and Shum, 2009, Levy and Levy, 2014, Meulbroek, 2005, Portes and Rey, 2005, Schoenmaker and Soeter, 2014, Tesar and Werner, 1995.

Chapter 12: Limits to Arbitrage: Amihud and Mendelson, 2001, Barberis and Tkalor 2003, Berk and DeMarzo, 2007, D'Avolio, 2002, De Long *et al.* 1990, Galai and Sade, 2006, Pasquariello and Vega, 2009, Sharpe and Alexander, 1990, Shleifer and Vishny, 1997.

Chapter 13: Market Sentiment: Baker and Wurgler, 2007, Barber, Odean and Zhu, 2009a, 2009b, Brown *et al.* (2003), Cao and Wei, 2005, De Long *et al.* 1990, Dolvin, and Pyles, 2007, Edmans *et al.* 2007, Frazzini and Lamont, 2008, Goetzmann and Zhu, 2005, Helliwell, and Wang, 2014, Hirshleifer and Shumway, 2003, Isen, 2011, Kamstra *et al.* 2003, 2012, Kaplanski, and Levy, 2010a, 2010b, Kaplanski *et al.* 2015, Kliger and Kudryavtsev, 2016, Kumar and Lee, 2006, Lee *et al.* 1991.

Chapter 14: Biases in Insurance, Savings and Pension Decision: Agnew *et al.* 2003, Benartzi, 2001, Benartzi and Thaler, 1999, 2001, 2007, Ben-Arab *et al.* 1996, Braun and Muermann, 2004, Burns, 2004. Chen *et al.* 2009, Choi *et al.* 2002, Choi *et al.* 2011, Cohen, 2009, Cummins *et al.* 1978. Darlin, 2009, Huberman and Jiang, 2006, Johnson *et al.* 1993, Kahneman and Tversty 1979, Mossin, 1968, Pashigian *et al.* 1966, Samuelson and Zeckhauser, 1988, Schoemaker, 1976, Shapira and Venezia, 2008a, 2008b, Skinner, 2007, Statman, 2017, Sydnor, 2010. Thaler and Benartzi, 2004, Thaler and Sunstein, 2009, Wakker *et al.* 1997.

Chapter 15: The Hot Hand: Aharoni and Sarig, 2012, Alter and Oppenheimer, 2006, Berk and Green, 2004, Bar-Eli *et al.* 2006, Boyle *et al.* 2011, Chevalier and Ellison, 1997, Gilovich *et al.* 1985, Gruber, 1996, Miller and Sanjurjo, 2015, Sirri and Tufano, 1998.

Chapter 16: Accounting Anomalies: Bartov *et al.* 2000, Bernard and Thomas 1989, Barberis *et al.* 1998, Bowman, 1980, 1982, 1984, Brick *et al.* 2012, 2015, Collins, Danid *et al.* 1998, De Bondt and Thaler 1985, 1987, Gong, and Hribar, 2003, Fiegenbaum and Thomas, 1988, Fiegenbaum, 1990, Foster *et al.* 1984, Hirshleifer *et al.* 2008, Hou *et al.* 2007, Jegadeesh and Titman, 1993, Jiang, 2007, Lev and Nissim, 2006, Lewellen, 2010, Livnat and Petrovits, 2009, Richardson *et al.* 2010, Sloan, 1996, Walther, 1997, Wu *et al.* 2007.

Chapter 17: The Existence and Disappearance of Anomalies, Seasonal and Calendar Effects: Abraham and Ikenberry, 1994, Amihud *et al.* 2001, Asness *et al.* 2015, Bickhchandani *et al.* 1992, Brockman and Michayluk, 1998, Chan *et al.* 2004, Chan and Lakonishok, 1993, Doyle and Chen, 2009, Flannery and Protopapadakis, 1988, French, 1980, Gultekin, and Gultekin, 1983, Kamara, 1997, Lakonishok and Maberly, 1990, Knetsch, 1989, Kahneman *et al.* 1991, Kamara, 1997, List, 2003, Malkiel, 1999, Moller and Zilca, 2008, Roll, 1983, Ritter and Welch, 2002, Rozeff and Kinney, 1976, Samuelson and Zeckhauser, 1988, Schwert, 2003, Venezia and Shapira, 2011, Ziemba, 2011.

References

Abraham, A., and Ikenberry, D., 1994, "The individual investor and the weekend effect", *The Journal of Financial and Quantitative Analysis*, *29*, 263–277.

Agnew, J., Balduzzi, P., and Sunden, A., 2003, "Portfolio choice and trading in a large, 401 (k) plan", *The American Economic Review*, *93*(1), 193–215.

Aharoni, Gil, and Oded H. S., 2012, "Hot hands and equilibrium", *Applied Economics*, *44*(18), 2309–2320.

Albert, J., 1993, "A Statistical analysis of hitting streaks in baseball: Comment", *Journal of the American Statistical Association*, *88*, 1184–1188.

Albright, S., and Christian, 1993a, "A Statistical analysis of hitting streaks in baseball", *Journal of the American Statistical Association*, *88*, 1175–1183.

Albright, S. C., 1993b, "A Statistical analysis of hitting streaks in baseball: Rejoinder", *Journal of the American Statistical Association, 88*, 1194–1196.

Allais, M., 1953, "Le comportement de l'homme rationnel devant le risque: Critique des postulats et axiomes de l'école Américaine", *Econometrica, 21*, 503–546.

Alpert, M., and Howard R., 1982, "A progress report on the training of probability assessors", in D. Kahneman, P. Slovic and A. Tversky, (eds.), *Judgment Under Uncertainty: Heuristics and Biases.* Cambridge: Cambridge University Press.

Alter, A. L., and Oppenheimer, D. M., 2006, "From a fixation on sports to an exploration of mechanism: The past, present, and future of hot hand research", *Thinking & Reasoning, 12*(4), 431–444.

Amar, M., and Y. Kroll, 2016, "Experimental exploration of the factors affecting investors' horizon in asset allocation decisions", in I. Venezia, (ed.), *Behavioral Finance: Where do Investors Biases Come From?* World Scientific Publishers, Singapore.

Amihud, Y., and Haim Mendelson, 1991, "Liquidity, asset prices and financial policy", *Financial Analysts Journal, 47*, 56–66.

Amihud, Y., Hauser, S., and Kirsh, A., 2001, "Allocations, adverse selection and cascades in IPOs evidence from Israel", *Journal of Finacial Economics*, 68.

Ariely, D., 2008. *Predictably irrational*, New York: HarperCollins.

Ariely, D., 2010. *The upside of irrationality*, Dan Ariely, USA.

Asness, C. S., Frazzini, A., Israel, R., Moskowitz, T. J., and Pedersen, L. H., 2015, *Size matters, if you control your junk.* Fama-Miller Working Paper.

Avery C., and P. Zemsky, 1998, "Multidimensional uncertainty and herd behavior in financial markets", *The American Economic Review, 88*, 724–748.

Baker, M., and Aldo S., 2007, *Behavioral Finance at JPMorgan*, HBS.

Baker, M., and J. Wurgler, 2007, "Investor Sentiment in the stock market". *Journal of Economic Perspectives, 21*, 129–151.

Bar Yosef, S., and I. Venezia, 2014, "An experimental study of overconfidence in accounting numbers predictions", *International Journal of Economic Sciences, 3*(1), 2014, 78–89.

Banerjee, A., 1992, "A simple model of herding behavior", *Quarterly Journal of Economics, 107*, 797–817.

Barber, B., and T. Odean, 1999, "The courage of misguided convictions", *Financial Analysts Journal, 55*, 41–55.

Barber, B. M., and Odean, T., 2000, "Trading is hazardous to your wealth: The common stock investment performance of individual investors", *The Journal of Finance, 55*, 773–806.

Barber, B. M., and Odean, T., 2001, "Boys will be boys: Gender, over-confidence, and common stock investment", *The Quarterly Journal of Economics*, *116*, 261–292.

Barber, B. and Odean, T., 2011, The Behavior of individual investors, Working Paper, Haas School of Business University of California, Berkeley.

Barber, B. M., Odean, T. and Zhu, N., 2009a, "Do retail trades move markets?", *Review of Financial Studies*, *22*, 151–186.

Barber, B. M., Odean, T., and Zhu, N., 2009b, "Systematic noise", *Journal of Financial Markets*, *12*(4), 547–569.

Barberis, N., Shleifer, A., and Vishny, R., 1998, "A model of investor sentiment", *Journal of Financial Economics*, *49*(3), 307–343.

Barberis, N., and Thaler, R., 2003, "A survey of behavioral finance", in Constantinides, G., M. Harris and R. Stulz, (eds.), *Handbook of the Economics of Finance: Financial Markets and Asset Pricing*, North Holland, Amsterdam, 1053–1124.

Bar-Eli, M., Avugos, S., and Raab, M., 2006, "Twenty years of "hot hand" research: Review and critique", *Psychology of Sport and Exercise*, *7*, 525–553.

Bartov, E., Radhakrishnan, S., and Krinsky, I. 2000, "Investor sophistication and patterns in stock returns after earnings announcements", *The Accounting Review*, *75*(1), 43–63.

Benartzi, S., 2001, "Excessive extrapolation and the allocation of 401(k) accounts to company stock", *Journal of Finance*, 1747–1764.

Benartzi, S., and Thaler, R., 1995, "Myopic loss aversion and the equity premium puzzle", *Quarterly Journal of Economics*, *110*, 73–92.

Benartzi, S., and Thaler, R. H., 1999, "Risk aversion or myopia? Choices in repeated gambles and retirement investments", *Management Science*, *45*(3), 364–381.

Benartzi, S., and Thaler, R., 2001, "Naïve diversification in defined contribution saving plans", *American Economic Review*, *91*, 79–98.

Benartzi, S., and Thaler, R. H., 2007, "Heuristics and biases in retirement savings behavior", *Journal of Economic Perspectives*, *21*, 81–10.

Ben-Arab, M., Briys, E. and Schlesinger, H., 1996, "Habit formation and the demand for insurance", *The Journal of Risk and Insurance*, *63*, 111–119.

Ben-David, I. and Doukas, J. A., 2006, Overconfidence, trading volume, and the disposition effect, evidence from the Trades of institutional investors, Working Paper, The University of Chicago.

Ben-David, I., Graham, J. R., and Harvey, C. R., 2007, Managerial overconfidence and corporate policies (No. w13711), National Bureau of Economic Research.

Bergman, N. K. and D. Jenter, 2007, "Employee Sentiment and Stock Option Compensation", *Journal of Financial Economics, 84*, 667–712.

Berk, J. B., and DeMarzo, P. M., 2007, *Corporate finance.* Pearson Education.

Berk, J., and Green, R., 2004, "Mutual fund flows and performance in rational markets", *Journal of Political Economy, 112*, 1269–1295.

Bernard, V. L., and Thomas, J. K., 1989, "Post-earnings-announcement drift: Delayed price response or risk premium?" *Journal of Accounting research*, 1–36.

Bernardo, A., and Welch, I., 2001, "On the evolution of overconfidence and entrepreneurs", *Journal of Economics and Management Strategy, 10*, 301–330.

Bickhchandani, S. D., Hirshleifer, D. and Welch, I., 1992, "A theory of fads, fashion, custom, and cultural changes as informational cascades", *Journal of Political Economy, 100*, 992–1026.

Bikhchandani, S., and Sharma, S., 2000, Herd behavior in financial markets, IMF Staff Papers *47*, 279–310.

Bodie, Z., Kane, A., and Marcus, A. J., 2013, *Essentials of investments.* McGraw-Hill.

Bowman, E. H., 1980, "A risk/return paradox for strategic management", *Sloan Management Review, 21*, 17–33.

Bowman, E. H., 1982, "Risk seeking by troubled firms", *Sloan Management Review 23*, 33–42.

Bowman, E. H., 1984, "Content analysis of annual reports for corporate strategy and risk", *Interfaces, 14*, 61–71.

Boyle, E., Shapira, Z., and Venezia, I., 2011, All streaks are not created equal: An analysis of sports announcer references to hot and cold streaks in the NBA, Working Paper, NYU Stern School of Business.

Braun, M., and Muermann, A., 2004, "The impact of regret on the demand for insurance", *Journal of Risk and Insurance, 71*, 737–767.

Breeden, D. T., Gibbons, M. R., and Litzenberger, R. H., 1989, "Empirical tests of the consumption-oriented CAPM", *The Journal of Finance, 44*(2), 231–262.

Brick, I., Palmon, O., and Venezia, I., 2012, "The risk-return (Bowman) paradox and accounting measurements", in Venezia, I., and Z. Wiener (eds.), *Bridging the GAAP: Recent Advances in Finance and Accounting*, World Scientific Publishing Co., Singapore 21–36.

Brick, I. E., Palmon, O., and Venezia, I., 2015, "On the relationship between accounting risk and return: Is there a (Bowman) Paradox?" *European Management Review, 12*(2), 99–111.

Brick, I., 2017, *Introduction to Corporate Finance*, World Scientific Publishing Co, London. Forthcoming.

Brockman, P., and Michayluk, D., 1998, "Individual versus institutional investors and the weekend effect", *Journal of Economics and Finance*, *22*, 71–85.

Brown, S. J., Goetzmann, W. N., Hiraki, T., Shirishi, N., and Watanabe, M., 2003, "Investor sentiment in Japanese and US daily mutual fund flows (No. w9470)". *National Bureau of Economic Research*.

Burns, W., 2004, *Circuit city stores*, Inc. Harvard Business School, Case no. 9-191-086.

Calvo, G. A., and Mendoza, E. G., 2000, "Rational contagion and the globalization of securities markets", *Journal of International Economics*, *51*(1), 79–113.

Camerer, C., and M. Weber, 1992, "Recent developments in modeling preferences: Uncertainty and ambiguity", *Journal of Risk and Uncertainty*, *5*, 325–370.

Cao, M., and J. Wei, 2005, "Stock market returns: A note on temperature anomaly", *Journal of Banking and Finance*, *29*, 1559–1573.

Cassar, G., and H. Friedman, 2007, "Does Overconfidence Affect Entrepreneurial Investment?" *Wharton Research Scholars Journal*.

Chan, L. K. C., and Lakonishok, J., 1993, "Institutional trades and intraday stock price behavior", *Journal of Financial Economics*, *33*, 173–199.

Chan, S. H. Leung, W. K., and Wang, K. 2004, "The impact of institutional investors on the monday seasonal", *The Journal of Business*, *77*, 967–986.

Chen T., Kalra, A., and Sun, B., 2009, "Why do consumers buy extended service contracts?" *Journal of Consumer Research*, *36*, 661–623.

Chevalier, J., and G. Ellison, 1997, "Risk Taking by Mutual Funds as a Response to Incentives," *Journal of Political Economy*, *105*, 1167–1200.

Chiappori P. A., Levitt S., and Groseclose, D. T. 2002, Testing Mixed-Strategy equilibria when players are heterogeneous: The case of penalty Kicks in Soccer, American Economic Review, *92*(4), 1138–1151.

Chiang, T. C., and Zheng, D., 2010, "An empirical analysis of herd behavior in global stock markets", *Journal of Banking and Finance*, *34*, 1911–1921.

Choe, H., Kho, B., and Stulz, R., 1999, "Do foreign investors destabilize stock markets? The Korean experience" *Journal of Financial Economics*, *54*, 227–264.

Choi, J. J., Laibson, D., Madrian, B. C., and Metrick, A., 2002, "Defined contribution pensions: Plan rules, participant choices, and the path of least resistance", in *Tax Policy and the Economy*, Volume 16 (pp. 67–114). MIT Press cambridge.

Choi, J. J., Laibson, D., and Madrian, B. C., 2011, $100 bills on the sidewalk: Suboptimal investment in 401 (k) plans, Review of Economics and Statistics, *93*(3), 748–763.

Christensen-Szalanski, J. J., and Bushyhead, J. B., 1981, "Physicians' use of probabilistic information in a real clinical setting". *Journal of Experimental Psychology: Human perception and performance*, *7*(4), 928.

Cipriani, M., and Guarino, A., 2008, "Herd behavior and contagion in financial markets", *The BE Journal of Theoretical Economics*, *8*(1).

Cipriani, M., and Guarino, A., 2005, "Herd behavior in a laboratory financial market", *The American Economic Review*, *95*(5), 1427–1443.

Cohen, L., 2009, "Loyalty based portfolio choice", *The Review of Financial Studies*, *22*, 773–806.

Collins, D. W., Gong, G., and Hribar, P., 2003, "Investor sophistication and the mispricing of accruals", *Review of Accounting Studies*, *8*(2–3), 251–276.

Constantinides, G. M., 1984, "Optimal stock trading with personal taxes: Implications for prices and the abnormal January returns", *Journal of Financial Economics*, *13*, 65–89.

Constantinides, G. M., 1990, "Habit formation: A resolution of equity premium puzzle", *The Journal of Political Economy*, *98*, 519–543.

Cooper, A. C., Carolyn Y. Woo, and W.C. Dunkelberg, 1988, "Entrepreneurs' Perceived Chances for Success", *Journal of Business Venturing*, *3*, 97–108.

Cooper, I. A., and E. Kaplanis, 1994, "Home bias in equity portfolios, inflation hedging and international capital market equilibrium", *Review of Financial Studies*, *7*, 45–60.

Coval, J. D., and Moskowitz, T. J., 1999, "Home bias at home: Local equity preference in domestic portfolios", *The Journal of Finance*, *54*, 2045–2073.

Coval, J. D., and Moskowitz, T. J., 2001, "The geography of investment: Informed trading and asset prices", *Journal of Political Economy*, *109*, 811–841.

Coval, Joshua D., and Shumway, T., 2005, "Do behavioral biases affect prices?", *The Journal of Finance*, *60*, 1–34.

Cummins, D., and Weisbart, S., 1978, The impact of consumer services on independent insurance agency performance. Glenmont, NY: IMA Education and Research Foundation.

Daniel, K. Hirshleifer, D., and Subrahmanyam, A., 1998, "Investor psychology and security market under- and Overreactions", *Journal of Finance*, *53*, 1839–1885.

Darlin, D., 2009, "Don't worry, be happy: The warranty psychology", *The New York Times*, November 8.

D'Avolio, G., 2002, "The market for borrowing stock", *Journal of Financial Economics 66*, 271–306.

De Bondt, W., and R. Thaler, 1985, "Does the stock market overreact?" *Journal of Finance, 40*, 793–808.

De Bondt, W., and R. Thaler, 1987, "Further evidence on investor overreaction and stock market seasonality", *Journal of Finance, 42*, 557–581.

De Long, J. B., Shleifer, A., Summers, L. H., and Waldmann, R. J. 1990a, "Noise trader risk in financial markets", *Journal of Political Economy, 98*, 703–738.

De Long, J. B., Shleifer, A., Summers, L. H., and Waldmann, R. J., 1990b, "Positive feedback investment strategies and destabilizing rational speculation". *The Journal of Finance, 45*, 379–395.

De Long, J. B., Shleifer, A. Summers, L. H., and Waldmann, R. J., 1991, "The survival of noise traders in financial markets", *The Journal of Business, 64*, 1–19.

Dolvin, S. D., and Pyles, M. K., 2007, "Seasonal affective disorder and the pricing of IPOs" *Review of Accounting and Finance, 6*, 214–228.

Doyle, J. R., and Chen, C. H., 2009, "The wandering weekday effect in major stock markets", *Journal of Banking & Finance, 33*, 1388–1399.

Driscoll, K., Malcolm, M., Sirull, M. And P. Slotter, 1995, "Gallup Survey of Defined Contributions Plan Participants", John Hancock Financial Services, November.

Dunn, E., and Norton M., 2012, Don't indulge. Be happy. New York Times.

Edmans, A. Garcia, D., and Norli, O., 2007, "Sports sentiment and stock returns", *Journal of Finance, 62*, 1967–1998.

Edwards, W., 1962, "Subjective probabilities inferred from decisions", *Psychological review, 69*(2), 109.

Ellsberg, D., 1961, "Risk, ambiguity, and the Savage axioms", *The Quarterly Journal of Economics, 75*, 643–669.

Ewijk, C. V., and de Groot H. L. F. and Santig, C., 2010, "A meta-analysis of the equity premium", *Tinbergen Institute Discussion Paper* TI2010, 078/3.

Fama, E., and MacBeth, J., 1973, "Risk, return and equilibrium: empirical tests", *Journal of Political Economy, 71*, 607–636.

Fama, E., and French, K., 1992, "The cross-section of expected stock returns", *Journal of Finance, 47*, 427–486.

Fama, E., and French, K., 1993, "Common risk factors in the returns on stocks and bonds", *Journal of Financial Economics, 33*, 3–56.

Fama, E., and French, K., 1996, "Multifactor explanations of asset pricing anomalies", *Journal of Finance, 51*, 55–84.

Fama, E. F., and French, K. R., 2014, A five-factor asset pricing model, Fama-Miller Working Paper. Available at SSRN: http://ssrn.com/abstract$=$2287202 or http://dx.doi.org/10.2139/ssrn.2287202.

Feldstein, M. and Horioka, C., 1980, "Domestic Saving and International Capital Flows", *Economic Journal, 90*, 314–329.

Fiegenbaum, A., 1990, "Prospect theory and the risk-return association: An empirical Examination of 85 industries", *Journal of Economic Behavior & Organization, 14*, 187–203.

Fiegenbaum, A., and H. Thomas, 1988, "Attitudes toward risk and the risk-return paradox: Prospect Theory Explanations", *Academy of Management Journal, 1*, 85–106.

Flannery, M. J., and Protopapadakis, A. A., 1988, "From T-bills to common stocks: Investigating the generality of intra-week return seasonality". *The Journal of Finance, 43*(2), 431–450.

Foster, G., Olsen, C., and Shevlin, T., 1984, "Earnings releases, anomalies, and the behavior of security returns", *Accounting Review*, 574–603.

Frazzini, A., and Lamont, O. A., 2008, "Dumb money: Mutual fund flows and the cross-section of stock returns", *Journal of Financial Economics, 88*(2), 299–322.

French, K. R., 1980, "Stock returns and the weekend effect", *Journal of Financial Economics, 8*, 55–70.

French, K. R., and Poterba, J. M., 1991, "Investor diversification and international equity markets", *The American Economic Review, 81*, 222–226.

Friedman, M., and Savage, L. J., 1948, "The utility analysis of choices involving risk", *The Journal of Political Economy*, 279–304.

Froot, O., and Seasholes, 2001, "The portfolio flows of international investors", *Journal of Financial Economics, 59*, 151–193.

Froot, K. A., Scharfstein, D., and Stein, J. C., 1992, "Herd on the street: Informational inefficiencies in a market with short-term speculation", *Journal of Finance, 47*, 1461–1484.

Galai, D., and Sade, O., 2006, "The "ostrich effect" and the relationship between the liquidity and the yields of financial assets", *The Journal of Business, 79*(5), 2741–2759.

Genesove, D., and Mayer, C. J., 2001, "Loss aversion and seller behavior: Evidence from the housing market", *The Quarterly Journal of Economics, 112*, 1233–1260.

Gervais, S., and Odean, T., 2001, "Learning to be overconfident", *The Review of Financial Studies, 14*, 1–27.

Gervais, S., and Goldstein, I., 2007, "The positive effects of biased self-perceptions in firms", *Review of Finance, 11*(3), 453–496.

Gervais, S., Heaton, J. B., and Odean, T., 2011, "Overconfidence, compensation contracts, and capital budgeting", *The Journal of Finance*, *66*(5), 1735–1777.

Gilovich, T., Vallone, R, and Tversky, A., 1985, "The hot hand in basketball: On the misperception of random sequences", *Cognitive Psychology*, *17*, 293–314.

Glaser, M., and Weber, M., 2007, "Overconfidence and trading volume", *The Geneva Risk and Insurance Review*, *32*(1), 1–36.

Gneezy, U., and Potters, J., 1997, "An experiment on risk taking and evaluation periods", *The Quarterly Journal of Economics*, *112*, 631–645.

Gneezy, U., Kapteyn A., and Portters, J., 2003, "Evaluation periods and asset prices in market experiment", *Journal of Finance*, *58*, 821–838.

Goel, A. M., and Thakor, A., 2008, "Overconfidence, CEO selection, and corporate governance", *The Journal of Finance*, *63*, 2737–2784.

Goetzmann, W. N., and Zhu, N., 2005, "Rain or shine: Where is the weather effect?" *European Financial Management*, *11*, 559–578.

Graham, J., 1999, "Herding among investment newsletters: Theory and evidence", *Journal of Finance*, *54*, 237–268.

Graham, J. R., Harvey, C. R., and Huang, H., 2005, "Investor competence, trading frequency, and home bias", *National Bureau of Economic Research*, (No. w11426).

Griffin, D., and Tversky, A., 1992, "The weighing of evidence and the determinants of confidence", *Cognitive Psychology 24*, 411–435.

Grinblatt, M. S., Masulis, R. W., and Titman, S., 1984, "The valuation effects of stock splits and stock dividends", *Journal of Financial Economics*, *13*(4), 461–490.

Grinblatt, M., and Keloharju, M., 2001, "How distance, language, and culture influence stockholdings and trades", *The Journal of Finance*, *56*, 1053–1073.

Grinblatt, M., and Keloharju, M., 2009, "Sensation seeking, overconfidence, and trading activity", *The Journal of Finance*, *64*, 549–578.

Grinblatt, M., Titman, S., and Wermers, R., 1995, "Momentum investment strategies, portfolio performance, and herding: A study of mutual fund behavior", *The American Economic Review*, *85*, 1088–1105.

Gruber, M., 1996, "Another Puzzle: The Growth in Actively Managed Mutual Funds", *Journal of Finance*, *51*, 783–810.

Gultekin, M. N., and Gultekin, N. B., 1983, "Stock market seasonality: International evidence". *Journal of Financial Economics*, *12*(4), 469–481.

Harris, L., and Gurel, E. (1986), "Price and volume effects associated with changes in the S&P 500 list: New evidence for the existence of price pressures", *The Journal of Finance*, *41*(4), 815–829.

Hayward, M. L., and Hambrick, D. C., 1997, "Explaining the premiums paid for large acquisitions: Evidence of CEO hubris", *Administrative Science Quarterly*, 103–127.

Heath, C., and Tversky, A., 1991, "Preference and belief: Ambiguity and competence in choice under uncertainty", *Journal of Risk and Uncertainty*, *4*(1), 5–28.

Heaton, J. B., 2002, "Managerial Optimism and Corporate Finance," *Financial Management*, *31*, 33–45.

Helliwell, J. F., and Wang, S., 2014, "Weekends and subjective well-being", *Social Indicators Research*, *116*, 389–407.

Hirshleifer, D., and Luo, G. Y., 2001, "On the survival of overconfident traders in a competitive securities market", *Journal of Financial Markets*, *4*, 73–84.

Hirshleifer, D., and Shumway, T., 2003, "Good day sunshine: Stock returns and the weather", *Journal of Finance*, *58*, 1009–1032.

Hirshleifer, D. A., Myers, J. N., Myers, L. A., and Teoh, S. H., 2008, "Do individual investors cause post-earnings announcement drift? Direct evidence from personal trades", *The Accounting Review*, *83*(6), 1521–1550.

Hong, J., and Stein, J., 1999, "A Unified theory of underreaction, momentum trading and overreaction in asset markets", *Journal of Finance*, *54*, 2143–2184.

Hou, K., Hirshleifer, D., and Teoh, S. W., 2007, "The accrual anomaly: Risk or mispricing?" Munich Personal RePEc Archive.

Huberman, G., 2001, "Familiarity breeds investment", *Review of Financial Studies*, *14*, 659–680.

Huberman, G., and Jiang, W., 2006, "Offering versus Choice in 401(K) plans: Equity Exposure and Number of Funds". *Journal of Finance*, *61*, 763–801.

Isen, A. M, 2011, "A Role for neuropsychology in understanding the facilitating influence of positive affect on social behavior and cognitive processes", In S. J. Lopez and C. R. Snyder, (eds). *The Oxford Handbook of Positive Psychology*, New York: Oxford University Press, 503–518.

Jegadeesh, N., and Titman, S., 1993, "Returns to buying winners and selling losers: Implications for stock market efficiency". *The Journal of Finance*, *48*(1), 65–91.

Jegadeesh, N., and Titman, S., 2001a, Momentum, University Of Illinois Working Paper.

Jegadeesh, N., and Titman, S., 2001b, "Profitability of momentum strategies: An evaluation of alternative explanations", *The Journal of Finance*, *56*, 699–720.

Jegadeesh, N., and Titman, S., 2002, "Cross sectional and time series determinants of momentum strategies", *Review of Financial Studies*, *15*, 143–157.

Jensen, M. C., 1978, "Some anomalous evidence regarding market efficiency", *Journal of financial economics*, *6*(2/3), 95–101.

Jiang, G., 2007, "Stock performance and the mispricing of accruals", *The International Journal of Accounting*, *42*, 153–170.

Johnson, E. J., Hershey, J., Meszaros, J., and Kunreuther, H., 1993. "Framing, probability distortions, and insurance decisions". In *Making Decisions About Liability and Insurance* (pp. 35–51). Springer Netherlands, the Netherlands.

Johnston, E. T., Kracaw, W. A., and McConnell, J. J., 1991, "Day-of-the-week effects in financial futures: An analysis of GNMA, T-bond, T-note, and T-bill contracts". *Journal of Financial and Quantitative Analysis*, *26*(1), 23–44.

Kahneman, D., and A. Tversky, 1979, "Prospect theory: An analysis of decisions under risk", *Econometrica*, *47*, 263–291.

Kahneman, D., Knetsch, J. L., and Thaler, R. H., 1991, "Anomalies: The endowment effect, loss aversion, and status quo bias", *The Journal of Economic Perspectives*, *5*, 193–206.

Kahneman, D., 2011. *Thinking, fast and slow*. Macmillan.

Kamara, A., 1997, "New evidence on the Monday seasonal in stock returns", *The Journal of Business*, *70*, 63–84

Kamstra, M., Kramer, L. A., and Levi, M. D., 2003, "Winter Blues: A SAD stock market cycle", *The American Economic Review*, *93*, 324–343.

Kamstra, M., Kramer, L. A., and Levi, M. D., 2012, "A careful re-examination of seasonality in international stock markets: Comment on sentiment and stock returns", *Journal of Banking and Finance*, *36*, 934–956.

Kaniel, R., Saar, G., and Titman, S., 2008, "Individual investor trading and stock returns", *The Journal of Finance*, *63*, 273–310.

Kaplanski, G., and Levy, H., 2010a, "Exploitable predictable irrationality: The FIFA world cup effect on the U. S. stock market". *Journal of Financial and Quantitative Analysis*, *45* (2010a), 535–553.

Kaplanski, G., and Levy, H., 2010b, "Sentiment and stock prices: The case of aviation disasters". *Journal of Financial Economics*, *95*, 174–201.

Kaplanski, G., Levy, H. Veld, C., and Veld-Merkoulova, Y., 2015, "Do happy people make optimistic investors?", *Journal of Financial and Quantitative Analysis*, *50*, 2015, 145–168.

Kidd, J. B., 1970, "The Utilization of Subjective Probabilities in Production Planning", *Acta Psychologica*, *34*, 338–347.

Kim, W., and S. Wei, 2002, "Offshore Investment Funds: Monsters in Emerging Markets?" *Journal of Development Economics, 68*(1), 205–224.

Kliger, D., and Kudryavtsev, A., 2016, "The availability heuristic and other psychological aspects of investors' reactions to company-specific events", in I. Venezia (ed.), *Behavioral Finance: Where do Investors Biases Come From?* World Scientific Publishers, London.

Knetsch, J. L., 1989, "The Endowment effect and evidence of nonreversible indifference curves", *American Economic Review, 79*, 1277–1284.

KrÄahmer, D., 2003, "Learning and Self-Confidence in Contests", Discussion Paper SPII 2003, 10, Wissenschaftszentrum, Berlin, http://ssrn.com/abstract=395702.

Kumar, A., and Lee, C., 2006, "Retail investor sentiment and return comovements", *The Journal of Finance, 61*(5), 2451–2486.

Kyle, A. S., and Albert Wang, F., 1997, "Speculation duopoly with agreement to disagree: Can overconfidence survive the market test?" *The Journal of Finance, 52*, 2073–2090.

Kyrychenko, V., and Shum, P., 2009, "Who holds foreign stocks and bonds? Characteristics of active investors in foreign securities." *Financial Services Review, 18*, 1–21.

Lakonishok, J., and Maberly, E., 1990, "The weekend effect: Trading patterns of individual and institutional investors", *The Journal of Finance, 45*, 231–43.

Lakonishok, J., Shleifer, A., and Vishny, R. W., 1992, "The impact of institutional trading on stock prices", *Journal of Financial Economics, 32*, 23–43.

Landier, A., and D. Thesmar, 2009, "Financial Contracting with Optimistic Entrepreneurs: Theory and Evidence", *Review of Financial Studies, 22*, 117–150.

Larkey, P. D., Smith, R. A., and Kadane, J. B., 1989, "It's okay to believe in the hot hand", *Chance, New Directions for Statistics and Computing, 2*, 22–30.

Lee, C., Shleifer, A., and Thaler, R. H., 1991, "Investor sentiment and the closed — end fund puzzle", *The Journal of Finance, 46*(1), 75–109.

Lichtenstein, S., Fischhoff, B., and Phillips, L., 1982, "Calibration of probabilities: The state of the art to 1980". D. Kahneman, P. Slovic, and A. Tverski (eds.) *Judgement under uncertainty: Heuristics and biases*, Cambridge University Press 1 Cambridge, pp. 306–334.

Leonhardt, D., 2003, "Caution is costly, Scholars say", *The New York Times*, July 30.

Lev, B., and Nissim, D., 2006, "The persistence of the accruals anomaly" *Contemporary Accounting Research, 23*, 193–226.

Levy, H., 1980, "The CAPM and beta in an imperfect market", *The Journal of Portfolio Management*, 5–11.

Levy, H., and Levy, M., 2014, "The home bias is here to stay", *Journal of Banking & Finance*, *47*, 29–40.

Levy, H., 2015, *Stochastic Dominance: Investment Decision Making under Uncertainty*, Springer, Netherlands.

Lewellen, J., 2010, "Accounting anomalies and fundamental analysis: An alternative view", *Journal of Accounting and Economics*, *50*, 455–466.

List, J. A., 2003, "Does market experience eliminate market anomalies?" *Quarterly Journal of Economics*, *118*, 41–72.

Livnat, J., and Petrovits, C., 2009, Investor sentiment, post-earnings announcement drift, and accruals. AAA.

Lobao, J., and A/P Serra, 2002. "Herding Behavior — Evidence from Portuguese Mutual Funds". Working Paper, University of Porto.

Lopes, L. L., 1981, "'Decision making in the short run", *Journal of Experimental Psychology: Human Learning and Memory*, *7*, 377–385.

Mackay, C., 1841, Extraordinary popular decisions and the madness of the crowds, London, Chapter 3.

Malkiel, B. G., 1999, *A random walk down Wall Street: Including a life-cycle guide to personal investing*, WW Norton & Company.

Malmendier, U., and Tate, G., 2005a, "Does overconfidence affect corporate investment? CEO overconfidence measures revisited", *European Financial Management*, *11*, 649–659.

Malmendier, U., and Tate, G., 2005b, "CEO overconfidence and corporate investment", *Journal of Finance*, *60*, 2661–2700.

Malmendier, U., Tate, G., and J. Yan, 2007, corporate financial policies with overconfident managers, Working paper, University of California, Berkeley.

Malmendier, U., and Tate, G., 2008, "Who makes acquisitions? CEO overconfidence and the Market's Reaction", *Journal of Financial Economics*, *89*, 20–43.

Mankiw, N. G., and Zeldes, S. P., 1991, "The consumption of stockholders and nonstockholders", *Journal of financial Economics*, *29*(1), 97–112.

Markowitz, H., 1952, "Portfolio selection", *The Journal of Finance*, 7(1), 77–91.

Markowitz, H. M., 1991, "Foundations of portfolio theory", *The Journal of Finance*, *46*(2), 469–477.

Maug, E. G., and Naik, N. Y., 1995, Herding and delegated portfolio management: The impact of relative performance evaluation on asset allocation.

Mayhew, B., and Vitalis, A., 2014, "Myopic Loss aversion and Market experience", *Journal of Economic Behavior & organization*, *97*, 113–125.

Mehra, R., and Prescott, E. C., 1985, "The equity premium: A Puzzle", *Journal of Monetary Economics*, *15*, 145–161.

Mehra, R., and Prescott, E. C., 2008, "The equity premium: ABCs", *Handbook of the Equity Risk Premium*, R. Mehra, (ed). Amsterdam: Elsevier.

Mehra, R., and Sah, R., 2002, "Mood fluctuations, projection bias and volatility of equity prices". *Journal of Economic Dynamics and Control*, *26*, 869–887.

Mehra, R., and Prescott, E. C., 2008, "The equity premium: ABCs", In R. Mehra(ed.), *Handbook of the Equity Risk Premium*, Amsterdam: Elsevier.

Meulbroek, L., 2005, "Company stock in pension plans: How costly is it?" *Journal of Law and Economics*, *48*(2), 443–474.

Michaely, R., and Womack, K. L., 1999, "Conflict of interest and the credibility of underwriter analyst recommendations", *Review of Financial Studies*, *12*(4), 653–686.

Miller, J. B., and Sanjurjo, A., 2015, Is it a fallacy to believe in the hot hand in the NBA Three-Point Contest? Bocconi University, Working Paper Series 548.

Moller, N., and Zilca, S., 2008, "The evolution of the January effect", *Journal of Banking & Finance*, *32*, 447–457.

Mossin, J., 1968, "Aspects of rational insurance purchasing", *Journal of Political Economy*, *76*, 553–568.

Neale, M. A., and M. H. Bazerman, 1990, Cognition and Rationality in Negotiation. New York: The Free Press.

Nofsinger, J. R., and Sias, R. W., 1999, "Herding and feedback trading by institutional and individual investors", *Journal of Finance*, *54*, 2263–2295.

Odean, 1998, Are investors reluctant to realize their losses? *Journal of Finance*, *53*, 1775–1798.

Odean, T., 1999, "Do investors trade too much?" *American Economic Review*, *89*, 1279–1298.

Oyer, P., and S. Schaefer, 2005, "Why do some Firms Give Stock Options to all Employees? An Empirical Examinations of Alternative Theories", *Journal of Financial Economics*, *76*, 99–133.

Palmon, O., Bar-Yosef, S., and Chen, R. R., 2008, "Optimal strike prices of stock options for effort averse executives", *Journal of Banking and Finance*, *32*, 2008, 229–239.

Palmon, O., and I. Venezia, 2012, "A Rationale for hiring irrationally overconfident managers", *Encyclopedia of Finance, 2nd edn.*, Springer Verlag.

Palmon, O., and Venezia, I., 2013, "Strike prices of options for overconfident executives", *Handbook of Financial Econometric and Statistics*, Springer Verlag.

Pashigian, B. P., Schkade, L., and Menefee, G. H., 1966, "The selection of an optimal deductible for a given insurance policy", *Journal of Business*, *39*, 35–44.

Pasquariello, P., and Vega, C., 2009, "The on-the-run liquidity phenomenon", *Journal of Financial Economics*, *92*(1), 1–24.

Portes, R., and Rey, H., 2005, "The determinants of cross-border equity flows", *Journal of International Economics*, *65*, 269–296.

Pratt, J. W., 1992, "Risk aversion in the small and in the large", In *Foundations of Insurance Economics* (pp. 83–98). Springer, Netherlands.

Raiffa, H., 1993, "Decision analysis: Introductory lectures on choices under uncertainty, 1968", *MD computing: computers in medical practice*, *10*(5), 312.

Richardson, S., Tuna İ., and Wysocki, P., 2010, "Accounting anomalies and fundamental analysis: A review of recent research advances", *Journal of Accounting and Economics*, *50*, 410–454.

Rietz, T. A., 1988, "The equity risk premium a solution", *Journal of monetary Economics*, *22*(1), 117–131.

Rigobon, R., 2002, "International financial contagion: Theory and evidence in evolution", *The Research Foundation of AIMR*, Charlottesville, VA, USA.

Ritter, J. R., and Welch, I, 2002, "A review of IPO activity, pricing, and allocations", *The Journal of Finance*, *57*(4), 1795–1828.

Ritter, J. R., 2003, "Behavioral finance", *Pacific-Basin Finance Journal*, *11*(4), 429–437.

Roll, R., 1986, "The Hubris Hypothesis of Corporate Takeovers", *Journal of Business*, *59*, 197–216.

Roll, R., and Ross, S., 1980, An empirical investigation of the arbitrage pricing theory, *Journal of Finance*, *35*, 1073–1103.

Roll, R., 1983, "Vas ist dat: The turn of the year effect and the return premia of small rms". *Journal Portfolo Management*, *9*, 18–28.

Ross, S., 1976, "The arbitrage theory of capital asset pricing", *Journal of Economic Theory*, *13*, 341–360.

Russo, E. and P.H. Schoemaker, 1992, "Managing Overconfidence", *Sloan Management Review*, *33*, 7–17.

Rozeff, M. S., Kinney, W. R., 1976, "Capital market seasonality: The case of stock returns", *Journal of Financial Economics*, *3*, 379–402.

Samuelson, P. A., 1963, "Risk and uncertainty: A fallacy of large numbers", *Scientia*, *98*, 108–113.

Samuelson, W., and Zeckhauser, R., 1988, "Status quo bias in decision making", *Journal of Risk and Uncertainty, 1*, 7–59.

Scharfstein, D. S., and Stein, J. C., 1990, "Herd behavior and investment", *The American Economic Review*, 465–479.

Schlarbaum, G. G., Lewellen, W. G., and Lease, R. C., 1978, "Realized returns on common stock investments: The experience of individual investors", *Journal of Business, 51*(2), 299–325.

Schoemaker, P., 1976, Experimental studies on individual decision making under risk: An Information processing approach. Doctoral Dissertation, University of Pennsylvania.

Schoemaker, P., and Kunreuther, H., 1976, "An Experimental Study of Insurance", *Journal of Risk and Insurance, 46*, 603–618.

Schoenmaker, D., and Soeter, C., 2014, *New Evidence on the Home Bias in European Investment*, DSF Policy Briefs, Duisenberg School of finance, No. 34.

Schwert, G. W., 2003, "Anomalies and market efficiency". *Handbook of the Economics of Finance, 1*, 939–974.

Shapira, Z., and Venezia, I., 2001, "Patterns of behavior of professionally managed and independent investors", *Journal of Banking and Finance, 25*, 1573–87.

Shapira, Z., and Venezia, I., 2008a, "Paying a premium: Why do consumers buy too much insurance", *STERN Business*, 36–39.

Shapira, Z., and Venezia, I., 2008b, "On the Preference for full-coverage policies: Why do people buy too much insurance?" *Journal of Economics and Psychology, 29*, 747–761.

Sharpe, W. F., and Alexander, G. J., 1990, *Investments*, 4. Englewood Cliffs, New Jersey (US): Prentice Hall.

Shefrin, H., and Statman M., 1984, "Explaining investor preference for cash dividends", *Journal of Financial Economics, 13*, 253–282.

Shefrin, H., and Statman, M., 1985, "The disposition to sell winners too early and ride losers too long: Theory and evidence", *Journal of Finance, 40*, 777–790.

Shefrin, H., 2002, *Beyond Greed and Fear*, Oxford University Press, NY.

Shiller, R., 1981, "Do stock prices move too much to be justified by subsequent changes in dividends?", *American Economic Review, 71*, 421–436.

Shiller, R. J., 2000, *Irrational exuberance*. Princeton University Press, New York.

Shleifer, A., 1986, "Do demand curves for stocks slope down?" *The Journal of Finance, 41*(3), 579–590.

Shleifer, A., and Vishny, R. W. 1997, "The limits of arbitrage", *The Journal of Finance, 52*, 35–55.

Siegel, J., and Thaler, R., 1997, "Anomalies: The equity premium puzzle", *The Journal of Economic Perspectives*, *11*, 191–200.

Sirri, E., and Tufano, P., 1998, "Costly search and mutual fund flows", *Journal of Finance*, *53*, 1589–1622.

Skinner, J., 2007, "Are you sure you're saving enough for retirement?", *The Journal of Economic Perspectives*, *21*(3), 59–80.

Sloan, R., 1996, "Do stock prices fully reflect information in accruals and cash flows about future earnings? (Digest summary)", *Accounting Review*, *71*(3), 289–315.

Slovic, P., *et al.*, 1977, "Preference for insuring against probable small losses: implications", *Journal of Risk and Insurance*, 245–258.

Staël von Holstein, C.S., 1972, "Probabilistic Forecasting: An Experiment Related to the Stock Market", *Organizational Behavior and Human Performance*, *8*, 139–158.

Solnik, B., and Bousquet, L., 1990, "Day-of-the-week effect on the Paris Bourse". *Journal of Banking & Finance*, *14*(2–3), 461–468.

Statman, M., Thorley, S., and Vorkink, K., 2006, "Investor overconfidence and trading volume", *Review of Financial Studies*, *19*(4), 1531–1565.

Statman, M., 2017, *Finance for Normal People*, Oxford University Press, Forthcoming.

Surowiecki, J., 2005, *The wisdom of crowds*. Anchor.

Sydnor, J., 2010, "(Over) insuring modest risks", *American Economic Journal: Applied Economics*, *2*(4), 177–199.

Tesar, L., and Werner, I., 1995, "Home bias and high turnover", *Journal of International Money and Finance*, *14*, 467–492.

Thaler, R., 1980, "Toward a positive theory of consumer choice", *Journal of Economic Behavior and Organization*, *1*, 39–60.

Thaler, R. H., and Johnson, E. J., 1990, "Gambling with the house money and trying to break even: The effects of prior outcomes on risky choice", *Management Science*, *36*(6), 643–660.

Thaler, R. H., and Benartzi, S., 2004, "Save more tomorrow™: Using behavioral economics to increase employee saving", *Journal of political Economy*, *112*, S164–S187.

Thaler, R., and Sunstein, C., 2009, *Nudge: Improving Decisions About Health, Wealth, and Happiness*, Penguin, New York.

The New York Times, 1987-12-26, "Group of 7, Meet the Group of 33".

Thompson, E. A., 2007, "The tulipmania: Fact or artifact?", *Public Choice*, *130*(1–2), 99–114.

Tversky, A., and Bar-Hillel, M., 1983, "Risk: The long and the short", *Journal of Experimental Psychology: Learning, Memory, and Cognition*, *9*, 713–717.

Tversky, A., and E. Shafir, 1992, "Choice under Conflict: The Dynamics of Deferred Decision", *Psycological Science*, *3*, 358–361.

Venezia, I., 2016 (Ed.), *Behavioral Finance: Where do Biases Come From?* Forthcoming, World Scientific Publishers, London.

Venezia, I., and Z. Shapira, 2007, "On the behavioral differences between professional and amateur investors after the weekend", *Journal of Banking and Finance*, *31*, 1417–1426.

Venezia, I., Nashikkar, A., and Shapira, Z., 2011, "Firm specific and macro herding by professional and amateur investors and their effects on market volatility", *Journal of Banking and Finance*, *33*, 1599–1609.

Vermalean, T., and Verstringe, M., 1998, Do belgians overreact? Working Paper, Catholic University of Louvain, Belgium.

Von Neumann, J., and Morgenstern, O., 1944, 2007, *Theory of Games and Economic Behavior*. Princeton university press, New York.

Voronkova, S., and Bohl, M., 2005, "Institutional traders' behavior in an emerging stock market: empirical evidence on polish pension fund investors". *Journal of Business Finance and Accounting*, *32*, 1537–1560.

Walther, B. R., 1997, "Investor sophistication and market earnings expectations", *Journal of Accounting Research*, *35*(2), 157–179.

Wakker, P., Richard T., and Tversky A., 1997, "Probabilistic insurance", *Journal of Risk and Uncertainty*, *15*, 7–28.

Wang, F. A., 2001, "Overconfidence, investor sentiment, and evolution", *Journal of Financial Intermediation*, *10*, 138–170.

Welch, I., 2000, "Herding among security analysts", *Journal of Financial Economics*, *58*, 369–396.

Wermers, R., 1999, "Mutual fund herding and the impact on stock prices", *Journal of Finance*, *54*, 581–622.

Wu, J. G., Zhang, L., and Zhang, X. F., 2007, Understanding the accrual Anomaly, NBER Working Paper 13525.

Wylie, S., 2005, "Fund Manager Herding: A Test of the Accuracy of Empirical Results Using UK Data", *Journal of Business*, *78*, 381–403.

Zapatero, F., 2016, "Reference based decisions in Finance", in I. Venezia (ed.), *Behavioral Finance: Where do Investors Biases Come From?* World Scientific Publishers, London.

Zarowin, P., 1989, "Does the stock market overreact to corporate earnings information?" *Journal of Finance*, *44*, 1385–1400.

Ziemba, W. T., 2011, "Investing in the turn-of-the-year effect", *Financial Markets and Portfolio Management*, *25*(4), 455–472.

INDEX

1/n, 193–194
1/n heuristic, 193
3Com, 168–169

A

Abnormal profits, 15
    cumulative abnormal returns,
        131, 133
Above normal, 10, 12, 14–15, 131,
    138, 142, 167, 171, 215, 217,
    223
Accounting, 5, 160, 220
    mental accounting, 59, 61–62,
        71–72, 86, 152, 154, 165,
        192–193
accountants, 101
Accruals
    accruals anomaly, 215–216, 221,
        224
Acquisitions/Mergers and
    acquisitions, 108–109
Adjusted
    risk-adjusted measures, 11
ADR, 168
Affect, 67–68, 92, 107, 129, 172, 181,
    200, 208, 216, 227
Allais
    Allais paradox, 39–41, 45, 51, 65
Alpha, 11–12
    Jensen's alpha, 11
Alternation, 210

Alternative, 20–24, 27, 46, 59, 65, 68,
    70, 97, 109, 142, 148, 173, 190, 199,
    208, 216, 225
Amateur, 83, 92, 94–95, 225
Ambiguity
    ambiguity aversion, 42
American, 91, 158, 168,
Analyst, 127
Analysts recommendation, 126
Anchoring, 59–61, 68, 187, 199–200
Announcement, 138, 142–144,
    215–216, 219, 222
Anomaly, 215–216, 221, 223–224,
    228–230
Appearance, 5, 54, 223
    disappearance, 5, 223, 238
Arbitrage, 5, 7, 10, 12, 17, 103, 167,
    170–175, 181, 185, 189, 216, 237
    arbitrage pricing theory (*see also*
        APT), 15–16
    performance based arbitrage (*see
        also* PBA), 167, 174
    limits to arbitrage, 5, 7, 167,
        170, 237
Arbitrageur, 10, 12, 167, 170–174,
    181, 216
Area, 3–5, 158, 209
Asset
    capital asset pricing theory (*see
        also* CAPM), 3, 8, 217
Atmospheric, 182

Attribute
    self-attribution, 101–102, 107,
       114, 140, 142, 144
Averse
    risk aversion, 19, 21, 29, 35, 70,
       75, 79, 147, 152, 155, 196, 199,
       201
    constant relative risk aversion
       (*see also* CRRA), 29, 31, 77,
       147, 196
Axiom
    rationality axioms, 32, 42

B

Baby
    baby bell, 162–163
Ball
    basketball, 52, 203–206, 211, 213
Base
    base rates, 55
Basketball players, 206
Basis points, 172
Bayesian
    Bayes rule, 55, 101, 121, 123, 130
Bearish, 178
Behavior, 4, 10, 13, 17, 32, 68, 78, 93,
    103, 106–107, 120, 129, 143, 148,
    170, 182, 193, 225
Behavioral, 3–9, 20, 36, 46, 58, 67, 77,
    84, 140, 152, 155, 161, 164, 195,
    202, 206, 213, 217, 223, 228
Believe
    belief, 9, 90–91, 99, 128, 139,
       188, 204, 208–209
Bell, 162–163
Below target, 220–221
Benchmark, 74, 127–128,
Benefit
    cost-benefit, 198, 201
    defined benefits, 189
    insurance benefits, 198
    tax benefits, 83–84, 86, 92, 111
Bernoulli's paradox, 24
Bet, 45, 149–152, 158
Beta, 9, 15, 135, 140, 217–218

Bias, 5, 49, 52–53, 56–57, 61, 76, 84,
    87, 90, 92–93, 98–99, 101–103, 113,
    130, 141, 157–163, 165–166,
    192–193, 203–205, 218, 230, 237
Bid-ask spread, 171–172
Bird in hand fallacy, 179
Block trades
    odd lot trades, 226
Bond, 22, 95, 96, 145–147, 153–154,
    168–169, 173, 179, 192, 229
Boston, 96, 209
Bowman paradox, 215, 220–222, 224
Box office, 62
Boy, 53, 206
Brexit, 129, 135–137
British, 6, 136
Bubble, 6–8, 115, 178
Bullet, 78–79
Bullish, 178
Bund, 173–174
Buy, 10, 12, 23, 29, 36, 60, 62, 86–87,
    92, 94, 96, 105, 107, 118, 120–125,
    127, 138–139, 142, 169, 170–173,
    178–180, 187, 194–202, 219,
    225–230, 232–233

C

Cancellation, 72–73
Capital
    capital markets, 4, 17, 79, 111,
       115, 177
Capital asset pricing model (*see also*
    CAPM), 3, 8–10, 14–17, 217
Cumulative abnormal returns (*see
    also* CAR), 131, 133
Cascade, 115, 120, 123–125, 127, 224,
    232–233
Cash
    cash flows, 47–48, 109–111, 168,
       177, 182
Cause, 8, 29, 53, 55, 87, 105, 111, 113,
    115–118, 120, 130, 144, 171–172,
    183, 185, 200, 219, 225–226
Certainty premium, 41–42
CEO, 108–109, 111

Chance, 21, 25, 52–53, 56, 60, 63, 66, 70, 78–79, 86, 99–100, 103, 105, 109, 122–124, 126–127, 150, 191, 196, 198, 203–204, 206, 208, 210–211, 213, 220
Characteristic, 116, 119
Charlatan, 126–127
Chilean Model, 155
Choice
    choice architecture, 35–37
Citigroup
    JP Morgan, 86, 171
Client, 91, 105, 155, 175, 199, 201, 232
Closed end fund, 177–181, 184–185, 224
Coding, 72
Cognitive, 4, 7, 39, 49, 51, 59, 86–87, 170, 187–189, 192, 202
Coin
    ducats, 26
Commission, 171–172, 197
Common
    common elements, 73
Company, 109, 112, 162, 164–165, 168, 192–193, 195–196, 198
Compensation, 74, 103, 112–114, 127–128, 145, 217
Confidence
    overconfidence, 5, 99–114, 140, 142, 144, 208, 218, 236
Confirmation
    confirmation bias, 101–102, 204
    confirming signals, 142
Conservative, 39, 51, 56–59, 141, 144, 218, 222
Consistent, 12–13, 31, 39, 41, 45, 68, 107, 119, 138, 140–141, 152–154, 179, 213, 220, 224, 228, 233
Consumer, 36, 146–149, 194, 197, 199, 201–202
Consumption, 15, 28, 47, 147–149, 188, 199
Continuity, 34
Contagion, 117–118, 120

Contribution, 3, 92, 101, 189, 192
Corporate, 4, 13, 36, 99, 103, 108, 111, 114, 141–143, 149
Correlation, 9, 85, 90–91, 105–109, 116, 138, 158, 160–161, 166, 185, 207–210, 213, 220–221
Country, 70, 92, 117–118, 120, 136, 158, 161, 183
Coverage, 60, 187, 195, 198, 200–201
full-coverage puzzle, 187, 194
Crash, 6, 8, 84, 115, 118, 178
Crisis, 6–8, 118–120, 129, 135, 161, 178
Critique, 13, 20, 37, 39, 45, 125, 129
Constant Relative Risk Aversion (*see also* CRRA), 29, 31, 77, 147, 196
Culture, 67–68, 100, 161

D

Damage, 196–197
Data, 13–14, 47, 52, 87, 106, 133, 169, 209, 226
Day of the week effect, 182, 223–224
Debt, 8, 110–111, 179
Deductible, 60, 194–201
December, 8, 90, 134, 228–230
Decision makers, 4, 13, 20, 23, 26, 29, 33, 39, 42, 51, 57, 61, 67, 71, 76, 84, 115, 129, 141, 146, 152, 199, 218
Default, 8, 33, 35, 190–191
Defense, 14, 208–209, 212
Destabilize, 115, 117–118, 128
Diminishing
    diminishing marginal utility, 27, 76
Disappearance, 5, 223, 238
Disaster, 78, 182–183
Discount, 47, 66, 87, 105, 107, 110, 147, 178, 181, 185
Disposition
    disposition effect, 5, 83–84, 89, 91, 93, 95, 98, 107, 235
Distribution
    symmetric distribution, 22

Diversification, 21, 157, 159–163, 165–166, 193
Dividend, 35–36, 47, 62, 110, 138, 143, 178–179, 181, 184
Domain, 69, 75, 79, 82, 152
Dot-com, 7, 178
Drift, 138, 142, 215–216, 222, 224
Duration, 92–94, 169
Dutch, 6, 39, 46, 68, 178
Dutch/shell, 39, 46, 168

E

Earnings surprise, 216–217, 219
Economic
    macroeconomic, 84
Economist, 6–7, 17, 19, 30
Editing, 69–72
Efficiency
    semi strong efficiency, 9
    strong efficiency, 9
    weak efficiency, 9
Efficient
    efficient market hypothesis, 3, 5, 8, 19, 46, 58, 129
    efficient markets, 5, 13–14, 17, 39
Election, 33–34, 74, 102, 199
Ellsberg paradox, 40–42, 45, 54, 58, 65
Efficient market hypothesis (*see also* EMH), 3, 5, 8, 19, 46, 58, 129, 139
Employee, 93, 112–113, 164–165, 189, 191, 194
Employer, 109, 113, 157, 163–165, 189–193, 202
Endowment, 155, 223, 230–231
    endowment effect, 223, 230–231
Enrollment
    automatic enrollment, 190–191
Equity
    equity premium puzzle (*see also* EPP), 145–146, 152, 155, 164, 195, 236

closed end fund puzzle, 177, 181
full-coverage puzzle, 187, 194
Europe
    European, 136, 158, 161
Evaluation, 8, 69, 71, 73, 79, 110, 148, 154, 161, 181
Event, 6, 8, 13, 53, 75, 84, 101, 130, 138, 143, 148, 182
Evolution, 3, 5, 101, 103, 113, 130, 159–160, 168, 223
Example, 4, 6, 8, 12, 14, 17, 30, 35, 53, 57, 63, 74, 111, 136, 147, 167, 173, 192, 198, 208, 223
Excess volatility, 39, 46–47
    excess returns, 132, 220
Excessive, 46, 58, 105–106, 114, 129, 152, 199
Exchange
    Chicago Board of Exchange, 76
    Exchange rate risk, 159, 161
    exchange rate, 159, 161
    New York Stock Exchange, 178
Existence, 13, 75, 117, 149, 161, 205, 221, 224, 238
Expect
    expected utility, 24, 26, 31, 42, 147, 149, 153, 195
    expected values, 25
    expectations, 126
Experience, 29, 67–68, 87, 200, 230–231, 233
Experiment, 14, 25–26, 33, 40, 45, 50, 53, 65, 69, 77, 88, 100, 125, 133, 154, 200, 206, 213, 230
Explanation, 25, 29, 101, 125, 142, 150, 180, 187, 195, 208, 215, 218, 224, 227, 230
Exploit, 104, 167–168, 172, 181, 183, 189, 216, 229, 233
Extreme factor, 79, 163

F

Factors
    factor analysis, 15
    Fama–French multi factor
        model, 17
    five factor asset pricing model,
        15, 17
    four-factor pricing model, 16
    multi-factor asset pricing, 3, 15
    non-diversifiable factors, 15
    robust minus weak factor, 17
Fallacy, 52, 179, 203, 205, 213
Feminist, 54–55
FG (field goal), 212
Finance
    behavioral finance, 3, 7, 10, 17,
        20, 29, 46, 88, 152, 180, 218
    corporate finance, 4, 36, 108,
        111, 114
    traditional finance, 8
Firm
    acquiring firm, 108
    employer's firm, 157
    firm's beta, 15
    firm's returns, 15
    firm's risk, 10
    firm's performance, 112
    firm's specific risk, 109
    regional firm, 162
Flow
    cash flows, 47–48, 109–110, 168,
        177
    fund flows, 178–180
Foreign
    foreign investment, 161
Foul shots, 208–209
Framing
    narrow framing, 62
Frankfurt, 173–174
Frequent, 102–103, 105, 107, 139,
    149–150, 155, 194
    infrequent, 102
Full
    full-coverage, 60, 187, 194,
        199–200

Function
    utility function, 22, 24, 26, 28,
        30, 77, 147, 152, 199
Fund
    fund manager, 52, 127, 162,
        203
    mutual fund, 21, 87, 92, 118,
        139, 162, 178, 180, 194, 207,
        229
    pension funds, 92
Fundamental
    fundamental value, 170–171
    fundamental analysis,

G

Gains
    capital gains, 36, 62–63, 84, 90
    paper gains, 89
    realized gains, 88–89
Gamble
    gambler's fallacy, 205
Game, 25, 104, 127, 149, 152, 183,
    205, 208, 211
Gender, 67–68
General, 3, 14, 21, 58, 71, 102, 146,
    158, 204, 229
German, 158, 173
Globalization, 157, 160
Group, 6, 16, 93–94, 116, 118, 193
Guarantee, 41, 78, 171, 173, 191

H

Habit
    habit formation, 74, 148, 199
Hot hand fallacy
    cold hand, 204, 211
    hot hand, 5, 52, 203–207, 209,
        213
Herd
    herding, 5, 115–117, 119, 128,
        236
    intentional herding, 116
    spurious herding, 116
Heuristic
    1/n heuristic, 193

High
    high minus low (book to
        market), 16
    high deductibles, 194, 202
    high accruals, 215
Historical
    history, 3, 5, 14, 168, 204
    historical returns, 149
    historical distribution, 154
Home
    home bias, 5, 157–158, 161, 193,
        237
    home stocks, 159
    housing market, 96
Horizon, 139–140, 146, 152, 155
Hospital, 53
Household, 8, 36, 163, 183, 187–188,
    191
Hubris, 108

I

Idiosyncratic risk, 9
Impact, 73, 112–114, 171–172, 174,
    178
Imperfect
    imperfect competition, 104
Implementation
    implementation costs, 169
Incentives, 113
Independence of Irrelevant
    Alternatives (*see also* IIRA), 34,
    42, 65, 193
Index
    fear index (VIX), 178–179, 184
    index inclusion, 39, 46
    large cap index, 16
    sentiment index, 184
    small cap index, 16
    S&P index, 16
Individual
    individual investors, 106, 149,
        153, 178, 219, 225–227
Information
    favorable information, 130–132,
        137

information aggregation, 103
information costs, 118
informational cascade, 232
insider's information, 9
low strength information,
    141–142
new information, 53, 55–57, 102,
    129, 136–138, 141, 218
prior information, 141
private information, 103, 142
public information, 9, 13, 142
Innovations, 103, 114
Internet
    internet survey, 105–106
Initial
    initial wealth, 28, 30–32
    initial beliefs, 56
Institutions, 8, 92, 119, 149, 155, 168,
    225, 233
    institutional investors, 117, 216,
        219, 225–227, 232
    institutional trades, 226–227
Insurance decisions, 23, 78
    full coverage insurance, 60, 195,
        199–200
    insurance policy, 195
Insure
    insured, 195–197, 199–201
    insurer, 195, 198, 200, 202
Intentional herding, 116
Intentional decisions, 116
International investment, 157, 159
    international diversification, 157,
        159, 166
    international home bias, 158, 161
    international markets, 118
Internet survey
    internet questionnaire, 106
    internet, 105–106, 160
Invest, 32, 104, 120, 123, 126, 128,
    146, 156, 158, 161, 165, 180, 187,
    194, 205, 207, 213, 232
Investment strategies
    foreign investments, 161
    investment banks, 232

investment company, 162
investment decisions, 84, 94–95,
    107, 111, 155, 163, 216
investment factor, 17
investment horizon, 146, 152–153
investment manager, 162, 213
investment rate, 110
investment results, 207
short investment horizons, 146,
    152
value of investment, 153, 164
Investor
independent investor, 94, 125
individual investor, 62, 106, 149,
    153, 178–179, 219, 225, 227
managed investor, 92, 94, 227
overconfident investors, 104, 107,
    142
professional investor, 4, 83, 92,
    119, 130, 161, 227
IPO
underpricing of IPO, 224, 233
Irrational
irrational behavior, 103, 195
Isolation
isolation effect, 59, 63–64, 73
Israel, 91–92, 115, 118, 169, 217, 227

J

January effect, 12, 134–135, 224,
    228–230, 233
Joint hypothesis, 13–14, 89, 148

L

Lifetime expected utility, 147, 149
Limits of arbitrage
limits to arbitrage, 5, 7, 167,
    170, 237
limitations, 25, 37, 206
limit, 143, 189
Liquidity, 48, 105, 159, 169, 225–226
Stock's liquidity, 48
Local home bias, 157–158, 161–163
local investment, 158
local stocks, 162

London, 173–174
Losers, 83–84, 86–87, 89, 91, 93, 96,
    98
Losses
loss aversion, 5, 76, 79, 145, 149,
    152, 192–193, 236
myopic loss aversion, 145, 149,
    192, 236
paper loss, 89, 97
Lottery, 25–26, 29, 60, 64
Low
low accruals, 215
low deductibles, 194–195, 199
low positions, 215
low sentiment, 183–185, 219
low-strength, 141–142
loyalty, 165

M

Managers
fund manager, 52, 127, 162, 203,
    206
investment managers, 162, 213
money managers, 92, 162, 205,
    207, 213
overconfident mangers, 102–103
Marginal
marginal productivity, 112
marginal utility, 27, 62–63, 76
Markets
book to market factor, 16
capital markets, 4, 17, 79, 111,
    115, 177
efficient market, 3, 5, 8, 13, 19,
    47, 58, 67, 129, 136, 170
financial markets, 4, 135, 161,
    218
market efficiency, 3–4, 8–9,
    12–14, 17, 19, 46, 91, 117, 128,
    229
market inefficiencies/anomalies,
    3, 12
market risk premium, 10–11
market sentiments, 182
market value, 8, 96, 135

stock market, 3, 6–7, 46–48, 92,
    95–96, 104, 118, 130, 135, 141,
    152, 164, 177, 180, 219, 231
Matching, 189, 192
Mean, 9, 17, 19–25, 32, 54, 57, 74, 99,
    104, 125, 128, 188, 218, 220–221
    mean–variance,19–24, 37
    mean–variance rule, 19–24
Measure, 10–11, 94, 99, 106, 109, 113,
    139, 147, 179–180, 182
Media, 67–68
Medical insurance, 78, 197–198
Mental accounting, 68, 71–72, 86,
    152, 154, 165, 192–193
Miscalibration, 99, 102, 106–107, 110
Mispricing, 167, 169–171, 178-180,
    184–185
    IPO mispricing, 179, 184
Momentum, 12, 16, 85, 138–140, 142
    momentum effect, 224
    strategies momentum, 139
Monday
    Black Monday, 6, 178
    Monday effect, 224
Monetary, 33, 72, 75, 151, 178
Money
    money managers, 92, 162, 205,
        207, 213
Month, 16, 90, 132, 134, 140, 150,
    153, 168, 184, 218, 231–232
Mutual funds, 21, 87, 92, 118–119,
    139, 162
Myopic
    myopic loss aversion, 145, 149,
        155, 192–193, 236
Myth, 204, 206, 213

N

National, 118, 157–159, 161, 182–183
NAV (*see also* Net Asset Value),
    180–181
NBA, 203, 205, 207, 209, 211
Negative
    negative domain, 69
    negative outcome, 69

negative correlation, 90–91, 185,
    204, 208, 220–221
negative effects, 108, 111
negative recency, 205
Noise
    noise traders risk, 169–170, 181
    noise traders, 169–171, 178, 181
Normal profits, 9–10, 12, 14–15, 167,
    171
Normal returns, 12, 14, 132, 134, 139,
    216–217, 220, 224, 229, 231–232
    above-normal profits, 10, 12,
        14–15, 215, 217, 223
Nudge
    nudging, 35–37
New York Stock Exchange, 178

O

Observations, 12, 53, 71, 88, 95, 110,
    124, 212
Odd-lot trades, 226
Opponents, 13–14, 105
Opportunity, 32, 174, 189
    arbitrage opportunity, 169, 171,
        173, 179
Optimal savings, 187–188, 190
Optimism
    optimistic, 102–103, 158, 178,
        219–220
    optimistic managers, 102–103
Option(s), 103, 112–113, 117, 204,
    229, 231
Overestimate, 100, 102, 107–109, 112,
    202
Overreaction, 5, 7, 55, 104, 129,
    131–136, 141, 144, 170, 222, 236
Overvaluation, 183–184

P

Palm, 102, 104, 113–114, 168, 221,
    236
Paradox
    Allais paradox, 39–41, 44, 49, 65
    Bernoulli's paradox, 24

Bowman paradox, 215, 221–222, 224

Ellsberg paradox, 40, 42, 44, 58, 65

St. Petersburg paradox, 24–25

Partial

partial ordering, 22

Participants, 4, 24, 33, 40, 44, 51, 54, 77, 100, 107, 130, 154, 188, 194, 200, 210, 230–231

Passive investments, 155–156

Payment, 97

dividend-paying firm, 63

expected payment, 195, 200

Performance based arbitrage (*see also* PBA), 167, 174

Performance-sensitive compensation, 103

Persistence, 7, 13, 103–105, 113, 169, 215, 223, 229, 233

Pessimistic, 170, 178, 199, 219–220

Phenomenon, 12, 29, 108, 123, 146, 162

hot hand phenomenon, 209

Planning

planning horizons, 155–156

saving plans, 155, 188, 191, 194

tax planning, 83–84

Point

reference point, 64–65, 72–73, 76, 79, 85, 87, 95, 148

three-point, 209–211

Policy

full-coverage policy, 195–196, 200–201

policy makers, 36, 188

Population, 89, 102, 199, 204

Portfolio

equity portfolio, 159

well-diversified portfolios, 11

Portugal, 117

Positive

positive correlation, 85, 106, 109, 138, 158, 208, 218

positive effect, 111, 161

positive earnings, 217, 219

Post-earnings-announcement drift (*see also* PEAD), 216

Precision, 99, 107

Prediction, 57, 70, 110, 184, 194

Preference, 23, 26, 29, 33, 36, 42, 51, 64, 120, 147, 163, 194, 200

Premium

certainty premium, 41–42

dividend premium, 178, 184

equity premium puzzle, 145, 155, 164, 195–196, 236

equity premium, 145–149, 153, 194–196, 236

risk premium, 5, 9–11, 145–146, 152, 181, 217

Present value

net present value (*see also* NPV), 30–32

Price, 6, 8

price impact, 171–172

stock prices, 13, 47, 76, 118, 132, 138, 141, 144, 182, 219

sub-prime, 7–8, 120, 135, 178

Probability, 23, 43, 45, 54, 65, 78

posterior probability, 55, 121, 123

prior probability, 56

Professional, 4, 67, 83, 91, 94, 98, 117, 119, 130, 161, 188, 201, 203, 205, 209, 227–228

Profitability measures, 3, 10

profitable, 52, 97, 100, 139, 216

Propensity to buy/sell, 227–228

Property

property owner, 97

properties, 22, 27–28, 57, 75, 178

Prospect

expected prospective value, 151, 153

prospect theory, 5, 7, 20, 29–30, 35, 46, 51, 59, 69, 72, 74, 85, 87, 147, 149, 152, 199, 220, 235

Proxy, 178–179
Psychological bias, 19, 46, 49, 87, 90,
    92, 218
Public information, 9, 13, 142
    public signals, 107, 142
Purchase, 10, 61–62, 78, 84, 86, 91,
    94, 97, 110, 122, 138, 143, 172, 195,
    201, 227, 232
    purchase price, 84–86, 91, 96
    purchase decision, 122, 201, 202
P/E ratio, 12, 130

R

Random, 26, 40, 44, 53, 56, 61, 97,
    129, 183, 204, 210, 229, 231
Ratio
    Sharpe Ratio, 11
    Lintner Ratio, 11
    P/E ratio, 12, 130
Rationality, 5–6, 10, 17, 19, 24, 32,
    39, 46, 66, 68, 83, 102, 108, 188
    investors rationality, 6
    irrationality, 83, 108
    rational behavior, 32, 49, 103,
        120, 195
    rational decision, 24, 27, 32, 37
    rationality axiom, 32, 42
Real estate market, 83, 95
    real estate, 6, 83, 95–96, 117
Realistic, 45, 50, 58
    unrealistic, 45, 50, 147, 199, 232
    reality, 142, 154
Realized gains/losses, 88–89
Reasonable, 21–23, 44, 196
    unreasonable, 22–23
Rebalancing, 90, 105
Recency bias, 204
    positive/negative recency, 205
Reflection principle, 69–70, 75
Region, 75, 77, 158, 161–163
Regret, 41, 45, 50, 86–87, 200
Relative strength, 139–140
Representativeness, 39, 51–59,
    140–141, 144, 203

Researcher, 6–7, 13–14, 29, 46, 49, 85,
    88, 116, 145, 148, 157, 169, 178,
    180, 195, 206, 217, 220, 229–230
Resident, 119, 163
Result
    investment result, 207
    superior result, 207
Returns
    above-normal returns, 12, 131,
        138
    expected returns, 9, 12, 15, 152,
        174, 218, 220
    normal returns, 9, 12, 14, 131,
        133, 138
    stock/asset/portfolio return, 16
Risk
    fundamental risk, 169–170
    idiosyncratic risk, 9
    market risk premium, 10–11
    noise traders risk, 169–170, 181
    positive risk-return, 220
    risk averse/aversion, 20, 25, 29,
        69, 120, 128, 148, 158, 179,
        199–200
    risk free interest, 10
    risk premium puzzle, 5
    risk premium, 5, 9–11, 146, 152,
        187, 217
    risk seeking, 29, 75–76, 79, 86,
        220
    riskless asset, 149, 153
    risky portfolio, 194
    risky project, 28
    risky stock, 152
    systematic risk, 9–11, 119, 140
Robust, 17, 87–88, 92, 109, 134, 194,
    224
Russian roulette, 78
Round trip, 92–95
Royal Dutch, 39, 46, 48, 168
Russian roulette, 78

S

Sample
    sample size, 53, 57

Saver, 188–191, 193, 202
Savings, 5–6, 28, 155, 158, 164,
    187–192, 202, 237
Seasonal effects, 134, 182
Segregation, 72–73
Self
    self-attribution, 101–102, 107,
        114, 140, 142, 144
    self-control, 35–36
    self-selection, 199
Sell
    seller, 84, 97, 170, 172
    selling, 10, 12, 84–86, 88, 92, 96,
        178–179
Sentiment
    market sentiment, 7, 170,
        177–183, 185, 219, 237
    investor sentiment, 177, 180, 219
Sequential decisions, 63–64, 125
Shareholders
    institutional shareholdings, 219
Shooter
    shooting, 208–211
Short, 178
    short-term, 111, 139, 174, 193,
        218
Shot, 52, 203–212
Siamese twins, 39, 46, 163
Signal
    correlated signals, 126
    good/bad signal, 127
    public/private signal, 107, 142
Simple deal, 94–95
Size
    anomaly, 12
    prize size, 45
    sample size, 53, 57
Slope, 183, 221
Small firm effect, 12, 232
Small probabilities effect, 59, 65
Sophisticated, 119, 140, 219
Stock split, 138, 143–144
Sport, 33, 39, 46, 168, 182, 203, 213
Spurious herding, 116
Stage, 71–72, 79

Startup, 111, 114
State, 35, 46, 78, 95, 162
Status
    status quo, 73, 230
Stock
    stockholder, 108, 113, 163, 179,
        221
Streak, 203–205, 210
Strength
    low/high strength information,
        58, 141–142
    relative strength strategy, 139
Substitution axiom, 65
Success
    success rate, 207–209, 211–212
Survey, 78, 105–106, 110, 178, 182,
    190, 194, 203
Survive, 78, 104
Systematic risk, 9–11, 119, 140
Status quo, 73, 230
    status quo bias, 230

T

Target firm
    above target firm, 221
    below target firm, 221
Tax
    tax benefits, 83–84, 86, 92, 111
    tax code, 83, 92
    tax considerations, 84, 90, 92,
        169
    tax payment, 83
    tax planning, 83–84
Team, 33, 101, 112, 158, 205, 208, 212
Tendency, 36, 60, 63, 87, 141, 156,
    158, 161, 200–201, 224–225
Theater, 61–62
Theory
    arbitrage pricing theory, 15
    Bernoulli's theory, 25
    cascades theory, 120, 125, 127,
        224, 232
    economic theory, 19, 24
    efficient market theory, 13, 67
    financial theory, 9

hot hand theory, 203, 205, 208, 211, 213
overreaction theory, 135
prospect theory, 5, 7, 20, 29, 32, 46, 51, 69, 73, 77, 85, 87, 153, 199, 220, 222, 235
traditional decision theory, 19, 73
utility theory, 5, 19–20, 24, 26, 28, 31, 35, 45, 51, 67, 72, 77, 146, 194–195, 200
Three-point, 209–211
Thumb Rule, 164
Trade, 48, 76, 87, 89, 104, 117, 119, 160, 169, 173, 180, 221, 225, 227–228, 230
Tradeoff, 221
Trader
noise traders, 169–171, 178, 181
overconfident trader, 104
Trading costs, 90–91, 229
Trading volume, 106–107, 120, 178, 184, 226–227
Traditional, 7–8, 19–23, 33, 73, 145, 168, 195
Transaction
transaction costs, 105, 155, 160, 171, 178, 216–218, 222, 229
Transitivity, 33
Trend, 159, 170, 210
Turn of the year effect, 224, 228
Two-step decision, 63
Typical, 20, 27, 77, 196–197

U

UK, 48, 117, 136, 146, 159, 189
Uncertain alternatives, 20, 25, 27
Uncertainty, 20, 25, 27, 125, 200
Underperform, 180
Underpricing of IPO, 224, 231, 233
Underreaction, 5, 129, 136, 138, 142, 218, 236
Urn, 40–43, 45, 51–52, 56
Utility
quadratic utility, 22

utility function, 22, 24, 26, 31, 62, 77, 147, 153, 196, 199
utility theory, 5, 19, 24, 28, 31, 45, 51, 58, 71, 73, 194
USA (*see also* US), 48, 83, 87, 90, 95, 146, 159, 162, 168, 177, 197–198, 206, 212

V

Value
absolute value, 198
actuarial value, 196, 201
correct value, 181
current value, 6
expected value, 20, 25, 60, 120, 150, 152, 194
fundamental value, 170–171
market value, 8, 96, 135
value anomalies, 224
value function, 69, 73–74, 151, 154
Variance, 19–21, 23–24, 37
Violation, 34, 39, 42, 44, 51, 65, 71, 193
Volatility Index (*see also* VIX (or) fear index), 178–179, 184
von Neumann and Morgenstern (*see also* VNM), 19, 235
Volatility
excess volatility, 39, 46–47
volatility index, 178

W

Wait, 35, 85, 91, 96–97, 171
Waiver, 196–197
Warranty, 197, 201–202
Weak efficiency, 9
Wealth, 19, 27, 30, 62, 74, 147, 188
Initial wealth, 28–32
Final wealth, 27–32, 72
Weather, 182
Weekend effect, 12, 182, 223–225, 227, 233
Weighting
weighted average, 74, 94

weighting of probabilities, 69
weighting function, 75, 77
Welfare, 27–28, 41, 112–113, 164
Well-diversified portfolio, 11, 164–165
Winning stocks, 93, 133
Winning firms, 135
Winner, 83–84, 87, 90, 93, 98, 133

Women, 101, 105, 107, 114, 209
Worker, 54, 112, 163, 188, 192, 202

Y

Year, 90, 155, 160, 197, 223, 228,
232
Yield, 23, 181, 215

Printed in the United States
By Bookmasters